THE
DOS 3.3
AND OS/2
HANDBOOK

A PRACTICAL USER'S GUIDE

THE
DOS 3.3
AND OS/2
HANDBOOK

A PRACTICAL USER'S GUIDE

Stephen Morris

HEINEMANN
NEW·TECH

Heinemann Newtech
An imprint of Heinemann Professional Publishing Ltd
Halley Court, Jordan Hill, Oxford OX2 8EJ

OXFORD   LONDON   MELBOURNE   AUCKLAND   SINGAPORE
IBADAN   NAIROBI   GABORONE   KINGSTON

First published 1989

British Library Cataloguing in Publication Data
Morris, Stephen, *1955 Nov. 14-*
    The DOS 3.3 and OS/2 Handbook: a Practical User's Guide.
    1. Microcomputer systems. Operating systems. DOS
    I. Title
    005.4'469

ISBN 0 434 91284 0

Produced by SC&E Morris Computer Services, Bodenham, Hereford

Printed and bound in Great Britain by
Butler & Tanner Ltd, Frome and London

Table of Contents

Part One   An Introduction to DOS 3.3 and OS/2

Part Two   The Operating System Commands

Part Three Batch Files

Part Four   Programming

List of Illustrations

Foreword

DOS 3.3 is the latest member of the family of operating systems for the IBM PC and compatibles. It is currently being supplied with many of the newer IBM PC compatibles, including the Amstrad portable. It is also one of the two alternative systems that can be used with the PS/2 series of computers.

OS/2, the other PS/2 operating system, is fully compatible with DOS 3.3 and incorporates almost all of its commands and utilities. It has the added advantage of being able to make full use of the large memory and multi-tasking capabilities of the PS/2. There is therefore a substantial, and growing, population of users of these two systems.

Since the systems are so similar, most of the text applies equally to both DOS 3.3 and OS/2. The new features of OS/2 are covered in their own separate sections. Apart from these few exceptions, the differences between DOS 3.3 and OS/2 are not particularly significant. Any minor differences between the operating systems are clearly marked in the text.

The handbook is aimed at both the new user and the experienced operator. Basic knowledge of computer hardware is assumed but the operating systems themselves are covered right from the very first steps. For the new user, the early chapters provide an introduction to the operating systems and show how the computer can be used at its most efficient.

The book will also be of interest to the more experienced user who is moving over from DOS 3.3 to OS/2. For many people the thought of transferring from one system to another is just as daunting as the original process of learning an operating system for the first time. This book shows you that the differences between DOS 3.3 and OS/2 are really quite small and that even the totally new aspects of OS/2 can be mastered quickly and with a minimum of disruption.

It is assumed that the new user will require a guide to the operating systems and their use while the experienced user needs more of a detailed reference guide. Therefore this handbook is divided into a number of sections.

Part 1 is aimed at the new user, introducing the concepts and basic structure of the operating systems. There should be sufficient information here to run applications programs and carry out simple housekeeping tasks.

Part 2 describes the full command set, so that the experienced operator can tailor the system to his own particular requirements and make more efficient use of the system. This section is in the form of a detailed reference, with the commands divided into a number of categories. In each case there are ample worked examples (so often missing in DOS reference manuals).

Part 3 covers batch files and their use, from simple files for the new user to full batch-file programming. This part is at the same two-level approach: an introduction to the subject and the more straightforward operations, followed by a full reference section, again with plenty of examples.

Part 4, the final part, takes us deeper into the heart of the operating system. This section covers, briefly, the way in which the operating systems actually work, and how we can use their more advanced functions within programs.

A system of cross-referencing is used throughout the book to assist the user in finding the information he or she needs as quickly as possible. However, it should be noted that the handbook is more than just a reference manual; it also provides an introduction for the beginner and is heavily based upon a practical approach to the operating system, providing operators with the knowledge they need to make more efficient use of their computers.

Every effort has been taken to ensure that the information given in this book is accurate and complete. However, in any work of this size there will inevitably be ommissions and errors, for which I apologise. Obviously I cannot take responsibility for any problems that may arise from use of the information contained in this book.

I would like to thank Emily Morris for all her work on the manuscript and Robin Kinge for his assistance during the preperation of the final text.

PART ONE

AN
INTRODUCTION
TO DOS 3.3 AND
OS/2

1. *Introduction to the Operating System*

The first section of this handbook is aimed at those who are new to the intricacies of computer operating systems. Much of the information given here will be familiar to those who have already worked with previous versions of MS-DOS or PC-DOS. For those who already understand the basic workings of the operating system, probably all that is required is a quick scan through these first few chapters.

This chapter provides some background information on DOS 3.3 and OS/2. It describes what they are and what they do, and gives a brief summary of their history. Perhaps most importantly, this chapter tells you why you need an operating system in the first place.

INSIDE THE COMPUTER

Many people see computers as highly intelligent, clever machines, capable of carrying out amazingly complex tasks and able to take over the more, mundane humdrum jobs or enhance the capabilities of the efficient operator. In part this is true but the real truth of the matter is not quite so straightforward. The fact is that the computer on its own can do nothing; it certainly contains some highly complex and clever electronics but these are only the skeleton around which the system is built. The electronic circuits themselves are capable of very little that is applicable to the real world. It is only the computer programs that transform this empty shell into a useful tool.

The computer is comprised of a number of components. These fall into two broad categories:

- The *hardware*, consisting of the machine itself, its keyboard, monitor, disk drives and system unit.

- The *software*, comprising the programs that give the computer instructions.

The hardware of the computer is able to carry out a range of operations, such as adding two numbers together or comparing two values to see which is greater. It may select from a series of operations depending on the outcome of such a comparison. However, although the hardware is able to combine these into many different operations, it needs to know what order to perform them in. This is the job of the software. A computer program is merely a list of instructions for the hardware, telling it in which order the instructions are to be executed.

These lists of instructions are stored in the computer's *memory*. When a program is run, the computer executes each instruction from the list in turn. Also stored in memory is the *data*, the information with which the program is to work and the results it produces.

To be of any use to us the computer must be able to perform four basic tasks:

■ Input. Information must be fed into the computer.

■ Storage. The programs and information that are fed in and the results that are created must be stored in the computer's memory.

■ Processing. The computer must carry out the instructions, using the input to produce results.

■ Output. The results that are produced by the program - messages to the user and so on - must be output in some way to the user.

Perhaps we should also add to this list the ability to store information away from the computer itself. This ability is not essential in every case, but without it many applications become almost impossible.

MEMORY

Computers, like people, have only a limited amount of memory. The middle of the range IBM PS/2 System 50, for example, has a memory that can hold up to seven million characters of information. This is the equivalent of about 10 average- sized books. This may seem a large memory but it is surprising how quickly it can be used up.

Units

There are a few basic units for measuring the capacity of a computer's memory. The smallest practical unit, as far as the user is concerned, is the *byte*. A byte of memory can store a single character for text-based programs, such as word processors; for number-based programs, such as databases, a byte holds a single value. For large values two or more bytes are needed.

Because the computer's memory is so vast the bytes are grouped together into *kilobytes* (abbreviated to K). 1K is approximately 1000 bytes (1024, to be precise). Similarly, 1000K is generally referred to as a *megabyte* or 1M. These same units are used for the capacity of disks and other storage devices.

Thus a double-density 3½" floppy disk may hold 720K while the System 50's memory is 1M (expandable to 7M) and hard disks are generally in the range 20M to 65M.

Types of Memory

Broadly speaking the computer has two types of memory:

■ *Read Only Memory (ROM)*, which is memory that is permanently fixed and cannot be changed.

■ *Random Access Memory (RAM)*, which is memory that can be accessed at any time and the contents of which can be changed.

The ROM, as it's name implies, can be read but cannot be written to. That is, you can see what is in the memory and the computer can carry out any instructions that it may contain but you cannot change the contents of that part of memory. This makes ROM fine for storing programs that are going to be used frequently but absolutely hopeless for any sort of data, or for programs that are only going to be used occasionally.

In fact, the ROM is a fairly small part of the computer's overall memory; the ROM is generally reserved for a few simple programs that are used to get the computer going.

RAM holds programs while they are running and stores their results.

External storage

Computers work in a very similar way to people. Because people have only a limited memory, when they want to remember something they write it down on paper and store it away somewhere for future use. When they need to recover that information, they find the paper and read the information back into their memories, ready for use. Alternatively, a person who wants to use some information from somebody else can pick up a book and read that information into his or her memory.

Computers operate in precisely the same way. When a program is created in a computer it can be stored away (on disk) for future use. The disk is the equivalent of a piece of paper, taking the information away from a computer. This program can later on be read back into the computer's memory. The same is true of data, the information stored by computers. We cannot hope that a computer will hold all the information that we need or create, so this too is stored away on disk for future use. Similarly, any new programs that are needed or data from another computer can be read in by getting a disk from some other source.

THE ORIGINS OF DOS AND OS/2

A computer's internal hard disk can store many megabytes of programs and data. There is no limit to the number of floppy disks we can have and therefore no limit to the amount of programs and data that can be stored away from the computer. If we are to maintain this information in any sort of sensible order we need a special set of programs; these programs form the *operating system.*

Part of the function of the operating system is to control the storage of programs and data on disk. It allows us to make copies of selected data, move data and so on. It is also the job of the operating system to maintain order in the computer's memory and control the way in which data is transferred to and from the external devices (printers, modems, etc.)

A BRIEF HISTORY

The most widely used operating system to-day is generally known as *DOS.* This is an abbreviation of PC-DOS (the operating system of the IBM PC) or MS-DOS (the operating system for IBM-compatibles).

DOS first made its appearance as PC-DOS, the operating system developed by Microsoft for the original IBM PC, in

DOS versions		
Version	**Year**	**Modifications**
1.0	1981	Original version for IBM PC and compatibles
1.1	1981	Minor bugs fixed
1.25	1982	Double-sided disks allowed
2.0	1983	Introduction of sub-directories
		First appearance of file handles
2.01	1983	International symbols introduced
2.10	1983	Minor bugs fixed
2.11	1983	Minor bugs fixed
2.25	1983	Extended ASCII character set
3.0	1984	High capacity floppy and hard disks allowed
3.1	1984	Networking capabilities
3.2	1986	3½'' disks allowed
3.3	1987	Support for PS/2
4.0	1988	Enhanced user interface
		New disk layouts

Figure 1.1 The history of DOS

1981 (see Figure 1.1). Shortly afterwards other manufacturers began to produce computers that were *IBM-compatible* (that is, they work in a similar manner to the IBM and data can be transferred between IBM's and compatibles with ease). The operating system was also copied, although on machines other than the IBM PC it was known as MS-DOS.

DOS 1 had some fairly severe limitations, not least because it could only store a limited number of programs or sets of data on each disk, no matter how small they were. This restriction was due to the size of the *directory*, the place where details of a disk's contents are stored.

Two years later, DOS 2 overcame these problems by the introduction of *sub-directories*, divisions of the original directory, so that the number of different items stored on disk became limitless. DOS 2 also introduced some major enhancements for programmers.

DOS 3 emerged in 1984. The first version, DOS 3.0, allowed much higher disk capacities for both floppy and hard disks. DOS 3.1 (which is rarely encountered these days) was the first version to provide support for networks while DOS 3.2 at last recognised the need for 3½" disks. With the shipping of the IBM PS/2 range of computers came the announcement of DOS 3.3, a version able to support some of these machines' enhanced capabilities.

Since then we have seen an even newer version, DOS 4.0, which has a greatly improved 'user interface' (a term which describes the way in which the user communicates with the computer).

OS/2 came on the scene in 1987, at the same time as DOS 3.3. This new operating system has been designed to take account of the PS/2's different modes of operation, although it still maintains compatibility with earlier versions of DOS.

THE NEED FOR OS/2

DOS has sufficed for many years and provided a satisfactory environment for the 8086-based IBM PC's and compatibles. However, it has its limitations, and with the newer 80286 and 80386 machines now flooding the market it has begun to outlive its usefulness.

The need for OS/2 arises from the restrictions of DOS. The most vital of these limitations are:

■ DOS can only run one program at a time.

■ DOS can only access 640K of user memory in normal operation. Even with special handling it has difficulty extending beyond one megabyte.

■ DOS has difficulty in accessing hard disks greater than 32M capacity.

Each of these points is considered below.

Foreground programs

DOS can only concentrate on one thing at a time. This was quite sufficient in the past when all we wanted to do was operate a single program but, with such a variety of sophisticated applications now available, the need to combine operations is becoming more necessary. For example, you might want to take results from a number of applications - word processor, spreadsheet and graphics - and combine them into a single desktop publishing task; alternatively, it is frustrating to have to sit idly by while the computer prints out results from a program or communicates with another machine across the telephone lines.

DOS made one minor attempt to overcome the printing difficulty with the PRINT program, an application that runs *in the background*; PRINT sends the contents of a list of documents to a standard printer while other work continues *in the foreground*. However, there is a tendency for PRINT to slow down the foreground program - especially if it has heavy disk-access needs - and it will only work with *ASCII files* (text files that have had all special codes for bold, italic and different fonts stripped out).

RAM maximum

Unadulterated versions of DOS cannot use more than 640K of RAM. This means that programs are confined to a comparitively small region of memory. While ten years ago even 64K seemed an unimaginable expanse of memory that could never possibly be filled, modern applications struggle to keep within 640K.

Even the addition of an Expanded Memory Driver (discussed later) often only brings the usable memory up to one megabyte.

Disk capacity

The 32M limit on hard disk capacity has been overcome to a certain extent by DOS 3.3, which allows larger hard disks to be divided up into more than one section, each with a maximum of 32M. Even this can be limiting when a single application (such as a desktop publishing package) can take 2M for the programs alone. A single publication may take up to 2M for its various files, so disk space soon disappears.

The OS/2 solution

OS/2 breaks through these arbitrary barriers. The first release of the operating system allows access to up to 16M of memory, which is enough for current applications (though OS/2 itself takes a minimum of 2M and history has shown that applications find ways of filling the space made available to them, no matter how great it may be).

As far as disk size is concerned, there is no real limit here and we can take as much as we like. The major problem arises from the management of such vast amounts of disk space. It is very easy to lose a few megabytes of programs or data by forgetting where they are. Efficient disk management becomes essential; this is the major task of every operating system and the majority of the commands described in this book are intended to keep data storage under control.

Finally, but most importantly, OS/2 does not restrict us to running a single program at any one time.

MULTI-TASKING

The process of running a number of programs simultaneously is called *multi-tasking*. To the user, it appears that the computer is doing several things at once; it may be printing a report, communicating with a mainframe computer and calculating the monthly cashflow while at the same time allowing the user to have full, unbridled access to the word processor.

In fact, the computer is still only performing one action at a time. It achieves this remarkable effect by spreading its time around each application in turn. First it sends a piece of data to the printer, next it transfers an item from the mainframe; it then picks up where it left off on the financial calculations, does a bit more work and stores away the result so far; finally the computer is made available to the user for word processing. What makes this run so smoothly is that each period allocated to any one application is very small. In the time taken to press a key the computer will have cycled round the various activities several times.

Because the main activity depends on the users, and the computer works at hundreds of times their speed, the majority of time in word processing will be spent waiting for the person at the keyboard to do something. So the wasted time in between key presses can be put to good use by the machine without creating any noticeable delay for the person operating the computer.

Even when the foreground program is fairly labour-intensive there should not be any real holdups, because of the speed of the 80286 and 80386 machines. (Multi-tasking on an 8086 - for example, with PRINT - can be rather tedious.)

The time allocated to each individual activity is called a *timeslice* and can be varied by the user. Lengths of timeslices

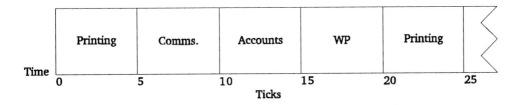

Figure 1.2 Allocating timeslices

are measured in clock *ticks*. The process of multi-tasking is demonstrated in Figure 1.2.

OPERATING MODES

DOS 3.3 and OS/2 operate in very different ways because of their approach to the use of computer time.

Real mode

In many respects, DOS has a very easy time when it comes to controlling what is happening in the computer. Since only one application is running there is no danger of any confusion over what program is accessing which device (with the possible exception of PRINT, which takes care of its own priorities when it comes to accessing printers and disk drives). Any DOS applications are said to operate in *real mode.*

Protected mode

For OS/2 the situation is much more complex and the dangers are more apparent. If all activities operated in real mode there would be absolute chaos, with the applications competing for use of individual devices and constantly overruling each other. Imagine the chaos if the word processor and accounts program were both trying to print out at the same time!

For this reason OS/2 applications must be protected from each other. In order to achieve this, no OS/2 application is allowed to work directly with the hardware. Unlike DOS, where a program could bypass the operating system altogether and send a piece of data directly to the printer, under OS/2 this is strictly forbidden.

All attempts to pass data to and from the internal and external devices (including the keyboard and screen) must be channelled through OS/2. OS/2 is then able to control all access to devices and make sure things do not get in a muddle.

For the user everything seems to run smoothly; for the programmer the more exotic practices of direct access allowed by DOS have been curtailed but the potential pitfalls have also been reduced.

This form of operation is known as *protected mode*.

DOS compatibility   Of course, the fact that programs must be specifically written to work in protected mode means that original DOS programs will not run directly in this mode. OS/2 allows for this by allocating one portion of its time to run real mode applications. You can only run one real mode program at a time - as with DOS - but at least all your old DOS applications can be safely transported to OS/2 and will still run quite happily.

MEMORY MANAGEMENT

OS/2 also has a fundamentally different approach to the use of memory. Under DOS, any application can determine the physical location of its programs and data in memory. This is clearly not possible under OS/2, where two applications may demand access to the same piece of memory.

Therefore OS/2 applies a concept known as *virtual memory*. Each application is allocated its own section of virtual memory; this memory does not actually exist so it can be as large as we like. When an application needs to use a section of memory, either to load a segment of program or to store data, OS/2 allocates a section of *physical memory* for that purpose. OS/2 takes care of all the problems of matching virtual memory with physical memory.

All memory is divided into 64K *segments* and allocated a segment at a time. Similarly, programs and data are divided into 64K segments. OS/2 only ever loads those segments that are needed at any one time. For example, it will not load the segment containing a word processor's printing program until we select the Print command.

If we have several programs running, physical memory eventually fills up. OS/2 then carries out a process known as

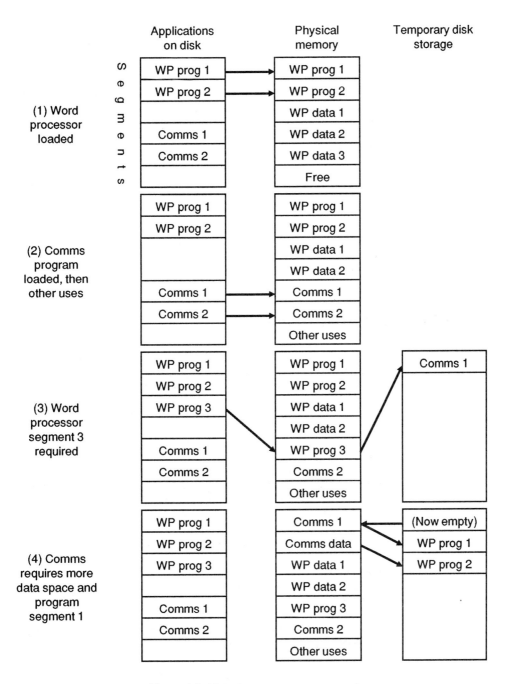

Figure 1.3 Virtual memory management

segment swapping. In order to load a new segment of program or data it first transfers a segment of memory to disk, where it is stored in a temporary file. OS/2 keeps track of what is stored where and will read the segment back into memory as required. This process is illustrated in Figure 1.3.

Most of the time this is of no concern to the user. It only becomes of interest if so many applications are running that the constant disk access slows down our activities to the point that they become unbearable.

Virtual devices

In a similar way, any access to a device is actually done via a *virtual device*. For example, programs can no longer write directly to the screen. Instead, OS/2 keeps a copy of the screen display in memory for each application. When a program writes to the screen its own version of the display is updated in memory. The physical screen only presents the display that has been created by a single application at any one time.

The same approach is used for all other devices, such as the keyboard and printer. In this way, OS/2 is far more in control of the computer than DOS could ever be.

We can now look at the actual operation of these two operating systems.

2. *Operating Systems Basics*

The basic principles of DOS have remained unchanged since its inception back in 1981. The way in which instructions are given to the operating system, the method of storing data and programs on disk, and the overall appearance of the operating system have hardly varied in all these years and through the several new versions that have come along.

There have been additions to DOS, of course. There are new commands and many of the original commands have been enhanced. The way in which DOS can be used by the advanced programmer has also changed quite considerably. There are many new functions available and there is a new, simpler method of accessing files on disk. However, these considerations are of little or no interest to the casual user. The important feature is that virtually anything learnt with the original DOS 1 still applies today.

Interestingly enough, OS/2 is almost identical in appearance and operation to DOS 3.3. There are many new concepts, an increased set of commands and - for the programmer - a whole new set of functions, but the overriding principles remain the same. This is perhaps a surprise; one might have expected Microsoft and IBM to take the opportunity of a new range of machines to completely revamp the operating system but they have not done so.

There are a number of reasons for this. First and foremost must have been the need to maintain compatibility with programs and data from DOS. It is still proving very difficult for the manufacturers to tempt existing users to come over to OS/2, even though all are assured that they can still run their existing DOS programs unchanged. In addition there is the need to provide the hesitant user with a similar entrance point to their programs. We all like to stick to programs, computers and operating systems that we know; talk to anyone about any feature of their computer system - hardware or software - and they will almost invariably extol the virtues of their particular system over all others.

Yet once you have mastered one system - whether it is a computer, application or operating system - the problems of transferring to something new are generally very mild compared to the trauma of learning the original system. Times taken to retrain are also only a fraction of those spent on the original training. This is because the basic principles - the part that is most difficult to grasp for the new user - remain the same. It is only the method by which results are achieved that change, and the human brain is remarkably adept at replacing one set of instructions with another. Nevertheless, the inherent dislike for change that exists in most people, especially those for whom computers remain a tool rather than a source of constant excitement and adventure, is always there. So, to persuade existing users to be converted is always going to be far harder than capturing new disciples from the uninitiated.

That said, it is a shame that more could not have been done to improve the appearance of the 'front end' of OS/2. It is true that some OS/2 machines are now being bundled with Presentation Manager - just as many DOS machines were supplied with Windows - but at the present time this does not show much promise of gaining wide acceptance amongst users.

This book covers only the standard command-line approach of DOS and OS/2 for communicating with the operating system. Those who wish to discover the enhancements provided by Windows and Presentation Manager will need to look elsewhere.

In this chapter we look at the basic principles behind this method of communication and the core of the instruction set, around which all other activities are based.

DISK TYPES

To be of any use to us the computer must be able to store information and programs in some permanent form; this generally takes the form of disks (of varying types) and tapes. These various devices are collectively referred to as *media*.

Most information is stored on disk, except in those cases where we are using a tape or other device for backup purposes. Leaving aside the less common types of media, the disks that are used fall into three basic categories:

■ *Floppy disks.* These are removable, low-capacity disks; in the case of IBM PC's, PS/2's and compatibles these are 5¼" and 3½" disks. These disks are extremely fragile and, on hard disk machines, are generally used only for backup purposes and for transferring data between machines.

■ *Hard disks.* These are very high capacity disks, built into the computer. They are non-removable and therefore cannot be exchanged when full. As a result a considerable amount of disk 'housekeeping' is required.

■ RAM disks. These are not real disks, but sections of memory that have been temporarily marked out for data storage and act in the same way as disks. Access is very fast; the main disadvantage is that when the computer is switched off all data is lost. They are fine for temporary storage of programs, particularly for floppy disk computers.

There are now also some removable hard disk units, where the hard disk can be exchanged. These behave identically to normal hard disks, with the advantage that there is no longer any restrictive limit on hard disk capacity; different hard disks can be loaded for different applications. The disadvantage is that the chances of hard disk failure are greatly increased, with the resultant loss of a vast amount of data.

Each type of disk is used for a different purpose, as described above, but the way in which they are used by the operating system is the same in each case.

DRIVE NAMES   All commands need to refer to a particular disk drive. As a general rule DOS does not care - or even know - which disk we have in a floppy disk drive. It is up to us to decide which disk to load and to put it in at the appropriate time. However, the operating system does need to know which drive we are talking about. It is no good saying we want a list of all files on a disk without telling the operating system where to look for the disk.

For this reason each drive is given a label, consisting of a single letter. The labels are used in a particular order by DOS:

■ Floppy drives are labelled A and B. However, if a computer has only a single floppy drive then this drive may be labelled as two separate *logical drives*, A and B, so that we can copy data from one floppy disk to another using the single drive. This concept is expanded upon later.

■ The hard disk is nominally labelled drive C. As we shall see, this disk may be *partitioned* into more than one logical drive, in which case the extra partitions are called D, E and so on.

■ A ram disk on a floppy machine is labelled C, while on a hard disk machine it will be D (or the letter after the last logical hard drive, if the disk has been partitioned).

■ If the computer is linked into a network then the extra drives that are available on the network will be allocated the next free letters.

Whenever a drive is referred to in a command the drive label is followed immediately by a colon (for example, 'A:' for the floppy drive). This label is referred to as the *drive specifier*.

FILES AND FILENAMES

Almost everything stored on disk, whether a program or set of data, is held in the form of a *file*. A file is just a convenient idea for a collection of information. Data files can be as large or as small as we like. The data in a file does not have to be related; it can be a collection of totally separate items. A large item of data (for example, the text for a report) can be split into a sequence of smaller files for convenience.

As we progress through the book we will come across many different types of file. The important feature is that each file contains a single, independent collection of data or programs.

NAMING FILES   Every file must be given a *filename* so that it can be identified. Filenames are made up of two parts:

■ The main part of the name can be up to eight characters long and should give an idea of what is contained in the file.

Character	Hex	Explanation
!	21	Exclamation
#	23	Hash
$	24	Dollar
%	25	Percent
&	26	Ampersand
'	27	Apostrophe
(	28	Open bracket
)	29	Close bracket
-	2D	Minus
0 - 9	30 - 39	Decimal numbers
@	40	At symbol
A - Z	41 - 5A	Upper case letters
∧	5E	Control
_	5F	Underscore
a - z	61 - 6A*	Lower case letters
{	7B	Open brace
}	7D	Close brace
~	7E	Tilde

* Lower case letters converted to upper case (41h - 5Ah)

Reserved Filenames

Filename	Use
CLOCK$	The system clock
COM1	Standard serial port
COM2	Second serial port
COM3	Third serial port
CON	Console (keyboard and screen)
KBD$	Keyboard
LPT1	Standard parallel port
LPT2	Second parallel port
LPT3	Third parallel port
NUL	Null device
POINTERS$	Pointers
PRN	Standard printer
SCREEN$	Screen

Figure 2.1 Valid filename characters

■ The file may have a optional *extension* (or *filetype*). This can be up to three characters long and should tell you what sort of file it is.

If the filename has an extension, then the two parts are separated by a full stop, with no spaces. For example, the FORMAT program, which has an EXE extension (indicating that it is an *executable* file) is written 'FORMAT.EXE'.

The filename may consist of almost any combination of letters and numbers, and the following characters:

! # @ $ % ^ & ' ( ) - _ { } ~

As a general rule it is better to stick to letters and numbers. Note that upper and lower case letters are treated the same, so 'LETTER.TXT', 'letter.txt' and 'Letter.Txt' all refer to the same file. There must be no spaces in the filename.

Certain three-letter names are reserved for particular devices and must not be used (see below).

We can identify the location of a file by inserting the drive specifier before the filename, as in:

```
A:FORMAT.EXE
```

The permissible characters and the reserved names are listed in Figure 2.1.

AMBIGUOUS FILENAMES

When running a program we only need to look at one file at a time. However, for many 'housekeeping' operations (when copying, renaming and deleting files) it is helpful to work with a number of files at a time. For example, we may want to copy all files with a TXT extension to a backup disk or delete any file starting with JAN. To do this both DOS and OS/2 provide two *wildcards*. These are special characters that can be included in the filename to indicate that we are looking for any files that match the name given.

The ? wildcard

The first wildcard is the '?' character. This can be placed anywhere in the filename and represents any other character at that position. It will also be matched by a blank (if it is in a position beyond the end of the name or extension). For example:

CHAPTER?.TXT	includes CHAPTER1.TXT, CHAPTER2.TXT and CHAPTER.TXT
???SALES.DAT	includes JANSALES.DAT, FEBSALES.DAT, etc.

For this command to be useful great care must be taken in devising names. For example, if filenames contain numbers we should use 02JAN.LET and DEPT05A.REG in preference to 2JAN.LET and DEPT5A.REG, since these files may have to be found by the specifications ??JAN.LET and DEPT??A.REG (and may need to be grouped with 18JAN.LET and DEPT11A.REG.

*The * wildcard*

Although the ? wildcard is helpful in some circumstances, by far the most useful wildcard is the '*' character. This is placed at the end of the main name, extension or both and represents any number of characters, indicating that we don't care what comes at the end. For example:

CHAP*.TXT	includes CHAPTER.TXT, CHAP01.TXT and CHAP.TXT
*.TXT	includes all files with a TXT extension
LETTER.*	includes LETTER.TXT, LETTER.DOC, LETTER
LET*.*	includes all filenames beginning with LET (such as LETTER.TXT and LET)
LET*.	includes all files that begin with LET but have no extension
LET*	is generally identical to 'LET*.' (but see the special case under the DIR command)
.	includes all files (with or without extensions)

We can combine these wildcards, as well. For example, ???SAL*.T* includes JANSALES.TXT and VERSAL.T.

FILE TYPES

As a general rule we can use the extension for any purpose we like. However, there are a few extensions that have a particular meaning for DOS and OS/2:

EXE	DOS or OS/2 executable program

COM	DOS command file (or program)
CMD	OS/2 batch file
BAT	DOS batch file
SYS	DOS or OS/2 device driver

Other conventions are frequently used but are not compulsory:

DAT	Data file
TXT	Text file
BAK	Backup file
ASM	Assembler file
OBJ	Object file (result of compiling a program)
BAS	BASIC file

Most applications have their own set of *default* extensions (that is, extensions that are automatically added unless we specify otherwise).

Note that there is also a general convention that any file with a '$' in the extension is a temporary file, created by an application. Such files are usually deleted by the program that created them but may be left on disk if the machine is switched off or reset without properly quitting the application. As a general rule the files can be deleted but always check first that they have no residual purpose.

DEVICES

It is worth nothing at this stage that we sometimes need to refer to a *device* rather than a file. For instance when copying a file we may want to direct the output to the printer rather than copying the file to another part of the disk.

In such cases we must use the special names that have been allocated to the devices. These were listed in Figure 2.1.

It is important to realise that these device names are associated with the computer's ports and internal connections, rather than the physical devices themselves. For example, 'PRN' refers to whatever device may be connected to the parallel port at the time. Usually this is a printer but it may also be a plotter or other parallel device.

The use of the device names is expanded upon in Chapter 11.

STARTING UP THE SYSTEM

When the computer is switched on it runs a set of *diagnostic programs,* which check the various components of the system.

The computer itself can do very little else on its own. Its fixed memory contains the diagnostic programs that check the system and others that allow it to read and run a program from disk, but that is all. Anything else must be achieved by the operating system and application programs. It is the operating system that allows us to inspect the contents of disks, to move data and programs around, send output to the printer and run applications.

Therefore the final task of the on-board programs, once they have completed their internal system checks, is to load the operating system into memory. The operating system then takes complete control until the computer is switched off.

This process of starting up the system for the first time when the computer is switched on is generally known as *booting* the system.

Hardware checks Whenever the system is booted it does a check on each part of the system. Any hardware faults that are detected are reported on the screen; usually the computer can then do nothing else until the fault has been corrected.

After the hardware tests, the user memory is checked. (This is the Random Access Memory, or RAM, that is available for the user's programs and data.) As the memory is checked it is usually counted through on the screen.

Finally, the various devices and components are initialised ready for use.

Loading the operating system

The next stage is to load the operating system. The computer first checks the floppy drive to see if it contains a suitable disk. If it does, the operating system is loaded from there; if it does not contain a suitable disk, the operating system is loaded from the hard disk.

The operating system may then ask for the date and time to be entered. Either enter these in the format shown, or just press Return. (See Chapter 6 for details of setting the date and time.) The way in which the operating system behaves at this stage is determined by a file that may be called either AUTOEXEC.BAT (DOS 3.3) or STARTUP.CMD (OS/2). This is a very useful file, which can be customised to suit our own needs, as described in Chapter 13.

SYSTEM RESET

There are occasions when we need to go back to the beginning and start again:

■ When we want to load a different operating system (for example, CP/M or a different version of DOS)

■ When we want to clear a memory-resident program out of memory (for example, to free that memory for a program that requires more space than is currently available)

■ When a program crashes and there is no other way of getting out of it

In these cases we need to read the operating system into memory and start again, as if the computer had just been switched on. This process is known as *rebooting* or *resetting the system*. It is achieved by pressing the set of three keys:

Ctrl-Alt-Del

The procedure is to press and hold Ctrl and Alt, and then press Del. (This is the Del key at the bottom of the number pad.) As soon as Del is pressed the internal programs perform their system checks again (though this time they do not do a memory check) and then load the operating system. Again, they first try to load from floppy disk before loading the hard disk system. You are then back where you started.

Note that when the need to reboot arises from a program crashing there are occasions (particularly when any sort of disk access is involved) when the crash is so complete that even a full reset will not do the trick. In such cases the only option is to switch off and start again. This is a very last resort; if, and when, it does become necessary, always wait at least ten seconds after switching off before switching on again, since the power surges that are generated can otherwise be harmful to the computer.

THE COMMAND LINE

The method by which communication between the operating system and user take place is generally referred to as the *user interface*. This rather ghastly term is simply an expression of the means of giving the computer instructions and getting back results. Unless you install one of the enhanced interfaces (such as Windows or Presentation Manager) the user interface for DOS and OS/2 is a rather clumsy yet effective one.

This approach is still based upon the old teletype systems that were used - and in many cases still are used - with mainframe computers. There the principle was that an instruction to the computer was typed on one line and immediately printed on paper. The paper advanced one line and the computer typed out its response. The paper moved up to a fresh line and the user could type another instruction, and so it went on. If any mistake was made, it was too late to correct it and the only way of overcoming it was to type a completely fresh instruction on the next new line. This was of course the only way of doing things; when everything was being done on paper there was no way of going back and making changes.

The method used by DOS and OS/2 is almost identical. In this case the screen is treated rather like the old teletype paper. All communication is done by the user typing an instruction and the operating system presenting its result. Each new instruction is typed on a new line and the operating system always starts a new line for its response. When the bottom of the screen is reached the display simply *scrolls* up to make space for new information. The top line scrolls off the screen and is lost from view. Just like the teletype, any instruction or piece of information higher up the display can be viewed but you can never move back up to it to make changes. Once it has scrolled off the top of the screen it is gone for good.

THE PROMPT   As soon as a command has been entered the operating system tries to execute the instructions it has been given. When it is ready to process the next command (either because it has completed the previous command or because the instruction was faulty) it informs the user by displaying a *prompt*. The prompt that appears on the screen depends on whether you are working with DOS or OS/2. The prompt is always displayed on the next line, starting on the left, and takes the forms:

        A>   (DOS)

        [A:\]   (OS/2)

This is the *default* prompt (that is, the prompt that is automatically used by the system until you specify otherwise). As a general rule the prompt will tell you which is the drive to be used as a default in commands (in the examples above it is drive A).

To avoid confusion, the prompt will be referred to as, for example, the 'A prompt' when it could be the prompt from either operating system (that is, either the A> prompt or the [A:\] prompt).

Immediately following the prompt is a small flashing line, called the *cursor*. The cursor shows you where the next character to be typed will be displayed.

ENTERING
COMMANDS
              When the prompt is displayed the operating system is waiting for you to enter a command. There are a few important rules to remember when entering commands:

■ Either upper or lower case letters can be used; both are treated the same.

■ Spaces are very important. (For example, there must be a space between a command and filename but there must be no space between a drive specifier and its associated filename.) Double spaces are ignored, as are any spaces at the start of the command.

■ The command is completed by pressing Return.

The operating system takes no action while the command is being typed. The Return key acts as a signal that the command is complete and ready for processing. Therefore, a command can be edited at any time before pressing Return. For example, to delete the last character press either Backspace or ←.

Any command can be up to 127 characters long, though this is usually far more than could ever be needed. If you reach this limit the computer will beep and accept no more characters.

Note that most commands in OS/2 are identical to those of DOS. The illustrations in this case may show either operating system in such cases; both forms are illustrated when there is any major difference. (Indeed, in some respects there are more differences between DOS 3.2 and DOS 3.3 then there are between DOS 3.3 and OS/2.)

The keyboard buffer

You can start typing the next command while the previous one is being processed. Anything typed at the keyboard is stored in the *keyboard buffer*, an area of memory set aside for storing keystrokes that are waiting to be used. As a general rule the maximum number of characters stored in the buffer is 15.

The keyboard buffer stores all keystrokes, including Backspace and Return, so you can correct any mistakes you believe you may have made or enter a series of short commands. Obviously you should take great care with the more drastic commands (such as those to delete a group of files) and only press Return when the command is displayed.

The command buffer

Whenever the prompt is displayed, ready for the next command, the operating system holds the previous command in memory in a *command buffer*. The function keys can be used to redisplay the command or edit it. This means that if you made a mistake in the previous command it can be corrected without having to be completely retyped. A second, similar command, can be entered by simply making changes to the first. This part of the operating system is sometimes called the *command editor*.

The keys available for editing are shown in Figure 2.2.

The most useful keys are those that redisplay previous characters from the buffer. Either the → key or function key

Key	Effect
→	Display next character
←	Remove last character
Backspace	Remove last character
Ins	Insert mode. Any new characters are inserted in the buffer
Del	Delete next character from buffer
F1	Display next character
F2	(Followed by character.) Display all characters up to character specified
F3	Display remainder of buffer
F4	(Followed by character.) Delete all characters up to character specified
F5	Replace buffer with new command line
Esc	Abandon changes to buffer
Return	Process command as shown

Figure 2.2 Keys for editing previous commands

F1 displays the next character from the previous command. F3 displays the remainder of the command.

Pressing Ins puts the command editor into *insert mode*. Any new character keys are inserted before the next character in the buffer. The editor remains in insert mode until another of the editing keys is used.

The Del key deletes the next character from the buffer. This can be a bit tricky since you cannot see what character you are deleting. Note that the Backspace and ← keys are used to remove the last character from the command but the character remains in the buffer; it is not permanently deleted, as is the case with Del. Thus the sequence Del and → skips a character while Backspace followed by → leaves the command line unchanged.

For example, suppose the previous command is:

```
DR BB: /W
```

This would result in an error message. The command could be corrected by the following sequence of key strokes:

```
→ Ins I → → Del F3
```

The command now reads:

```
DIR B: /W
```

Note that any new characters are not inserted in the buffer. For example, type the following:

```
B ← →
```

The character displayed is not 'B' but whatever character was waiting in the buffer.

Lesser-used keys are F2, which displays all characters up to a specified character, and F4, which permanently deletes a group of characters in a similar way.

For example, first enter the command:

```
DIR C:*.COM /W
```

For a wide listing of all files on drive C you need the command:

```
DIR C:*.* /W
```

This can be created from the first command by the keys:

```
F2 C F2 C *(space) F4 / F3
```

When the command is complete you have three options:

■ Return enters the command that is displayed and the command is immediately processed.

■ Esc abandons the new command and restores the command buffer to its previous state. All insertions and deletions are lost. A '/' is added to the old command and the cursor moves down a line.

■ F5 stores the new command, as currently shown, in the command buffer. The old command is lost and the new

(1)   Prompt is displayed

	Command buffer:	DIR C:*.* /W
	Command line:	(Empty)

(2)   Edit with F2 * F2 * E Ins X E F3

	Command buffer:	DIR C:*.* /W
	Command line:	DIR C:*.EXE /W

(3)   Replace buffer with F5

	Command buffer:	DIR C:*.EXE /W
	Command line:	(Empty)

(4)   Edit with → → → → F4 / F3

	Command buffer:	DIR C:*.EXE /W
	Command line:	DIR /W

(5)   Abandon changes with Esc

	Command buffer:	DIR C:*.EXE /W
	Command line:	(Empty)

(6)   Edit with F2 / F3

	Command buffer:	DIR C:*.EXE /W
	Command line:	DIR C:*.EXE

(7)   Accept command with Return

	Command buffer:	DIR C:*.EXE
	Command line:	(Empty)

Figure 2.3 Operation of the command buffer

command can be re-edited. An '@' symbol is placed at the end of the old line and the cursor moves down to a new line.

Any editing changes are only temporarily held on the displayed command line.

This process is demonstrated in Figure 2.3.

Obviously you would not use most of these editing keys (except → and F3) for simple commands but they are useful for more complex commands. These keys are well worth mastering at an early stage.

The current drive

Much of the time we include the drive specifier in all commands, so that there is no doubt which drive we are talking about. However, DOS always has a *current drive* (sometimes called a *default drive*). This is the drive to which all commands will refer unless we specifically give a different drive specifier.

Initially, when the system is first started, the current drive is the drive used to boot the computer (A if a floppy disk was used, otherwise C).

A different current drive can be selected by entering the drive specifier as a command. For example, if the current drive is A we can make the hard disk the current drive by entering:

    C:

The new prompt will be either C> or [C:\]. To change back to the floppy drive enter:

    A:

Changing the current drive makes our other commands much simpler, as we shall see later. However, making an assumption that you are working with a particular drive can also be quite dangerous; deleting everything on the current drive is quite disastrous when you discover that the default drive is C and not A as you had thought! So, when excluding the drive specifier from the command, be particularly cautious. (It is also worth noting that drive specifiers should almost always be used in batch file commands, which are described later.)

Interrupting commands

When you have entered a command the operating system immediately carries out the required action. Sometimes it is necessary to halt a command or program before it finishes naturally, either because you have selected the wrong command or because it is doing something you don't want it to do.

As a general rule you can interrupt a command by pressing the combination of keys Ctrl and Break. Use Ctrl like a Shift key; hold it down and then press Break, releasing both keys together. The same effect is usually achieved by pressing Ctrl and C. The operating system shows that you have interrupted a process by displaying '^C'.

Executable files   If a file has a BAT, CMD, COM or EXE extension then it is called an *executable file*. This means that the program or instructions it contains can be executed by typing the name of the file at the command line. There is no need to type the extension. For example, to run a disk copying program called DISKCOPY.COM or DISKCOPY.EXE it is only necessary to enter:

```
DISKCOPY
```

The system searches the current drive for any file with a suitable extension and runs it.

Order of   Sometimes there will be a conflict; the same name may have
precedence   been used for both a BAT and COM file, for example, or it may be the name of an internal DOS or OS/2 command. In such cases the operating system decides which program to run according to a strict order of precedence. Programs are selected in the following order:

■ Internal commands

■ COM files

■ EXE files

■ BAT or CMD files

This means that some care must be taken in the naming of executable files. A batch file called BACKUP.BAT, which is supposed to run the program BACKUP.COM would in fact never be run itself.

Internal and   Many commands are part of the operating system itself and
external commands are read into memory when the system is started; these are *internal* commands. Other commands - the *external* commands - are held in separate files, with a COM or EXE extension, and are only read into memory when they are needed. For example, DISKCOPY is read from the file DISKCOPY.EXE when you want to copy a disk; after the copy has been completed that part of memory is re-used by the next program.

In the case of external commands you may have to tell the operating system where to find the file by including the drive specifier.

For example, if the current drive is A and DISKCOPY.EXE is on C the command would be entered as:

```
C:DISKCOPY
```

The 'Bad command or file name' message often indicates that the location of the command must be specified.

The main reference section in Part 2 indicates whether each command is internal or external.

Syntax

Commands generally consist of more than one part. First there is the command itself, then there is the file, drive or other item to which it applies. For example, the DIR command displays the directory - a list of files - for a disk. The command is often followed by a description of the files to be listed; for example, all EXE files are listed by:

```
DIR *.EXE
```

The number of items that are allowed after the command name varies with each command. This is the *syntax* of the command.

Parameters

Many commands allow the use of *parameters*. These usually take the form of a '/' character followed by a single letter (upper or lower case). Their effect is to modify the command in some way. For example, the /P parameter of the DIR command results in the list being displayed a screenful (or 'page') at a time. It is not essential for there to be any space between the command and the parameter but it is better practice to include a space, as follows:

```
DIR *.EXE /P
```

Often a command has more than one parameter added.

Error messages

If anything is wrong with the way in which the command has been entered, the operating system responds with an error message. For DOS, the messages are illustrated by the examples:

```
Bad command or file name

File not found

File cannot be copied onto itself
```

OS/2 has a slightly different form of error message. The three errors above would be indicated in OS/2 by the messages:

```
SYS1041: The name specified is not reconized as
an internal or external command, operable
program or batch file.

SYS0002: The system cannot find the file specified

SYS0023: The file cannot be copied onto itself.
```

(The number is for reference only; Chapter 13 shows how this message can be used to get more helpful information, using the HLPMSG command.)

Such messages are usually followed by the prompt. When this happens, check the command very carefully for errors. Check that it has been typed correctly, that there are no extra or missing spaces, and that the files mentioned actually exist (if it is necessary for them to exist for the command to work). The error message should give some hint of what is causing the problem but DOS and OS/2 error messages are notoriously unhelpful.

In some circumstances (usually with a disk error) the error message is followed by a request for further action (Figure 2.4). For DOS, this takes the form:

```
Abort, Retry, Ignore, Fail?
```

You can try to rectify the error and then press the first letter of one of the options:

■ 'Abort' abandons the action altogether

■ 'Retry' attempts to repeat the command

■ 'Ignore' carries on as if nothing had gone wrong

■ 'Fail' causes the command to stop that particular action

```
C:\>copy autoexec.bat prn:

Not ready error writing device PRN
Abort, Retry, Ignore, Fail? a

C:\>dir a:


Not ready error reading drive A
Abort, Retry, Fail? f
 Volume in drive A has no label

Not ready error reading drive A
Abort, Retry, Fail? a

C:\>
```

Figure 2.4 DOS error messages

```
Session Title: OS/2 Command Prompt

    SYS0029: The system cannot write to the specified device


        Return the error to the program
        End the program
        Retry the operation
        Ignore the error and continue
```

Figure 2.5 OS/2 error messages

It is not usually wise to choose the 'Ignore' option. The 'Fail' option may result in abandoning one part of the command but trying to continue with the next activity (for example, it may try to list the next part of the directory) while 'Abort' usually halts a command altogether.

OS/2 responds with similar options:

```
Return the error to the program
End the program
Retry the operation
Ignore the error and continue
```

These are the equivalent of Fail, Abort, Retry and Ignore respectively (see Figure 2.5). A response is selected by moving the highlighting bar up and down with the ↑ and ↓ keys, and then pressing Return.

In some cases the operating system requires confirmation that it is to continue with the action:

```
Are you sure (Y/N)?
```

Press 'Y' and Return to continue or 'N' to abandon. (Use either upper or lower case letters.)

THE OS/2 PROGRAM SELECTOR

If we are to have more than one application running at a time in OS/2 then we need some way of starting and stopping programs and of moving between them. Each application that is running is termed a *session*. Access to these is through the OS/2 *Program Selector*.

If you started up with DOS then the A> or C> prompt will be displayed and there is no way of activating the Program Selector. On the other hand, if you booted up with OS/2 the [A:\] or [C:\] prompt will be displayed.

You can select the Program Selector at any time by pressing Ctrl-Esc (press and hold Ctrl, then press Esc). The Program Selector menu is displayed. At its simplest it takes the form of a list of options (Figure 2.6); some implementations of OS/2 will provide more sophisticated displays but their use is

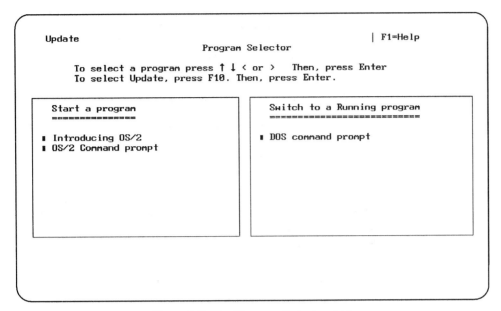

```
  Update                                              | F1=Help
                        Program Selector

        To select a program press ↑ ↓ < or >   Then, press Enter
        To select Update, press F10. Then, press Enter.

   ┌─────────────────────────────────┐   ┌─────────────────────────────────┐
   │  Start a program                │   │  Switch to a Running program    │
   │  ═══════════════                │   │  ═══════════════════════════    │
   │                                 │   │                                 │
   │  ▪ Introducing OS/2             │   │  ▪ DOS command prompt           │
   │  ▪ OS/2 Command prompt          │   │                                 │
   │                                 │   │                                 │
   │                                 │   │                                 │
   │                                 │   │                                 │
   │                                 │   │                                 │
   │                                 │   │                                 │
   └─────────────────────────────────┘   └─────────────────────────────────┘
```

Figure 2.6 The Program Selector menu

similar. In such cases you can usually press function key F1 to get additional on-screen help.

The display is in two parts. On the left is a list headed 'Start a Program'. These options are used to run a particular program or start up a new OS/2 session. On the right are the programs that are already running. There is always one called 'DOS Command Prompt'. This is the real mode application. You can never have more than one real mode application and this application will always exist.

Any new applications will be listed below this as they are started.

SELECTING OPTIONS

You can select any option from the Program Selector by moving through the list with the ↑ and ↓ keys and pressing Return when the required option is highlighted.

The real mode option

If you select the real mode option the DOS A> or C> prompt is displayed. You are then free to enter normal DOS 3.3 commands or run any DOS application. At any time you can get back to the Program Selector by pressing Ctrl-Esc (even if you have left the DOS application running). When you next select the real mode option the screen will be as you left it - if there was an application running, it will not have carried on updating while you were away.

Protected mode options

To start your first protected mode option, highlight 'OS/2 Command Prompt' and press Return. The OS/2 prompt is displayed. You can enter any OS/2 commands or run an OS/2 application. As soon as you have set the OS/2 program running you can jump back to the Program Selector by pressing Ctrl-Esc. The new session will have been added to the list. If you left the session still displaying the prompt, the new session will be listed as 'OS/2 Command Prompt'.

You can add other applications to the list on the left. Press function key F10 and then Return. Four options are provided. Select one of these by highlighting the option with the ↑ and ↓ keys, then press Return. The first option lets you add a new item to the list; the second deletes an item; the third changes the information stored about these items; and the fourth redisplays the program selector.

You can now start another OS/2 application, enter more OS/2 commands (in a new OS/2 session) or select an existing option. The number of OS/2 sessions that can co-exist is limited only by the speed of the machine you are using and how slow you are prepared to let the overall system become.

Switching between sessions

If there are a number of sessions active we need to jump from one to another to see how far our applications have got or to transfer data between them.

There are two basic methods of switching from one session to another:

■ Press Ctrl-Esc to return to the Program Selector, then highlight the option and press Return.

■ Press Alt-Esc to jump straight to the next session in the list.

The Alt-Esc option is very useful for cycling through the sessions. Each time you press this combination you will get a new display. Pressing Alt-Esc in the last protected mode application takes you back to the DOS real mode session.

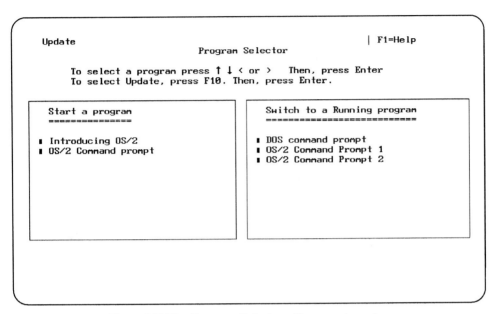

```
 Update                                          | F1=Help
                         Program Selector
       To select a program press ↑ ↓ < or >   Then, press Enter
       To select Update, press F10. Then, press Enter.

  ┌──────────────────────────────┐  ┌──────────────────────────────┐
  │  Start a program             │  │  Switch to a Running program │
  │  ===============             │  │  ============================│
  │                              │  │                              │
  │  ▪ Introducing OS/2          │  │  ▪ DOS command prompt        │
  │  ▪ OS/2 Command prompt       │  │  ▪ OS/2 Command Prompt 1     │
  │                              │  │  ▪ OS/2 Command Prompt 2     │
  │                              │  │                              │
  │                              │  │                              │
  │                              │  │                              │
  │                              │  │                              │
  │                              │  │                              │
  └──────────────────────────────┘  └──────────────────────────────┘
```

Figure 2.7 The Program Selector with several sessions

ENDING A SESSION

Remembering that you can have more than one protected mode session running, and that one or more of these applications will eventually terminate, the result will be that there will be more than one 'OS/2 Command Prompt' listed in the list. It doesn't matter which is which; they all behave identically.

When you have a spare session there are two options: use it to run another application or close it down. To close down a session, select the a running 'OS/2 Command Prompt' option and, at the OS/2 prompt, enter the command:

    EXIT

Do not forget to press Return. You are immediately returned to the Program Selector and the item will have been deleted from the list.

It is good practice to always close down all applications before switching off the machine or resetting it. Never leave an application running, since there is a danger that any data you were working on will be corrupted.

Remember that when the system is reset all sessions are lost.

We are now ready to look at the way in which files are stored on disk.

3. *Working with Disks*

Before any disk can store data it must be prepared for use. This preparation may involve a number of stages, depending on the type of disk. It is also essential to make copies of all important floppy disks, such as the original system disks and any disks containing application programs. This chapter describes these various operations.

DISK STRUCTURE

A disk is simply a flat surface liberally covered with magnetic material that is capable of storing information. A new disk has no structure to its surface, however. Before it can be used the operating system needs to mark out the areas that are to be used for storing files.

The disk drive has a read/write head (rather like the head on a tape recorder) that sits just above the surface of the disk. As the disk spins a circular *track* of data passes underneath the head; any data can be read from the track or new data written onto it. The drive head can move in towards the centre or out to the edge of the disk but there are only a limited number of positions at which it can read data. Therefore, each disk has a fixed number of tracks; in the case of a floppy disk this is either 40 or 80, while hard disks will have several hundred tracks (Figure 3.1).

These tracks have to be identified and cleared of any data before new files can be transferred to them; this process is known as *formatting*.

Terminology
There is a great deal of jargon associated with disk layouts. Although it is not essential to be fully conversant with all of these names it helps to have an idea of what some of them mean, especially those that are likely to crop up in the operating system messages.

We have already seen that each disk can have a number of tracks, marked out as a series of concentric circles. The outermost track is labelled as track 0. These tracks are usually created on both *sides* of the disk; although older computers may have *single-sided drives*, most new computers are fitted with *double-sided drives*, which have read/write

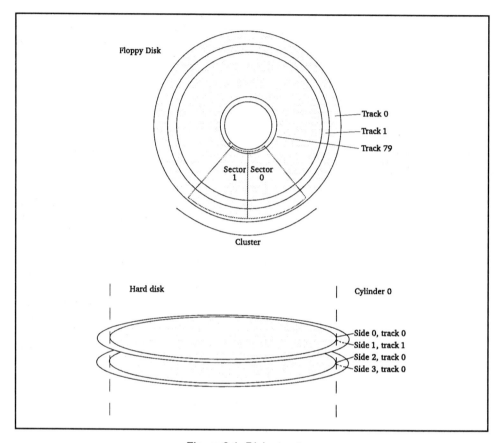

Figure 3.1 Disk structure

heads on both sides of the disk. (Note that when there is more than one side the heads always move in unison, so data may be read first from one side and then from the other, without moving the heads. For this reason, data is always stored a track at a time, on alternate sides of a disk.)

While floppy disks only have two sides, hard disks (or *fixed disks* or *Winchesters* as they are sometimes called) generally consist of more than one actual disk, with the disks placed one above the other. The separate disks are called *platters*. The most common hard disks have two platters and therefore four sides, with four read-write heads that all move in unison. All tracks with the same number (which are physically one above the other) are grouped together to form a *cylinder*.

For convenience, each track is divided up into a number of sections of data, called *sectors*. The operating system usually reads and writes data from a number of sectors at a time; these groups of consecutive sectors (usually two or four) are referred to as *clusters*.

All of these terms are used by the operating system, particularly in its error messages.

THE FLOPPY DISK FORMAT COMMAND

The way in which disks are prepared depends on whether they are floppy disks or hard disks. We will look first at the procedure for floppy disks.

Formatting of floppy disks is done by the *FORMAT* command. This is an external command; if formatting on a floppy disk system, the FORMAT program will be found on the main operating system disk. Make sure that this disk is *write-protected* before you start; that is, the notch on the side of a 5¼" floppy disk should be covered or you should be able to see through the hole at the bottom of a 3½" disk (see Figure 3.2). When a disk is write-protected, no changes can be made to it, so it is safe from accidental damage.

Load the disk and type the command:

```
FORMAT A:
```

The 'A:' indicates that it is the disk in drive A, the main floppy drive, that is to be formatted. (Note that on some older machines, such as the original Apricot Xen, drive A is the hard disk; check that drive A on your machine is the floppy drive, otherwise the results can be quite disastrous!)

Although you can enter the command without a drive specifier it is not a good idea to do so, as you may inadvertently format the wrong disk.

Enter the command by pressing Return. If the FORMAT program cannot be found an error message is displayed. Replace the disk with a different one from the set of originals. In the case of DOS you can repeat the command by pressing

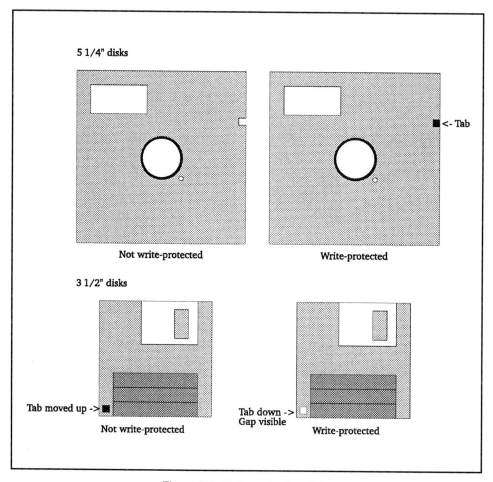

Figure 3.2 Write-protecting disks

function key F3 and Return. For OS/2 you must select 'Retry the operation' from the menu that is displayed.

You are instructed to load a new 'diskette' (that is, a floppy disk) and press 'Enter' (another name for the Return Key); see Figure 3.3. Make sure, before you start, that the disk is completely blank or redundant. Formatting is a drastic process, which writes to every sector of the disk and therefore destroys any data that is already there. (To check whether a disk is actually empty, use the DIR command described in the next chapter.) To interrupt the program press Ctrl-Break.

```
[C:\]format a:
Insert a new diskette for drive A:
and press ENTER when ready

Formatting has been completed.

Enter up to 11 characters for the volume label,
or press Enter for no volume lable. DATADISK

    1457664 bytes total disk space
    1457664 bytes available on disk

Format another (Y/N)?n
[C:\]
```

Figure 3.3 The FORMAT command

Once you have pressed Return the formatting process begins and, although it can be interrupted, there is no point doing so. All of the most important information, detailing the files stored on the disk and their locations, is stored on track 0, which is the first track to be formatted. The data on a partially-formatted disk is almost impossible to recover.

Formatting takes some time, so be patient. As a general rule the tracks or cylinders are counted through as they are formatted, though the precise way in which the messages are displayed varies from one implementation of the operating system to another.

Once the disk has been formatted you are asked a question similar to:

```
Format another diskette (Y/N)?
```

The precise message varies slightly from one version of DOS to another, and is different again for OS/2. Press 'Y' to repeat the process with another disk or 'N' to end the program; then press Return.

It is generally a good idea to format all new disks in one go. This avoids confusion later over which disks have been formatted and also saves the frustration of discovering that you have no usable disk at some critical point in an application.

The disk is now completely blank and ready for storing programs and data.

Bad sectors

Very occasionally, FORMAT will discover a part of the disk which is unusable, due to some imperfection in the disk surface. Since the operating system always works in terms of complete sectors, this means that the entire sector containing the imperfection is of no use, no matter how small it may be. These are called *bad sectors*, and while they may be permissable on hard disks they are not acceptable on floppies. The format process will fail, with a suitable message. Sometimes the error is so minor that if you try reformatting the disk the slight variations in positioning of the head will bypass the fault and the disk will format correctly. If the problem recurs, however, the disk is obviously unsafe for use and should be discarded.

If a series of disks refuse to format it is more likely to be a drive fault, rather than disk failure, so the drive should be serviced.

System disks

As described earlier, if you want to start up the computer from floppy disk then you must use a *system disk*.

A system disk is one that has the special system files on it. These files have to be copied in a special way and although it is possible to add them later to a completely blank disk (see SYS in Chapter 7) it is usual to include them as part of the formatting process.

To prepare a new system disk enter the command:

```
FORMAT A: /S
```

Remember to leave spaces between the three parts of the command.

This command instructs the operating system to format the disk and then copy across the system files. Such a disk can be used to boot up the computer. If you have a hard disk machine you will generally start up from the hard disk, so most floppy disks will be non-system disks.

You can check whether or not a disk is a system disk using the CHKDSK command (see Chapter 7).

PREPARING HARD DISKS

The procedures for hard disks are somewhat more complex. Whereas floppy disks may only take files created by a single operating system, hard disks, because of their high capacity, may be divided up into a number of different areas, either so that different operating systems can be used or to make it easier to handle such vast quantities of data.

Each of these areas can be formatted in a different way. Before any subdivisions can be made, however, the entire hard disk must be prepared for use. The procedures for getting a hard disk up and running therefore fall into three stages:

1. Format the entire hard disk.

2. Divide the disk into separate areas.

3. Format each individual area.

These three operations must be carried out in strict sequence, as described below.

THE HARD FORMAT PROGRAM

The first stage - that of formatting the entire hard disk - is known as a *hard format* or *low-level format*. During a hard format the tracks are marked out on the disk, data is written to every sector and any existing data is destroyed. Hard formatting is rarely done more than once.

For obvious reasons, the preparation of the hard disk must be done from programs on floppy disk. The system should therefore be booted from floppy disk, using the original system disk.

As soon as the A> or [A:\] prompt is displayed you can format the hard disk. Before you begin, make absolutely certain that there is nothing of any importance on the hard disk. Once

```
C:>hdformat

DISK FORMAT UTILITY
This routine erases all data
Are you sure you want this?
(Y)es or (N)o


Head: 1 Cylinder: 19
```

Figure 3.4 The HDFORMAT command

you start formatting there is no way of saving anything off the disk. Any programs put there by your dealer will be lost, for instance. Indeed, most dealers and manufacturers format their hard disks before they are sent out, so this stage may never be necessary. Unless you are certain that the disk requires formatting you should skip this section.

The command to format the entire disk varies from one machine to another, but the principles are the same. Suppose, for example, that the program is *HDFORMAT*. This program is activated as follows:

```
HDFORMAT
```

Once the program has been loaded into memory a dire warning is displayed (Figure 3.4):

```
This routine erases all data
Are you sure you want this?
(Y)es or (N)o
```

Only if you are absolutely sure that the hard disk does not contain unrecoverable files should you press 'Y' and Return.

Formatting a hard disk takes several minutes, but the cylinders are counted through as they are formatted.

Bad sectors

When the format program discovers bad sectors - and there are always a few on hard disks - it repeats the format process on that sector several times before giving up and moving on to the next one.

When the format is complete the program displays details of the amount of space available, including the number of bad sectors. Anything up to 1% in bad sectors is acceptable (about 320K on a 32M hard disk). It is rare to find this amount, however, and anything greater should certainly be a cause for concern. Hard disks almost always have some bad sectors because it is not economically viable to produce perfect hard disks.

Bad sectors are marked as such by the hard format program so that they can never be used to store data. You can always check the number of bad sectors with the CHKDSK command, described in Chapter 7.

CREATING PARTITIONS

Under DOS 3.3 and OS/2 the hard disk can be split into several *partitions*. Each partition consists of a group of consecutive cylinders. There may be a single partition, covering the whole disk, or a number of partitions of varying sizes.

Each partition is treated as if it were a separate disk. Therefore the partitions do not all have to use the same operating system. For example, you could have one partition for OS/2 and another for DOS 3.3, though there would be little point. It is more likely that you would use part of the disk for a totally different operating system, such as Xenix.

The first partition that is created is called the *primary partition*. In addition you may have one or more *extended partitions*.

Logical drives

The partitions on the hard disk are treated as totally separate drives.

The primary partition is automatically labelled as drive C. Each extended partition can be further subdivided into more than one *logical drive*, if required. These extra drives are labelled from D onwards.

```
IBM Personal Computer
Fixed Disk Setup Program Version 3.30
(C)Copyright IBM Corp. 1983,1987

FDISK Options

Current Fixed Disk Drive: 1

Choose one of the following:

        1. Create DOS partition
        2. Change Active Partition
        3. Delete DOS partition
        4. Display Partition Information


Enter choice: [1]
```

Figure 3.5 The FDISK main menu

```
Create DOS Partition

Current Fixed Disk Drive: 1


        1. Create Primary DOS partition
        2. Create Extended DOS partition
        3. Create logical DOS drive(s) in
             the Extended DOS partition


Enter choice: [1]



Press ESC to return to FDISK Options
```

Figure 3.6 Creating a partition

To the system they are logically different even though they are on the same physical drive. (This is similar to the situation with a single-floppy system, where the floppy drive can be treated as two distinct logical drives.)

The FDISK command

The partitions and logical drives are set up by the *FDISK* command, which is again to be found on the original floppy disk. FDISK is run simply by entering the command:

```
FDISK
```

Unlike the other commands we have encountered so far, FDISK is based on a menu system (Figure 3.5).

Note that the way in which FDISK operates may vary from one implementation to another.

Select option 1 to create a primary DOS partition (Figure 3.6). The program shows you how much space there is on the disk that is yet to be allocated to partitions. You must now enter the number of cylinders required for the primary partition. (To calculate the capacity of each cylinder divide the total disk capacity by the number of cylinders; for example, a 32M disk with 305 cylinders has 110K per cylinder.) The primary partition cannot be larger than 32M.

FDISK suggests using the maximum number of cylinders; to accept this default just press Return. Otherwise, enter a new value. Unless your hard disk is more than 32M, or you want to use more than one operating system, it is probably best to have just a single partition.

The partitioning process is over very quickly. In fact, all FDISK does is store the necessary information on a particular part of the disk dedicated to this purpose. When this is done the details of the partitions created so far are displayed; press Esc to return to the menu.

If there is any space left on the disk you may repeat the process, by selecting option 1 again, to set up an extended partition. Note that DOS 3.3 and OS/2 allow up to four partitions; earlier versions of DOS were not so generous. However, there is generally little point in having more than two partitions. Extended partitions can be any size.

Logical drives

The program offers you the opportunity to set up logical drives for any extended partitions. The extended partition can be further subdivided, in much the same way as the disk was originally partitioned, with each logical drive taking up a specific number of cylinders. At this stage the logical drives are labelled D, E and so on. Each logical drive cannot exceed 32M in size.

Before allocating logical drives it is a good idea to try and decide what the drives will be used for and roughly what proportion of the disk is needed for each.

Active partitions

Before a partition can be used it must be made *active*. All new partitions are *non-active*. Active partitions are those that can be accessed; DOS and OS/2 allow only two active partitions at any time.

Select option 2 from the FDISK main menu to make each partition active.

Other FDISK options

You cannot change partitions or logical drives except by deleting them and starting again (using option 3). When you do so, all existing data is lost. At any time you can use FDISK to look at the way in which the disk can be partitioned (option 4).

The full FDISK options are shown in Chapter 5.

Press Esc to leave the FDISK main menu; the system is automatically rebooted when you leave the program.

FORMATTING PARTITIONS

Before you can use any of the new partitions they must be formatted. This is a *high-level format*, which simply marks out the sectors on each track. It does not write to every byte of the disk, as the hard format program does.

In this case the same FORMAT command is used as for floppy disks. (Note that FORMAT, when used on floppy disks, performs both a low-level and high-level format.) The syntax of the command is the same:

```
FORMAT C: /S
```

This command formats the primary partition and copies the system files onto it. When the formatting has been completed the system can be booted from the hard disk.

In a similar way you must format each of the logical drives in the other active partition (if there is one).

The disk is now ready to accept program and data files. As a general rule, the original disks will include an installation program to copy on all the other operating system programs and associated files. The procedure varies from one machine to another, though it should be fully documented in the computer's User Manual. The installation should set up the disk so that any command typed at the C prompt is automatically located, no matter where it may have been stored. If this is not the case (that is, the commands described below result in a 'Bad command' message) then you will have to set up the disk yourself using the PATH command described in Chapter 13.

THE VOLUME LABEL

All disks - floppy and hard - have a *volume label*. This is a name, up to 11 characters long, used to identify the disk. It is particularly useful for floppy disks, where it provides a quick means of checking whether or not a disk is the one required. For example, you may have two sets of data files with the same names (such as those created by a payroll package); the volume label can be used to distinguish between the sets of data in those cases where the paper labels stuck on the disks are ambiguous. Its use for the hard disk is somewhat limited.

The volume label is shown at the top of all directory listings.

Labels when formatting

There are two ways of giving a disk a label. The first is to add the /V parameter to the command line when formatting:

```
FORMAT A: /V
```

In this case, formatting concludes with the message:

```
Volume label (11 characters, ENTER for none)?
```

The name can be up to eleven characters long, using the same characters as for filenames, with no spaces. Press Return on its own if you do not want to give the disk a volume label. Try to select a label that tells you something about the contents of the disk (such as PAYROLL1989 or LETTERS_2).

The LABEL command

The disk volume name can be changed later using the LABEL command. To change the label on the disk in the current drive, enter:

    LABEL

If the A> or [A:\] prompt is displayed the current label of the disk in drive A is displayed and you are prompted for a new name. Type the new name and press Return.

Press Return on its own to delete the label altogether. In this case you are asked for confirmation that this is really what you want to do:

    Delete current volume label (Y/N)?

Press 'Y' and Return to delete the label.

To change the label of a disk in a particular drive (and to be certain that the current drive is the one you think it is) enter the command in the form:

    LABEL A:

To bypass the messages altogether (except when deleting the label), include the name in the command:

    LABEL A:PAYROLL1989

There must be no space between the drive specifier and the label.

The VOL command

You can display the volume label of any disk at any time with the *VOL* command. To show the volume label of the current drive (for example, drive A) enter:

    VOL

The operating system responds with:

```
Volume in drive A is PAYROLL1989
```

or:

```
Volume in drive A has no label
```

To identify the disk in a particular drive enter:

```
VOL C:
```

OS/2 offers an enhancement, under which the labels of more than one disk can be displayed by a single command:

```
VOL A: C:
```

The greatest use of this command is in batch files, some examples of which are given later.

COPYING DISKS

Floppy disks are generally of a very high quality (especially if you are prepared to spend a little more by buying branded disks with a 'lifetime guarantee'). Even so, floppy disks are a very fragile medium and susceptible to damage at any time. However high the quality, there is always a danger that a disk will become corrupt for no apparent reason, no matter how careful you have been. For this reason it is important to always take *backup copies* of floppy disks.

In particular, you should always make backups of any original disks (such as the original system disks and those of any application programs). You should do this even if you have copied all the information onto the hard disk. Sooner or later the hard disk will develop problems; the average time before a major fault occurs is generally estimated as about three years. When this happens you need to be sure you can recover all programs from floppy disk.

The program to copy floppy disks is called DISKCOPY and is put into effect with the command:

```
DISKCOPY
```

If the DISKCOPY.EXE (or possibly DISKCOPY.COM) program is not on the current drive you may have to include the drive specifier:

```
A:DISKCOPY
```

Once the program has been loaded into memory, it responds with the request:

```
Enter drive letter for source
```

(There will be some variations in these messages, depending on the particular version of DISKCOPY that is being used.) The *source* disk is the disk to be copied. Usually this is drive A. Type 'A' and Return. The program continues with:

```
Enter drive letter for target
```

The *target* disk is the disk on which the copy is to be made. On a double-floppy system this will usually be drive B (the right-hand drive); on a single-floppy system you must use drive A again. Type the drive letter and press Return.

Some versions of DISKCOPY insist on the drives being specified in the command, as follows:

```
DISKCOPY A: A:
```

The program now asks for the disk (or disks) to be loaded in the drive:

```
Insert source diskette in drive A

Insert target diskette in drive B

Press any key when ready
```

The request for drive B will be absent if copying from A to A.

Load the original disk in drive A, having first ensured that it is write-protected and, on a double-drive computer, a redundant or blank disk in drive B.

DISKCOPY now copies the contents of part of the disk into memory. It cannot perform the copy in a single operation because the memory available to it is not generally sufficient.

```
[C:\]diskcopy a: b:

Insert the source diskette in drive A:

Insert the target diskette in drive B:

Press Enter to continue

Copying 80 tracks
9 sectors per track, 2 side(s).

Formatting while copying

Copy has ended.
Copy another diskette (Y/N)?  n

[C:\]
```

Figure 3.7 Copying disks using two drives

On a double-drive system this data is transferred to the new disk in drive B, and the process is repeated until all of the disk has been copied.

If the new disk has not been formatted or is from another system then it is automatically formatted as part of the copying process (Figure 3.7).

If there is anything wrong with either disk the program will stop with a suitable warning message.

Single-drive systems

On single-drive systems you are asked to load the target disk in drive A and press any key to continue. When the first part of the disk has been copied you are asked to load the source disk again, and so it continues until all of the disk has been transferred (Figure 3.8). Take great care when copying on a single drive; the program will not be able to tell if you get the disks muddled up.

Completing the copy

In both cases, you are asked if you want to copy another disk. Enter 'Y' to repeat the process with another disk or 'N' to end the program.

```
[C:\]diskcopy a: a:

Insert the source diskette in drive A:

Press Enter to continue

Copying 80 tracks
9 sectors per track, 2 side(s).

Insert TARGET diskette in drive A:

Press any key when ready . . .

Insert SOURCE diskette in drive A:

Press any key when ready . . .

Insert TARGET diskette in drive A:

Press any key when ready . . .

Insert SOURCE diskette in drive A:

Press any key when ready . . .
```

Figure 3.8 Copying disks using a single drive

Note that DISKCOPY produces a complete replica of the original. The copy will only be a system disk if the original contained the system files. All data will be stored in the same order and in the same locations. Any corrupt data is also copied across without modification. Sometimes it can be more useful to copy on a file-by-file basis (see XCOPY in Chapter 5).

You can specify the drives to be used for copying by including the drive specifiers in the original command line:

DISKCOPY A: B: (double-drive systems)

DISKCOPY A: A: (single-drive systems)

The first parameter specifies the source disk, the second identifies the target.

When you have formatted some blank floppy disks, made copies of all original disks and partitioned the hard disk, you are ready to start setting up directories and working with files.

4. *Using Directories*

The number of files stored on any disk rapidly escalates, especially if it is a hard disk. These files would become unmanageable if we did not have some method of subdividing them.

This chapter looks at the operating system's *sub-directories*, how they are created, deleted and otherwise managed, and how they affect the syntax of all commands.

THE ROOT DIRECTORY

The operating system keeps track of what is held on disk by storing details of files in the *directory*. Each disk has one main directory, called the *root directory*. This directory is created when the disk is formatted.

The directory can be listed on screen with the DIR command. To list the directory of the disk in the current drive, enter the command:

```
DIR
```

The directory begins with the volume label and the name of the directory (Figure 4.1). For example, 'A:\' indicates that it is the root directory of drive A.

This is followed by a list of all the files in the directory. For each file there are five items. The first and second columns hold the filename and extension (padded with spaces if necessary). The third column shows the size of the file in bytes.

The last two columns list the date and time at which the file was created or last changed. Every time you make a change to a file, no matter how small, the date and time are updated. The date may be in either British format (day then month) or American format (month before day), depending on how the system has been customised. (Details of how to change this are given in Chapter 13.) Similarly the time may use either the 12-hour clock (with an 'a' or 'p' to indicate 'a.m.' or 'p.m.' respectively) or the 24-hour clock.

```
A>dir

 Volume in drive A is GROWLOG
 Directory of  A:\

GLPSFG3 EXE    79152   3-04-89  12:00p
GLSET9   EXE    54240   3-04-89  12:00p
GLRDGTR3 EXE    75504   3-04-89  12:00p
GLDLMAN3 EXE    76304   3-04-89  12:00p
GLEDIT3  EXE    55120   3-04-89  12:00p
GLLIST3  EXE    55040   3-04-89  12:00p
GLPLOT3  EXE    21936   3-04-89  12:00p
GROWLOG  BAT       28   4-04-89   9:55p
MULTI    EXE    33917  21-07-88   6:01p
READ     ME      3200  21-07-88   6:01p
        10 File(s)    999424 bytes free

A>
```

Figure 4.1 The root directory

At the bottom of the list are the number of files in the directory and the amount of free space left on disk.

To list the directory of any disk other than the current drive, add the drive specifier to the command:

    DIR C:

This command lists the directory of drive C.

Listing by page

Frequently, the directory is so long that it scrolls up over the top of the screen. There are two ways of listing the directory a section at a time. The first is to enter the command, then press Ctrl and S (or Ctrl and NumLock) as the directory scrolls up. This combination of keys interrupts most processes and, in the case of the directory, makes it pause. The listing can be resumed by pressing any other key.

However, this method is a bit hit and miss. Though useful for those occasions when you realise that a display is about to disappear, there is another, more certain method. Adding /P

```
ABIOS      SYS         49  10-21-87   12:00p
ANSICALL   DLL       3637  10-21-87   12:00p
BKSCALLS   DLL       5704  10-21-87   12:00p
BMSCALLS   DLL       2576  10-21-87   12:00p
BVSCALLS   DLL      31744  10-21-87   12:00p
CLOCK01    SYS       2762  10-21-87   12:00p
CLOCK02    SYS       3188  10-21-87   12:00p
CMD        EXE      57648  10-21-87   12:00p
COMMAND    COM      25564  10-21-87   12:00p
CONFIG     SYS         90  10-21-87   12:00p
COUNTRY    SYS      14632  10-21-87   12:00p
CPISPFPC   DLL     108598  10-21-87   12:00p
DISK01     SYS      18616  10-21-87   12:00p
DISK02     SYS      20329  10-21-87   12:00p
DOSCALL1   DLL       8709  10-21-87   12:00p
DMPC       EXE       2472  10-21-87   12:00p
DTM        DLL       2222  10-21-87   12:00p
F80000     BIO       9216  10-21-87   12:00p
F80100     BIO       8704  10-21-87   12:00p
FC0400     BIO       6656  10-21-87   12:00p
FC0500     BIO       9216  10-21-87   12:00p
FORMATS    TBL        590  10-21-87   12:00p
HARDERR    EXE      16288  10-21-87   12:00p
Press any key when ready . . .
```

Figure 4.2 Listing the directory by pages

to the command results in the directory being listed a 'page' at a time, as follows:

    DIR A: /P

The directory of the floppy disk is listed until it fills the screen, at which point it pauses with a message to press any key to continue (Figure 4.2).

Wide listings

Sometimes we want just a list of files and are not too concerned about the other details. In this case we can get a 'wide' listing of the directory by adding the /W parameter to the command:

    DIR A: /W

This results in a list with the names and extensions of five files in each row (Figure 4.3).

Listing groups of files

The ambiguous file specifications described earlier can help to reduce the size of a directory listing. For instance, all files on the current drive with a COM extension can be listed with:

```
[C:\]dir a: /w

 Volume in drive A has no label.
 Directory of  A:\

ABIOS     SYS   ANSICALL DLL   BKSCALLS DLL   BMSCALLS DLL   BVSCALLS DLL
CLOCK01   SYS   CLOCK02  SYS   CMD      EXE   COMMAND  COM   CONFIG   SYS
COUNTRY   SYS   CPISPFPC DLL   DISK01   SYS   DISK02   SYS   DOSCALL1 DLL
DMPC      EXE   DTM      DLL   F80000   BIO   F80100   BIO   FC0400   BIO
FC0500    BIO   FORMATS  TBL   HARDERR  EXE   ISPD     MSG   ISPM     MSG
KBD01     SYS   KBD02    SYS   KBDCALLS DLL   KEYBOARD DCP   MONCALLS DLL
MOUCALLS  DLL   MSG      DLL   NLS      DLL   OSO001   MSG   PRINT01  SYS
PRINT02   SYS   QUECALLS DLL   SCREEN01 SYS   SCREEN02 SYS   SESMGR   DLL
SHELL11F  AIF   SHELL11F AII   SHELL11F CNF   SHELL11F EXE   SHELL11F LIB
SHELL11F  PRO   SPOOLCP  DLL   STXTDMPC DLL   SWAPPER  EXE   VIOCALLS DLL
VIOTBL    DCP   4201     DCP   5202     DCP
       53 File(s)    366592 bytes free

[C:\]
```

Figure 4.3 A wide directory listing

```
DIR *.COM
```

A wide listing of all files on drive C with names that start with 'LET' can be displayed with:

```
DIR C:LET*.* /W
```

All files that have no extension are listed with:

```
DIR *.
```

There is also a special case, that applies to the DIR command only:

```
DIR *
```

This command lists *all* files, regardless of whether or not they have an extension.

You can check for the existence of a particular file by specifying the file directly:

```
DIR C:LETTER.DOC
```

```
[C:\]dir *.bat a:*.bat c:con*.*

 Volume in drive C has no label.
 Directory of  C:\

AUTOEXEC BAT        99   3-29-89    4:06p
CONFIG   BAT        84   3-16-89    5:24p
              4 File(s)     1433600 bytes free


 Volume in drive A has no label.
 Directory of  A:\

AUTOEXEC BAT        99   3-29-89    4:06p
              1 File(s)    365056 bytes free


 Volume in drive C has no label.
 Directory of  C:\

CONT          <DIR>       2-22-89    3:40p
CONFIG   BAT        84   3-16-89    5:24p
         2 File(s)   1433600 bytes free
```

Figure 4.4 OS/2 Multiple directory listings

If LETTER.DOC does not exist in the directory of drive C, or if any other directory command does not find any matching files, the volume label is followed by the message:

```
File not found
```

Other combinations are available when sub-directories are introduced, as described below.

Note that any attempt to read the directory of an unformatted disk results in a 'Sector not found' message. A similar message is displayed if the drive is empty. In such cases press 'A' to abort the command.

OS/2 enhancements

OS/2 introduces a new enhancement to the DIR command, allowing more than one file specification on the command line. For example:

```
DIR *.BAT A:*.BAT C:CON*.*
```

In this case we would get three consecutive listings: all the files with a BAT extension on both the current drive and drive

Disk type	Capacity	Entries in root directory
Single-sided, double-density, 8 sectors/track	160K	64
Double-sided, double-density, 8 sectors/track	320K	112
Single-sided, double-density, 9 sectors/track	180K	64
Double-sided, double-density, 9 sectors/track	360K	112
Quad density	720K	224
Hard disks	>10M	No practical limit

Figure 4.5 Disk capacities

A, and all files on drive C beginning with 'CON' (see Figure 4.4). If the specifications refer to the same directory the listings are amalgamated into a single list.

DISK CAPACITY   The total capacity of a disk depends on its type. Those with the lowest capacity are the *double density* disks; 5¼" disks have a capacity of 360K while similar 3½" disks hold 720K. *High density* or *quad density* disks hold 1.2M (5¼") or 1.44M (3½"). Hard disks are generally named according to their capacity (10M, 20M, 32M etc.).

A very small amount of space is taken up by the directory and related information. However, for system disks the space used by the system files can be quite substantial. The capacities of various disk formats are shown in Figure 4.5.

Note that in the case of floppy disks space is always used in units of 2048 bytes, no matter how small the file may be. For example, adding a 100-byte file to a disk reduces the bytes free by 2048, even though the file size is shown as 100. This is because the operating system always works a cluster at a time. For hard disks the cluster size may vary.

The way in which disk space is currently allocated (including system files, bad sectors, etc.) can be found with the CHKDSK command described in Chapter 7.

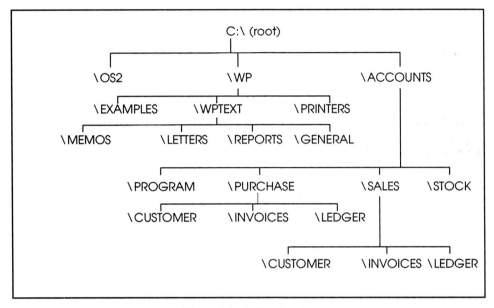

Figure 4.6 A directory tree

SUB-DIRECTORIES

There is a limit to the number of entries the root directory can hold. This is because the amount of space allocated to the directory is fixed when the disk is formatted. For most floppy disks the number of entries cannot exceed 112; the number varies for other disk formats (Figure 4.5).

Very long directories also cause problems because it is difficult to locate a particular file and keep the directory in good order.

Clearly 112 entries is insufficient for a high density disk, let alone a hard disk. For this reason the concept of *sub-directories* was introduced in DOS 2.00. A sub-directory is simply another directory containing a collection of files in the same way as the root directory. The sub-directory is given a name which is stored as an entry in the root directory.

Each sub-directory may, in turn, contain other sub-directories; these can hold further levels of sub-directory, and

```
[C:\]dir c:

 Volume in drive C has no label.
 Directory of  C:\

COMMAND  COM     25564  21-10-87   12:00p
OS2             <DIR>    4-04-89    9:46p
ACCOUNTS        <DIR>    4-04-89    9:49p
WP              <DIR>    2-03-90    2:17a
CONFIG   SYS       59    4-04-89    8:44p
AUTOEXEC BAT       56    4-04-89    9:33p
COUNTRY  SYS    11254   24-07-87   12:00a
KEYBOARD SYS    19735   24-07-87   12:00a
     8 File(s)   41323008 bytes free

[C:\]
```

Figure 4.7 An example hard disk directory

so on. In this way the root directory and sub-directories form a *directory tree*, as illustrated in Figure 4.6.

In the example, the root directory includes an \OS2 sub-directory, which contains all of the operating system's external command files, as well as various other information relating to the operating system. (On hard disk systems that only have DOS 3.3 there will usually be a \DOS or \MSDOS sub-directory for similar files.) The root directory in the example also contains two other sub-directories, \WP and \ACCOUNTS. In practice, hard disks soon fill up with many more sub-directories. The root directory also contains a number of other files, as illustrated by the listing in Figure 4.7.

Any sub-directories in the directory listing are identified by '<DIR>' in the column where the file size is usually listed.

Normally we want to keep the root directory as uncluttered as possible, so only use it to store files which really cannot go anywhere else. In the example, the only files left in the root directory are those that are needed when the system is first started up and others which are used to run the application programs. Anything that is not essential has been moved into other sub-directories.

For this approach to be a success it is necessary to set up the system to make the best of these conventions; this is done with the procedures outlined in Chapters 13 (System Customisation) and 16 (Introduction to Batch Files).

The \WP sub-directory contains all the files needed for a word-processing program. In addition, it has three sub-directories of its own:

\EXAMPLES   Example text files

\WPTEXT   A sub-directory for storing all the user's text files

\PRINTERS   Files needed to set up various printers

\WPTEXT is itself further subdivided. It holds a number of template files, used as the basis for any new documents, and a number of self-explanatory sub-directories to hold the documents that have already been created.

In a similar fashion, \ACCOUNTS is further divided to provide sub-directories for different aspects of the accounts data.

There is no specific limit to the number of directory levels, though more than about four levels tends to become unpractical for most applications and most of the time it is better to stick to a single level.

In fact, a sub-directory is simply a special type of file, which has a structure that is identical to the root directory. For this reason, there is no theoretical limit to the length of a sub-directory; it can have as many entries as we like. In practice, however, it makes sense to keep each directory to a sensible size, otherwise file-handling can become rather cumbersome.

As a general rule each application is given its own directory and the data it creates will either be in a sub-directory of this or will be in another sub-directory of the root directory. Often these sub-directories are automatically created for you as part of an application's installation process.

Some programs - such as desktop publishing packages - create large numbers of data files for each particular application; in these cases it is worth setting up a sub-directory for each individual project that uses the package (for example, for each publication).

Sub-directory names

The same rules are applied to the naming of sub-directories as to files; the main part of the name can be up to eight characters long and there is an optional extension of up to three characters. In fact, the extension is rarely used in sub-directory names. As for filenames, it is better to stick to numbers and letters, and there must be no spaces. Since sub-directories also have an entry in another directory, they cannot have the same name as any other file or sub-directory in that directory. Two sub-directories in different locations can share a name (as in the two different LEDGER sub-directories in the previous example), as can files in different directories.

Directory paths

In order to identify a particular file or directory, we need to specify its location, usually relative to the root directory. To do this, sub-directory names start with a '\' when they appear in commands. (Note that this rule changes when we use the 'current' directory described below.) In particular the root directory is identified by a '\' on its own. For example, any references to the root directory of drive C will appear as:

```
C:\
```

A file in that directory can be completely specified by adding its name:

```
C:\AUTOEXEC.BAT
```

When this piece of text is included in a command the operating system recognises that we are referring to the file named AUTOEXEC.BAT in the root directory of drive C.

If drive C is the current drive, the drive specifier is not essential and the file can be identified by:

```
\AUTOEXEC.BAT
```

For files in a sub-directory we need to use a *directory path*, which consists of all the sub-directories that must be passed through in order to reach the file. Consecutive directories are separated by the '\' symbol. For example, the main word-processing directory can be identified by:

```
C:\WP
```

To identify a particular file, add the full filename and extension at the end. The file SPELL.EXE in that directory is completely specified by:

```
C:\WP\SPELL.EXE
```

This provides a complete *file specification*. Other examples include:

```
C:\WP\EXAMPLES
```
The \EXAMPLES sub-directory of \WP

```
C:\WP\EXAMPLES\LETTER.DOC
```
The file LETTER.DOC in the above directory

```
C:\ACCOUNTS
```
The \ACCOUNTS directory

```
C:\ACCOUNTS\LEDGER\LG88.DAT
```
The file LG88.DAT, contained in the \LEDGER sub-directory of \ACCOUNTS

If the drive specifier is omitted the current drive is assumed:

```
\OS2
```
The \OS2 directory on the current drive

```
\OS2\FORMAT.EXE
```
The FORMAT.EXE program file in the \OS2 directory of the current drive

When trying to run programs or external commands that are not in the current drive it may be necessary to insert the directory name before the command name. For example:

```
C:\OS2\FORMAT A:
```

This is only essential if entering 'FORMAT' on its own results in a 'Bad command' message; there will be no need for this if the PATH command has been properly applied (see Chapter 13).

```
[C:\]dir c:\wp

 Volume in drive C has no label
 Directory of  C:\WP

 .              <DIR>      4-04-89   8:46p
 ..             <DIR>      4-04-89   8:46p
 LETTERS        <DIR>      4-04-89   8:46p
 SPELL    EXE    37888    27-04-88   4:17p
 WP       EXE   155088    23-09-88   5:00a
 RULER    DOC     1024    23-09-88   5:00a
 WP       HLP     1990    20-01-89   5:21p
 DIARY    DOC     3712    23-09-88   5:00a
 TEXT     DOC     5760    23-09-88   5:00a
 PTR      EXE   204288    27-04-88  11:32a
 PTR      HLP   139898    27-04-88  11:32a
 WINDOW   DOC      384    23-09-88   5:00a
 TABLE    DOC     1024    23-09-88   5:00a
         13 File(s)  28325888 bytes free

[C:\]
```

Figure 4.8 A sub-directory listing

Simpler paths can be used when we specify a current directory, described below.

DISPLAYING SUB-DIRECTORIES

The contents of any sub-directory can be displayed on screen using the DIR command, and specifying the directory path. For example, the contents of the \WP directory can be shown with the command:

```
DIR C:\WP
```

This listing starts with two special entries:

```
    .               <DIR>
    ..              <DIR>
```

All sub-directory listings start with these two entries (Figure 4.8). The '.' entry supplied refers to the sub-directory itself and is of little use to us. The '..' entry refers to the *parent directory*; that is, the directory which contains this sub-directory as an entry. This is an important feature of the operating system. The entry in the parent directory tells the operating system what the sub-directory is called and where

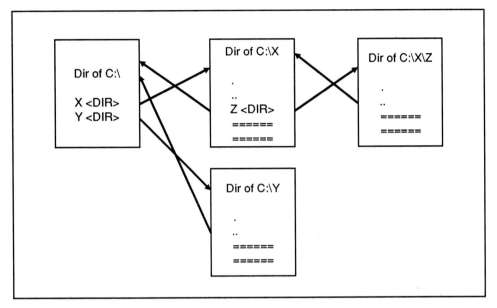

Figure 4.9 Linked directories

on disk it is located; the '..' entry in the sub-directory stores details of the location of the parent. Since all sub-directories are linked in this way the operating system can move either up or down the directory tree to locate any file. This process of linking directories is illustrated in Figure 4.9. More uses for the '..' entry are given later.

Note that the number of files shown at the bottom of the directory listing includes these two special entries.

Sub-directory listings can include ambiguous file specifications and all the usual parameters, such as:

```
DIR C:\WP\LETTERS\*.DOC /P
```

This example yields all files with a DOC extension in the \LETTERS sub-directory of the \WP directory of drive C, listing them a page at a time.

THE CURRENT DIRECTORY

In the same way that there is a current drive (that is, the one to which all commands apply unless specified otherwise), so there is a *current directory*. This is the directory which all commands will affect unless we state otherwise.

There is a different current directory for each drive in the system. Initially, the current directory is the root directory in each case. The current directory can be altered with the *CHDIR* (CHange DIRectory) command. This command is usually abbreviated to *CD*.

The command should be followed by the path of the directory that is to become current. For example, to make \WP the current directory, enter:

```
CD C:\WP
```

Any operations on drive C now refer to the \WP directory unless we state otherwise. For example, this directory can now be listed with:

```
DIR C:
```

(The 'C:' can be omitted if C is the current drive.) For drive A, the root directory is still the current directory.

To change the current directory of the current drive, simply omit the drive specifier:

```
CD \WP\LETTERS
CD A:\OS2
```

These two commands set the directories for the current drive (to \WP\LETTERS) and drive A (to \OS2). To change back to \WP on the current drive repeat the previous command:

```
CD \WP
```

Any references to sub-directories of the current directory can be abbreviated to only that part of the path from the current directory onwards. In such cases, however, the '\' at the beginning must not be included (see Figure 4.10). For instance, with \WP as the current directory, the DOC files in the \LETTERS sub-directory can be listed with:

```
DIR C:LETTERS\*.DOC
```

```
C>cd a:\os2

C>cd \wp

C>dir c:letters\*.doc

 Volume in drive C has no label
 Directory of  C:\WP\LETTERS

DIARY    DOC    11290   3-17-87  12:00p
         1 File(s)   1372160 bytes free

C>cd letters

C>dir *.doc

 Volume in drive C has no label
 Directory of  C:\WP\LETTERS

DIARY    DOC    11290   3-17-87  12:00p
         1 File(s)   1372160 bytes free

C>
```

Figure 4.10 The current directory

Again, if C is the current drive the command can be abbreviated to:

    DIR LETTERS *.DOC

The complete sub-directory can be displayed with:

    DIR LETTERS

\LETTERS can be made the current directory with:

    CD LETTERS

Take care when using these abbreviated forms, however, as you will not get the result you expect if the current drive or current directory are not as you think.

Checking the current directory

There are two ways of checking that you are in the current directory. One is to enter the CD command with no parameters. The operating system returns the current directory of the current drive (see Figure 4.11). Alternatively, the drive can be specified:

```
C>cd
C:\

C>cd \wp

C>cd
C:\WP

C>cd a:
A:\

C>cd a:\bats

C>cd a:
A:\BATS

C>cd letters

C>cd
C:\WP\LETTERS

C>
```

Figure 4.11 Checking the current directory

```
CD A:
```

This results in the current directory of drive A being displayed.

An alternative is to change the prompt to include the current directory. This is done with the *PROMPT* command:

```
PROMPT $P$G    (DOS 3.3)
```

```
PROMPT [$P]    (OS\2)
```

A full explanation of this command is given in Chapter 6.

Using the parent directory

When the current directory has been set, the '..' parent directory name comes into its own. This code can be included in any command as if it were a normal sub-directory name. For example, if \WP is the current directory we can list its parent directory (that is, the root directory) with:

```
DIR ..
```

All BAT files in the current directory's parent can be listed with:

```
DIR ..\*.BAT
```

We can make the parent directory the current directory with:

```
CD ..
```

Repeated use of this form of the command takes us back up through the directory tree until we reach the root directory, no matter where we start.

CREATING SUB-DIRECTORIES

Sub-directories can be created quite easily using the *MKDIR* ('MaKe DIRectory') command, usually abbreviated to *MD*. This command must include the name of the directory to be created.

For example, to create a new sub-directory called \QUOTES in the \WP directory, the command could be:

```
MD C:\WP\QUOTES
```

This command will fail, with a 'Cannot create directory' error message, if there is already a file or directory called 'QUOTES' in the \WP directory.

If drive C is the current drive and \WP the current directory, this command can be shortened:

```
MD QUOTES
```

Again, it is important to be sure of exactly where you are in the current drive and omit the '\'.

Having created a directory you can make this the current directory by pressing 'C' and function key F3, followed by Return.

You can check that the directory has been satisfactorily created with DIR. The directory is then ready to accept new files and/or sub-directories.

DELETING DIRECTORIES

Eventually some of the directories we create will outlive their usefulness. Other directories may be created accidentally in the wrong place. In such cases the redundant or unnecessary directories must be deleted. This is done with the *RMDIR* ('ReMove DIRectory') command, or *RD*.

Before a directory can be deleted it must satisfy the following conditions:

■ The directory must not contain any files or other sub-directories

■ The directory must not be the current directory

To ensure that the directory is empty use DIR to inspect its contents. Use the DEL command described in the next chapter to delete any unwanted files, and RD to delete any further level of sub-directory.

The syntax for the command is identical to MD:

```
RD  C:\WP\QUOTES

RD  QUOTES
```

The first version can be used from anywhere; the second assumes that C is the current drive and \WP the current directory.

DISPLAYING
THE DIRECTORY
TREE

It is very easy to get 'lost' when using a hard disk, especially one with many sub-directories. Locating a particular file or group of files can be very time consuming and take a great many DIR commands, especially if there are many similarly-named directories. DOS and OS/2 provide an external command, *TREE*, to deal with this problem. TREE displays all of the disk's directories, with the option to include the files as well.

Since TREE is an external command, the current directory must be the \DOS, \OS2 or other directory containing the file TREE.COM unless a suitable PATH command has been used. To display the directory tree of drive A, use the following commands:

```
CD \OS2
TREE A:
```

These commands assume that drive C is the current drive and that the operating system commands are held in a directory

```
[C:\]tree

Directory path listing

Path: \QB

Subdirectories:  BATS


Path: \QB\BATS

Subdirectories:  None


Path: \BATS

Subdirectories:  None


Path: \WP
```

Figure 4.12 Listing the directory tree

called \OS2 (see Figure 4.12). If the current drive is drive A, the directory of this drive can be shown with:

```
CD C:\OS2
C:TREE
```

To include the files in the listing add the /F parameter:

```
C:\OS2\TREE A: /F
```

This command lists all files on the disk in drive A, along with their sub-directories. The command can be used from anywhere, regardless of which is the current drive or directory.

In all these cases the display is rather functional. If TREE is used on its own the sub-directories are just listed one after the other, in the order in which they are found (so all sub-directories of a single directory are grouped together after their parent); the operating system always works down to the tip of each 'branch' of the tree in turn.

If the /F parameter is included the listing becomes almost impossible, since all files are included in a long list under each directory name. It is rather like doing a succession of DIR commands but without the additional information on file size, date and time. There is no simple way to slow this display down, other than some clever fingerwork with the Ctrl-S keys.

As an alternative you can use the MORE command to display the information a page at a time or FIND to locate a particular group of files; these two commands are explained in Chapter 10 but the syntax of the commands should take this sort of format:

```
TREE C: | MORE

TREE C: /F | FIND "DOC"
```

The second example is the closest we can get to an ambiguous filename with FIND. The command would locate all names containing the text 'DOC', such as LETTER.DOC, DOCUMNT1 and HADDOCK.STK, regardless of whether these are files or directories.

Various other commands affect the use of disks and directories. These are all detailed in the full descriptions in Chapters 7 and 8.

5.   *File Handling*

With so many directories on a hard disk - and it is inevitable that there will be a great many, if the disk is used properly - it is important to keep a very careful check on your files. Even a high-capacity hard disk can soon fill up if you do not perform regular *housekeeping* tasks. Unwanted files must be deleted, misplaced files copied and files that do not conform to the current naming conventions must be renamed. The same is true even if you only have a floppy disk system.

This chapter looks at the various operating system commands affecting files.

COPYING FILES

We may want to make a copy of a file for a number of reasons:

■ To copy it from a hard disk to a floppy disk for security

■ To copy it to a different directory

■ To safeguard a file when we are about to carry out some fairly drastic operation on it

■ To use one file as the basis for another, similar file

All of these things can be done with the *COPY* command. COPY is an internal command so it doesn't matter which is the current drive or directory. The command must be followed first by the specification of the file (or files) to be copied, then the destination of the file and its new name. Ambiguous filenames can be used in both parts of the command.

Copying to floppy disk

First let us look at the case where we want to copy files from hard disk to floppy for security reasons. Hard disks are generally very safe places to keep data but occasionally they develop problems. It is also very easy to accidentally wipe files off a hard disk. For these reasons it is important to make copies of all important files, away from the hard disk, on floppy disks.

Copies should be made on a regular basis and all floppies must be clearly marked. For more disciplined copy practices

```
[C:\WP\LETTERS]dir a:

 Volume in drive A has no label.
 Directory of  A:\

SYS0002: The system cannot find the file specified.

[C:\WP\LETTERS]copy contents.lst a:
        1 file(s) copied

[C:\WP\LETTERS]dir a:

 Volume in drive A has no label.
 Directory of  A:\

CONTENTS LST      786   3-02-90   3:08p
     1 File(s)   1456640 bytes free

[C:\WP\LETTERS]
```

Figure 5.1 Copying a single file

you can use either XCOPY or BACKUP (described later in this chapter).

To copy a particular file to floppy disk (for example, one named CONTENTS.LST), the command is:

```
COPY CONTENTS.LST A:
```

This command copies the file CONTENTS.LST from the current directory of the current drive to the current directory of drive A, giving the copy the same name as the original (Figure 5.1). The original file is always left intact after a COPY command.

If you are not in the correct directory or drive to start with, this can be included in the specification:

```
COPY C:\WP\BOOK\CONTENTS.LST A:
```

Similarly, if you are not sure that the correct directory has been selected on drive A, and the file is to be copied to the \BACKUPS directory, use the command:

```
COPY C:\WP\BOOK\CONTENTS.LST A:\BACKUPS\CONTENTS.LST
```

The filename at the end is not strictly speaking necessary. However, it is a wise precaution to take when copying to a sub-directory. (Otherwise, if \BACKUPS did not exist as a directory on drive A the file would be given the name BACKUPS; by including the full specification the operating system will respond with an error message if the \BACKUPS directory does not exist.)

In a similar way, a file can be retrieved from floppy disk:

```
COPY A:\BACKUPS\CONTENTS.LST C:\WP\BOOK
```

Again, the filename should be added at the end if you are not absolutely certain that \BOOK exists.

The COPY command always assumes that the current drive and directory are being used, unless stated otherwise, and that the copy is to be given the same name. Therefore, if \BACKUPS is the current directory on drive A, the current drive is C and the current directory on C is \WP\BOOK, the command given above can be cut right down:

```
COPY A:CONTENTS.LST
```

The last part of the command can be omitted altogether because the command assumes that the destination of the file is the current drive and directory (C:\WP\BOOK) and that the same name is to be used.

Note that any existing file of the same name is automatically overwritten. The command does not ask for confirmation that this is to be done.

If several files are to be copied you can use ambiguous filenames:

```
COPY C:*.LST A:
```

This command copies all LST files from the current directory of drive C to the current directory of drive A. As the files are copied their names are listed on the screen and the number of files copied is given at the end (see Figure 5.2).

```
Volume in drive C has no label.
Directory of   C:\WP\LETTERS

CONTENTS LST       786   3-02-90   3:08p
CUSTOMER LST       301   3-02-90   3:08p
ADDRESS  LST     11290   3-17-87  12:00p
     3 File(s)   1359872 bytes free

[C:\WP\LETTERS]copy *.lst a:
CONTENTS.LST
CUSTOMER.LST
ADDRESS.LST
        3 file(s) copied

[C:\WP\LETTERS]dir a:

 Volume in drive A has no label.
 Directory of   A:\

CONTENTS LST       786   3-02-90   3:08p
CUSTOMER LST       301   3-02-90   3:08p
ADDRESS  LST     11290   3-17-87  12:00p
     3 File(s)   1444352 bytes free
```

Figure 5.2 Multiple copies

Copying between directories

Copying from one directory to another is just as simple. For example, suppose that we want to copy all files with a DOC extension from \WP\LETTERS to \WP\LETTERS\CORRES. This is done with the command:

```
COPY C:\WP\LETTERS\*.DOC C:\WP\LETTERS\CORRES\*.DOC
```

Again this command can be abbreviated if C is the current drive and \WP\LETTERS the current directory:

```
COPY *.DOC CORRES
```

As before, you must make sure that \CORRES exists as a sub-directory of \WP\LETTERS; otherwise the first DOS file will be copied and given a filename of CORRES, the copy of the second DOC file will overwrite the first and so on. With any command like this it is always safest to get a listing of the directory to make sure the copy was completed successfully:

```
DIR CORRES\*.DOC
```

If you use exactly the same syntax as for the COPY command you will be certain that the correct command was used. To be really certain that you have the same syntax use the function keys after the COPY command as follows:

```
D I R F4 C Del F3
```

Alternatively, the space bar can be used to blank out the unwanted characters in the middle of the command. If you go too far, use ← to rub out the unwanted spaces.

Copying directories

All files in a directory can be copied, either by specifying '*.*' as the file specification or by just giving the directory name:

```
COPY C:\WP\LETTERS A:\BACKUPS
```

This copies the entire contents of LETTERS to the \BACKUPS directory on drive A.

Copying and renaming

Before carrying out any major operation on a file (such as changing the style of a document) it is a good idea to make a copy of the file before you start. You cannot have two copies of the same file in one directory with the same name but you can give the new file a different name. For example, to copy the file ELLIS.DEC to a new file in the same directory, giving it an OLD extension, use the command:

```
COPY ELLIS.DEC ELLIS.OLD
```

(Note that many applications automatically create backup files when saving; for example, WordStar generally creates files with a BAK extension.)

If any part of the name is to be the same, the wildcards can be used:

```
COPY ELLIS.DEC *.OLD
```

This has exactly the same effect as the previous command.

Similarly, all files with a DEC extension can be copied to identical files with an OLD extension:

```
COPY *.DEC *.OLD
```

To copy all LET files that have a name starting with 'DO' and rename them with names that start 'BA', use:

```
COPY DO*.LET BA*.*
```

The first two characters of each file are changed but the rest of the name remains unchanged. The wildcards in the first file specification are used to identify files to be copied, those in the second specification determine which parts of the name stay the same. In the example, DOG.LET is copied to BAG.LET (and any previous version of this file is overwritten).

Using files as templates

In a similar way to the above, an existing file can be used as the basis for a new file. For example, if you have one standard letter you can make a copy of it and then edit it to create a second, similar file. Such a standard file is usually called a *template*. When word processing, for example, it is useful to have a set of standard templates as a basis for all future documents.

Suppose that you have a set of templates stored in the \WP\TEMPLATE directory, and want to create a document called JONES.LET from a template file called STANDARD.LET. This can be done with the command:

```
COPY \WP\TEMPLATE\STANDARD.LET \WP\LETTERS\SMITH.LET
```

You are then ready to use the word processor to personalise SMITH.LET.

Using logical drives

If you have only a single floppy disk, you can still copy from one floppy disk to another. In this case the single floppy drive is treated as two separate *logical* drives. The operating system will tell you to put in the disks for drives A and B as they are required.

For example, if CONTENTS.LST exists on the root directory of one floppy disk and is to be copied to the root directory of another, you can use the command:

```
COPY A:CONTENTS.LST B:
```

In this case the 'A' and 'B' can be taken to refer to the original and copy disks respectively. When the command is entered the operating system copies the file into memory. It then requests the copy disk:

```
Insert diskette for drive B: and strike
any key when ready
```

Swap the disks over and then press any key. The file is copied from memory to the second disk. When the copy has been completed, you are asked to put the original disk back in:

```
Insert diskette for drive A: and strike
any key when ready
```

The operating system always tries to end up with the original disk back in the floppy drive.

COPY summary   To summarise, any file or group of files can be copied to any drive and directory, and any part of the name may be left the same or changed. The command assumes the current directory of the current drive is to be used, unless we specify otherwise; anywhere wildcards are used in the destination name it is assumed that that part of the name is to stay the same; if the name is omitted, the original name is used for the copy.

Other, more complex versions of COPY exist for combining files or creating and printing files (see Chapters 9 and 12).

RENAMING FILES

We often need to change the names of files. This may be necessary to ensure that existing files fit in with some naming convention, or to make life easier when carrying out other file operations.

The command is an internal one, *RENAME*, which is generally abbreviated to *REN*.

The syntax is very similar to that for COPY. The command is followed by the name (or names) of the file to be renamed and then the new name. For example, to rename a file called CONTENTS.LST as PRELIMS.LST, (assuming that the file is in the current directory and drive) enter:

```
REN CONTENTS.LST PRELIMS.LST
```

```
[C:\WP\LETTERS]dir *.lst

 Volume in drive C has no label.
 Directory of  C:\WP\LETTERS

CONTENTS LST      786   3-02-90   3:00p
CUSTOMER LST      301   3-02-90   3:00p
ADDRESS  LST    11290   3-17-87  12:00p
     3 File(s)   1359072 bytes free

[C:\WP\LETTERS]ren contents.lst prelims.lst

[C:\WP\LETTERS]dir *.lst

 Volume in drive C has no label.
 Directory of  C:\WP\LETTERS

PRELIMS  LST      786   3-02-90   3:00p
CUSTOMER LST      301   3-02-90   3:00p
ADDRESS  LST    11290   3-17-87  12:00p
     3 File(s)   1359072 bytes free

[C:\WP\LETTERS]
```

Figure 5.3 Renaming a file

Checking the directory before such an operation can be helpful (Figure 5.3). However, since the file itself is not affected there is no danger that another file will be over-written. The command issues an error message if a file of that name already exists.

It may be necessary to specify the drive and directory of the file to be renamed. Wildcards can be used in the new name for those parts that stay the same. Thus the command above could equally well have been entered as:

```
REN C:\WP\BOOK\CONTENTS.LST PRELIMS.*
```

There is no need to give a drive or directory in the new name since the file must stay in the same directory. (Use COPY if a file is to be copied and moved, or use the procedures in Chapter 16 to move a file completely, deleting the original.)

Wildcards can be included in the original specification if more than one file is to be renamed:

```
REN CON*.LST *.BAK
```

In this case all files that begin with 'CON' and have a LST extension are renamed, with the main part of the name staying the same but the extensions all changing to BAK (for example, CONTENTS.LST becomes CONTENTS.BAK).

DELETING FILES

Unless we take care to keep on top of the housekeeping tasks, disks soon fill up with unwanted and redundant files. These files can be erased with the *DEL* command. This internal command also sometimes appears as ERASE.

The syntax is similar to COPY, except that only one file specification is needed (see Figure 5.4). For example, to delete a particular file in the current directory enter:

```
DEL CONTENTS.BAK
```

To delete all BAK files in the current directory of drive A, enter:

```
DEL A:*.BAK
```

Deleting all files   All files can be deleted with the '*.*' specification:

```
DEL C:\WP\BOOK\*.*
```

In this special case, the program responds with a request for confirmation:

```
Are you sure (Y/N)?
```

Only press 'Y' and Return if you want all files in that directory to be deleted.

A complete directory can be deleted by just entering the directory name:

```
DEL BOOK
```

This deletes everything in the \BOOK sub-directory of the current directory, although you are prompted for confirmation before the deletions take place. The directory itself remains intact until deleted with the RD command.

```
[C:\WP\LETTERS]dir *.bak

  Volume in drive C has no label.
  Directory of  C:\WP\LETTERS

CONTENTS BAK       787    3-02-90    2:15a
CUSTOMER BAK       302    3-02-90    2:15a
ADDRESS  BAK     11290    3-17-87   12:00p
     3 File(s)   1343488 bytes free

[C:\WP\LETTERS]del contents.bak

[C:\WP\LETTERS]dir *.bak

  Volume in drive C has no label.
  Directory of  C:\WP\LETTERS

CUSTOMER BAK       302    3-02-90    2:15a
ADDRESS  BAK     11290    3-17-87   12:00p
     2 File(s)   1345536 bytes free

[C:\WP\LETTERS]
```

Figure 5.4 Deleting files

OS/2 allows you to delete more than one group of files at a time by including several specifications on the command line.

Note that when the operating system 'deletes' a file it does not actually do anything to the file itself. All that happens is that the entry in the directory is marked as being deleted. Various programs exist that will recover an erased file. However, any new files that are created will re-use the directory entry and the new data will use the space occupied by the deleted file. Therefore it is possible to recover the contents of a deleted file but only if no other major changes have been made to the contents of the disk in the meantime.

DISPLAYING THE CONTENTS OF FILES

We often need to find out exactly what a file contains. In many cases - for example, when a file contains a program, or data that has been stored in a compacted form - it is impossible to inspect the contents of the file directly.

```
[C:\]type c:\autoexec.bat
@echo off
PATH=\;\OS2;\SYSTEM;\BATS;\QB
keyb uk
echo on

[C:\]
```

Figure 5.5 Displaying the contents of a file

In some cases files will have been stored as *ASCII* files. ASCII is a standard, international code for representing text. The contents of such files can be displayed directly on the screen with the *TYPE* command (see Figure 5.5). For example, the contents of the file AUTOEXEC.BAT in the root directory of the hard disk can be displayed with the command:

```
TYPE C:\AUTOEXEC.BAT
```

As with other commands, the drive specifier and directory path can be omitted if the file is in the current directory.

For very long files the display scrolls off the screen. The display can be made to pause either with the Ctrl-S combination or by adding the MORE command (see Chapter 12).

Attempting to use TYPE with program files - such as DOS's COMMAND.COM - results in a screenful of strange symbols (and the computer beeps every time it comes across a particular character in the code). You will have more success with documents created by word processors, though even here there will be many strange characters; word processors tend to put special codes in the text to indicate where there

```
[C:\]type \config.sys \autoexec.bat
rem CONFIG.SYS
country=044
codepage=437,850
devinfo=kbd,uk,\keyboard.dcp
devinfo=scr,ega,\viotbl.dcp

rem AUTOEXEC.BAT
@echo off
PATH=\;\DOS;\SYSTEM;\BATS;\QB
keyb uk
echo on

[C:\]
```

Figure 5.6 Typing a list of files

are different type styles, margins and so on. Even so, this is a useful exercise if you want to find out roughly what is in a file.

OS/2 enhancements

OS/2 provides two major enhancements for TYPE. Firstly, the file specification can include wildcards. For example, all BAT files in the root directory can have their contents listed with the command:

    TYPE *.BAT

In this case the listings all appear one after another, so it is helpful if the name is included at the start of each file.

The second enhancement allows more than one file specification in the command line (Figure 5.6). For example, the two ASCII files needed when the system is booted can be listed with:

    TYPE \CONFIG.SYS \AUTOEXEC.BAT

Any practical number of file specifications can be included on the command line, and any of these can be ambiguous specifications.

BACKING UP FILES

No matter how much care you take with your disks it is inevitable that some files will eventually get lost. Disks are a very insecure place to keep data, regardless of whether they are floppy or hard disks, and human error accounts for a great many files being accidentally deleted or overwritten. To guard against this, and reduce any potential damage to a minimum, it is essential to make regular backup copies of all important files.

Original program disks should be copied with the DISKCOPY command which was described in Chapter 3.

It is usual to make a customised disk for each application, set up for a particular hardware configuration, to use in your day-to-day work. This working copy should also be backed up so that any damage to the original does not mean you have to go through the installation and customisation procedures again to make a new copy. If the installed program can fit on a single disk if can be copied with DISKCOPY; otherwise you must use BACKUP, which is described below.

Original program disks and original working disks should be stored well away from the computer, preferably in a different room or building, to minimise the risk of their being used by accident. You should only ever use backup copies of these disks.

As far as data files are concerned, these should be copied at regular intervals. The more you stick to a regular routine, the more likely it is that your data will be recoverable after any loss of files.

The way in which you backup your data will depend on the type of data. Word-processing documents, for example, should be copied to backup disks with the COPY command. For more complex file structures, such as accounts data, you should use the BACKUP command.

XCOPY

Before looking at BACKUP, it is worth considering the *XCOPY* ('eXtended COPY') command. XCOPY has the same syntax as COPY but also allows for a number of parameters. This is a useful command for copying a group of files, especially if you only want to copy files that have changed; it is also better than COPY when files are in different levels of sub-directory.

XCOPY is an external command, so you may need to tell the operating system where it is by including the drive and/or sub-directory in front of the command; before doing so it is worth trying the command on its own to see if it produces a 'Bad command' message.

At its simplest, XCOPY can be typed with an identical syntax to COPY:

```
XCOPY *.DOC A:
```

This copies all DOC files from the current drive and directory to the floppy disk.

Partial backups

It is not necessary to always back up all the files in a directory or group. While you will want to make a complete backup of a directory from time to time (say, at the end of a month or a week, depending on how frequently the data is changed), much of the time you will only want to copy those files that have changed.

Whenever a file is modified in any way the operating system marks it as such, by setting a special *archive attribute* in the directory. Whenever a file is copied with BACKUP or XCOPY the archive attribute may be cleared again. Therefore after a complete backup all of the files in the directory or group will have had this attribute cleared.

Later on (say, the next week or following day, depending on the procedure selected) it is only necessary to copy those files that have changed. These will be obvious to the operating system because their archive attributes will have been set.

To copy only the changed files add the /M ('modified') parameter:

```
XCOPY C:\WP\LETTERS\*.* A: /M
```

This command copies those files in C:\WP\LETTERS that have been modified in any way since XCOPY or BACKUP were last used.

Copying sub-directories

If the directory from which you are copying includes sub-directories, their contents can also be copied, using the /S parameter:

```
XCOPY C:\WP\LETTERS A: /S

XCOPY C:\WP\LETTERS A: /M /S
```

The first command makes a complete copy of the files in \WP\LETTERS, including any sub-directories of \LETTERS and the files in those sub-directories. If the sub-directories do not exist on drive A they are automatically created. The second command works with the same set of files but only copies those that have changed.

Complete backups

You can copy the entire contents of a disk with a command in the form:

```
XCOPY A:\*.* B: /S
```

If the disks in drive A and B are of the same type (both system disks or both non-system disks) you will end up with a complete copy of the original but with no fragmentation of files. (For a discussion on fragmentation see CHKDSK in Chapter 7.)

Various other parameters are also available, as detailed in Chapter 9.

BACKUP

Many of the more recent commercial applications produce extremely large files that fill most of a floppy disk. Some even create files that are too large to fit on a single floppy. In such cases, where backing up a set of programs to individual floppies is either too tedious or impossible because of the file sizes, it is necessary to use the *BACKUP* command.

BACKUP takes the contents of a directory or a group of files and copies them to one or more floppy disks, filling the disks completely. The advantage is that the user does not have to worry about where the copies are to be stored or how large the files are. The disadvantage is that it can be quite time-consuming to extract a file from the backups (since the

```
[C:\]backup c:\wp\letters a:

Insert backup diskette 01 in drive A:
Warning! The files in the root directory
of target drive A: will be erased

Press Enter to continue or Ctrl+Break to cancel.

The files are being backed up to drive A.

Diskette Number 01

\WP\LETTERS\ADDRESS.BAK
\WP\LETTERS\CUSTOMER.BAK
\WP\LETTERS\DIARY.DOC
\WP\LETTERS\BANK.LET
\WP\LETTERS\PRINTER.LET
\WP\LETTERS\ROBIN.LET
\WP\LETTERS\WILLIAMS.LET
\WP\LETTERS\ADDRESS.LST
\WP\LETTERS\CUSTOMER.LST
\WP\LETTERS\PRELIMS.LST
\WP\LETTERS\ADDRESS.TMP
```

Figure 5.7 The BACKUP command

files are stored in a special way and can only be recovered using the RESTORE command). However, since this command is really used just as a precautionary measure it should not be necessary to recover files from the backups very often.

Before using the BACKUP command you need to get a good supply of disks ready. Although BACKUP can be used to back up the entire hard disk, this is not generally practical. If 720K floppy disks are being used it would take about 45 disks to back up a 32M hard disk. Many files should not need to be copied. The majority of the disk will probably contain original operating system files and program files. Copies of all of these should already exist on the floppy disk originals and backups. That just leaves the data.

Hopefully, the data has been sensibly organised, so that the data files are in different sub-directories to the program files, and files created by separate applications are in different sub-directories to each other. Each separate directory can be backed up individually. The advantage here is that it is easier to restore the data for a single directory than for the entire hard disk.

BACKUP is an external command, so its location must be specified if no PATH has been specified. The drive, directory or ambiguous specification of the files to be backed up must be given, along with the name of the drive containing the backup disks. For example, to backup all of the files in the \WP\LETTERS directory to one or more floppy disks in drive A, enter the command:

```
BACKUP C:\WP\LETTERS A:
```

If only those files with a LET extension are to be copied the command becomes:

```
BACKUP C:\WP\LETTERS\*.LET A:
```

In either case, BACKUP responds with a request for you to load the first floppy disk in drive A, and a warning that any existing files on the disk will be destroyed (Figure 5.7). All files are erased, even if only a few files are being copied, since BACKUP completely rewrites the floppy disk's directory.

Load a formatted disk and press Return. The program copies across as many files as it can until the disk is full. The disk is completely filled, even if that means copying just part of a file. BACKUP then asks for backup disk number 02 to be loaded. When you have loaded the second disk and pressed Return, BACKUP continues copying from where it left off.

This process continues until all the files specified have been copied. As each disk is completed the name of the directory being copied and the backup number should be written on its label.

At any stage the BACKUP process can be interrupted by pressing Ctrl-Break but the backup disks will only be of any use if the BACKUP finished normally, without error or interruption. The command will fail if a backup disk is unformatted (when you should use the /F parameter, described below).

Note that you can also back up to a hard disk drive; in this case the operating system creates a sub-directory called \BACKUP to hold the files that are copied.

Partial backups   In the same way as for XCOPY, you can copy only those files that have been modified, by adding the /M parameter.

However, whereas for XCOPY you could overwrite the old backups, with this command it is not so straightforward, since the files are not copied in the normal way.

Obviously a different set of disks should be used for this process, as you still need to keep the original backups in case you need to restore the entire directory.

Other parameters constrain BACKUP to copy only files that were created after a specific date or time (see Chapter 9).

Adding to the backups

If only a few files are being backed up each time then it may be worth adding these to the existing backup disks, using the /A parameter:

```
BACKUP C:\WP\LETTERS A: /M /A
```

In this example, all modified files are added to the current backup disk. (Again, this should not be the original backup disks but the disks for those files that have changed.)

Backing up sub-directories

If the directory being backed up contains sub-directories these can also be copied, using the /S parameter (as for XCOPY). The sub-directories are automatically created on the backup disks.

Unformatted disks

DOS 3.3 introduced a new parameter, /F, which instructs BACKUP to format the floppy disks before copying files to them. This avoids the frustration of discovering that you do not have enough formatted disks ready part-way through a backup, though it does increase the time taken to make the backup. All disks are formatted, whether they need it or not. (Note that the FORMAT program is needed and must be in the current directory or a directory pointed to by the PATH command.)

The BACKUP log

It is useful to keep a record of the files that have been backed up, and to have an idea of where they were backed up to and when the backups took place. This is all done automatically for you if you add the /L parameter to the command. (This is another parameter that was introduced with DOS 3.3 and has been carried across to OS/2; perhaps surprisingly, OS/2 has not added any of its own parameters to the BACKUP command.)

```
[C:\]type backup.log

8-03-1990  5:02:38
001   \WP\LETTERS\ADDRESS.BAK
001   \WP\LETTERS\CUSTOMER.BAK
001   \WP\LETTERS\DIARY.DOC
001   \WP\LETTERS\BANK.LET
001   \WP\LETTERS\PRINTER.LET
001   \WP\LETTERS\ROBIN.LET
001   \WP\LETTERS\WILLIAMS.LET
001   \WP\LETTERS\ADDRESS.LST
001   \WP\LETTERS\CUSTOMER.LST
001   \WP\LETTERS\PRELIMS.LST
001   \WP\LETTERS\ADDRESS.TMP
9-03-1990  5:18:18
001   \WP\LETTERS\BANK.LET
001   \WP\LETTERS\PRINTER.LET
001   \WP\LETTERS\ROBIN.LET
001   \WP\LETTERS\WILLIAMS.LET
[C:\]
```

Figure 5.8 Displaying BACKUP.LOG

BACKUP creates a file called BACKUP.LOG in the directory that is being backed up, if it does not already exist; if there is such a file, the new backup information is added to it. You can inspect the contents of this file with the TYPE command:

```
TYPE BACKUP.LOG
```

All files that have been backed up are listed, along with the backup disk number, date and time of backup (Figure 5.8).

RESTORE   There is only any point in copying files with BACKUP if you can restore them to the hard disk when needed. This becomes necessary in the following circumstances:

■ When files are accidentally deleted or overwritten

■ When files are corrupted

■ When the hard disk develops a fault and has to be reformatted

```
[C:\]restore a: c:\wp\letters\*.*

Insert backup diskette 01 in drive A:
Press Enter when ready.


The files were backed up 09-03-1990.

Files will be restored from drive A:
Diskette 01
\WP\LETTERS\ADDRESS.BAK
\WP\LETTERS\CUSTOMER.BAK
\WP\LETTERS\DIARY.DOC
\WP\LETTERS\BANK.LET
\WP\LETTERS\PRINTER.LET
\WP\LETTERS\ROBIN.LET
\WP\LETTERS\WILLIAMS.LET
\WP\LETTERS\ADDRESS.LST
\WP\LETTERS\CUSTOMER.LST
\WP\LETTERS\PRELIMS.LST
\WP\LETTERS\ADDRESS.TMP
\WP\LETTERS\BANK.LET
\WP\LETTERS\PRINTER.LET
```

Figure 5.9 Restoring files

- When a new operating system is being installed (again requiring reformatting)

- When an entire directory of data is to be installed on a different computer

The only way of recovering files created by BACKUP is through BACKUP's companion command, *RESTORE*. The syntax of the RESTORE command is similar to that of BACKUP, this time the name of the backup drive (from which the files are to be copied) coming before the name of the directory where the recovered files are to reside.

For example, to restore the files backed up from the \WP\LETTERS directory, enter:

```
RESTORE A: C:\WP\LETTERS\*.*
```

RESTORE asks you to load backup disk number 01 and press Return (Figure 5.9). After the files have been copied off the first floppy disk you are asked to load disk number 02, and so on until all files have been recovered.

If you have been using two or more sets of backup disks (for instance, one set for weekly backups, another for daily backups of modified files) then the disks must be restored in the order in which they were backed up. For example, the weekly backups must be restored first (so that the directory will be restored to the same state as the previous week), followed by the daily backups (so that any modified files will replace the out-of-date versions that have just been restored). If a different backup is used on each day of the week for the modified files then all of these disks must be restored, starting with the oldest disk. If the disks are restored in any other order there is a danger that the files that are eventually left on the hard disk will not be the most recent versions.

Modified files

RESTORE has its own set of parameters. Two of these relate to modified files. The /M parameter checks the directory of the hard disk and restores from floppy only those files that have been changed (or 'modified') since the last backup was made. This means that any changes are lost.

The converse of this is the /P parameter which issues a prompt whenever it encounters a file on the hard disk that still has the archive attribute set. This means that the file has changed and has not been copied onto a backup disk by BACKUP or XCOPY. You are asked to press 'Y' if this file is to be overwritten or 'N' if you want to keep it intact.

There are also parameters for restoring only those files that were changed after (or before) a particular date or time (see Chapter 9).

Deleted files

The /N parameter restores only those files that are no longer contained in the sub-directory on hard disk.

This is a useful option if a group of files has been accidentally deleted.

It can also be applied if you only want to replace particular files (for example, if you have made changes to a set of files and then decide that you want to return to the original versions). In this case you must first delete from the hard disk the files to be replaced before invoking RESTORE with the /N parameter.

Restoring sub-directories

If you backed up the sub-directories of a directory, as well as its files, using the /S parameter, then you will need the same parameter when restoring the files.

Note that the parameters available for BACKUP and RESTORE vary from one version of the operating system to another, and that you should never mix the commands from different versions.

Backup summary

Three different commands can be used to back up your data:

■ COPY simply copies individual files or groups of files.

■ XCOPY copies in the same way as COPY but with some enhanced features, such as the ability to copy only modified files.

■ BACKUP copies one or more directories, as well as individual files, and provides a range of options for copying only specific categories of files.

Backed up files can be recovered by COPY if they were created with COPY or XCOPY; use RESTORE if the files were created by BACKUP.

6.   *Basic Commands*

Now that we have seen how the operating system organises files on disk we can look at some of the more basic commands that affect the operation of the system.

This chapter considers commands for clearing the screen, setting the date and time, changing the prompt and checking on the operating system version number. Finally, it concludes with a quick reference summary of all the commands encountered so far.

CLEARING THE SCREEN

Sometimes it is useful to be able to clear the screen and start afresh. Anything on the screen will eventually disappear as it is scrolled off the top but if you want to blank out the display altogether, this can be done with the *CLS* command:

```
CLS
```

There are no parameters for this command. The effect is to completely clear the screen and then display the prompt and cursor in the top left-hand corner. This instruction is particularly useful in the batch files described in Chapter 16.

THE DATE AND TIME

Most systems are able to maintain the current date and time in some form of battery-backed memory. However, the date and time must be set in the first place and will need to be changed if the batteries run out or are dislodged. For those systems that do not have any battery-backed memory the date and time must be set each time the system is started.

It is important to ensure that the correct date and time are held by the system before you start any operations that involve changing files. When new files are created the date and time of their creation are stored in the directory; when they are subsequently modified the date and time of the modification replaces the creation date and time. These values are important for two main reasons:

■ If you have two versions of a file the date and time tell you which is the most recent.

■ Commands such as BACKUP, RESTORE and XCOPY can use the date and time to determine which files to copy.

Obviously the time does not have to be accurate to the second; an approximation will do.

Note that COPY, RENAME and similar commands do not affect the date and time attached to the files. When a file is copied, the copy has the same date and time as the original; it is only when the file is changed that these are updated.

In some circumstances you are automatically requested to enter the date and then the time whenever the system is started up or reset. For details of how to change this feature, see the sections on AUTOEXEC.BAT and STARTUP.CMD in Chapter 16.

Setting the date　　You can change the system date or just check the current date by entering:

```
DATE
```

The operating system responds by displaying the current date and a request for a new date (Figure 6.1). The date is in the following format:

```
Current date is Thu 24-08-1989
Enter new date (dd-mm-yy)
```

If you are just finding out the current date, press Return without entering a new date. The date then remains unchanged.

If you want to change the date the format will depend upon the way in which the system has been customised. For the British format the day should be followed by the month; for the American format the month comes first (this is also the default if the system has not been customised at all). The format is indicated by the operating system as either '(dd-mm-yy)' or '(mm-dd-yy)'.

The day and month can be entered as one- or two-digit numbers; you can pad them with a 0 if you like but this is not

```
[C:\]date
The current date is: Mon 12-03-1990
Enter the new date: (dd-mm-yy) 38-3-90

SYS1036:
The system cannot accept the date entered.

Enter the new date (dd-mm-yy) 8-3-90

[C:\]time
The current time is: 11:06:18.83
Enter the new time: 9:o8

SYS1044:
The system cannot accept the time entered.

Enter the new time: 9:08

[C:\]date
The current date is: Thu  8-03-1990
Enter the new date: (dd-mm-yy)

[C:\]time
The current time is:  9:08:06.47
```

Figure 6.1 Entering the date and time

essential. The year can either be a two- or four-digit number. The three parts of the date must all be entered; they can be separated by a dash, full stop or oblique stroke. You must not try to enter the day of the week; this is automatically calculated for you.

For example, suppose that you wish to change the date to 8th March, 1990. Any of the following formats is acceptable (assuming the British format is used):

```
8-3-90
08-03-90
8-3-1990
08.3.90
8/03/1990
```

This list only includes some of the possibilities; any combination of formats is permissable.

If there is anything wrong with the date the system responds with a message such as:

```
Invalid date
```

If this happens you can either try again with a new date or press Return to leave the original date unchanged.

The date should be in the range 1st January, 1980 to 31st December, 2099. For years after 2079 you must enter the year as a four-digit number. If the system has lost the current date (for example, because the batteries have been removed) it is automatically set as 1-1-1980 when the computer is switched on. All dates are counted from this point; you cannot enter an earlier date.

If the system has no battery-backed memory the date and time must be entered whenever the system is reset.

The *DATE* command provides a useful means of discovering the day of the week for any date up to the end of the next century. Use the command to change to the selected date, then enter the command again to change it back to the current date. The second time the command is invoked the day of the week is shown for the required date.

The date can also be changed in a single operation by adding the new date as a parameter on the command line:

```
DATE 8-3-90
```

Any of the date formats previously described are acceptable.

Setting the time

The time can be set in a similar fashion to the date, using the *TIME* command:

```
TIME
```

The system responds with the current time:

```
Current time is 09:17:23.45
Enter new time
```

The time is shown in the format:

hours:minutes:seconds.hundredths

The operating system's attention to detail is rather excessive; it is very rare that we need to know the time to the nearest hundredth of a second!

If the command has been entered to find out the current time then the time can be left unchanged by just pressing Return. Otherwise a new value must be entered.

Fortunately, the new time does not have to be entered with such accuracy. Only those parts of the time that are important need be given; any parts that are missing are automatically set to 0. The hour can be padded with a 0 but this is not essential; the minutes and seconds must be 2-digit numbers, so should be padded with 0's if necessary. The first three parts of the time must be separated by colons. The time must be entered using the 24-hour clock, even if times in directory listings are shown with the 12-hour clock.

If the time is requested whenever you start up the system then it is probably good enough to set it to the nearest hour.

Acceptable time formats include:

```
9:37:30  Half a minute past 9:37 a.m.
08:30    8:30 a.m.
14:22    2:22 p.m.
12:00    Midday
00:00    Midnight
9        9 a.m.
```

If the time is wrong in any way the system responds with an 'Invalid time' message and the time must be re-entered.

If there is no battery-backed memory the time is always set to 00:00:00.00 (midnight) when the system is first started or reset.

The time can be entered in a single command:

```
TIME 9
```

This sets the time to 9 a.m.

The new time takes effect as soon as the Return key is pressed. Therefore for the time to be absolutely accurate you should enter the new time (rounded up to the next minute) and, using a watch, press Return when the minute is reached. Such fanaticism is really only warranted if the time is battery-backed, and if the computer is to be used for checking the time. Purists should note that the times on directory listings are only given in terms of hours and minutes anyway.

Setting the time with such accuracy can be justified if you use any application which constantly displays the current time, when the wrong time can be misleading.

CHANGING THE PROMPT

When the system is started up the prompt is fairly basic but not very informative. It tells us which is the current drive but nothing else.

The prompt can be changed in a number of different ways with the *PROMPT* command. The command must be followed by the text that is to be used for the prompt; this text is then displayed instead of the default prompt. For example, to change the prompt to 'Ready.', enter the command:

```
PROMPT Ready.
```

After each command the operating system now responds with:

```
Ready.
```

The cursor flashes immediately after the full stop (Figure 6.2).

DOS and OS/2 also provide means for including the current drive and directory, the date and time, and various other items in the prompt. This is done by inserting a '$' followed by a single-character code. For example, the current drive is represented by '$n' while the '>' symbol is signified by '$g'. So the default DOS prompt can be set in either DOS or OS/2 with the command:

```
PROMPT $N$G
```

A more useful version includes the '$p' code, which represents the current directory path, including the drive:

```
PROMPT $P$G
```

In this case the prompt changes each time CD changes the current drive. This is perhaps the most useful form of prompt,

```
[C:\]prompt Ready.

Ready.
Ready.prompt $n$g

C>
C>prompt $p$g

C:\>
C:\>prompt $t

 9:16:59.80
 9:17:00.13prompt $t$h$h$h

 9:17:13
 9:17:13prompt Date: $d$_Time: $t$_$p$g

Date: Thu  8-03-1990
Time:  9:17:55.33
C:\>
Date: Thu  8-03-1990
Time:  9:17:55.87
C:\>
```

Figure 6.2 Changing the prompt

since it helps avoid confusion over which is the current drive when trying to carry out file housekeeping tasks.

The date and time can be included with the codes '$d' and '$t'. For example, to show the current time, enter:

```
PROMPT $T
```

The response is a new prompt, which shows the current time:

```
11:10:08.23
```

Since you do not usually need this degree of detail, you can use the '$h' code, which represents the 'backspace' character and deletes the last character of the prompt:

```
PROMPT $T$H$H$H
```

The prompt now appears as:

```
11:11:13
```

125

The prompt can be moved down a line with $ followed by the underscore character. Text and codes can be mixed together. For example:

```
PROMPT Date: $D$_Time: $T$_$P$G
```

This results in a three-line prompt that is different whenever it appears:

```
Date:   Thu 8-3-90
Time: 11:15:23.15
C:\WP\>
```

The full set of special codes is given in Chapter 10.

The OS/2 prompt   The default OS/2 prompt is different to that of DOS:

```
PROMPT [$P]
```

OS/2 uses the standard DOS prompt for its real mode session and maintains a different prompt for each protected mode session. Any change made to the prompt in one session does not affect the prompts in other sessions.

The prompt can be totally blanked out with '$' followed by any character that has no special meaning:

```
PROMPT $X
```

Such a code is, perhaps, more useful in adding a space between the prompt and the command. Since any spaces at the end of the PROMPT command are usually ignored, the user's instructions generally follow immediately after the prompt, with no spaces. For example, suppose that we want to display the date and then a space. The command would be:

```
PROMPT $D $X
```

Be warned, however, that PROMPT is often a prime target for the office practical jokers.

At any time the prompt can be restored to its default by entering the command on its own.

OPERATING SYSTEM VERSION NUMBER

If you have booted up from floppy disk for any reason it is useful to be able to tell which version of the operating system you are using. This may be necessary for a number of reasons:

■ Some applications will only operate under specific versions of the operating system (for example, they may specify a minimum of DOS 3.2).

■ Some commands are not available in earlier versions of the operating system or their options may be significantly reduced (for example, XCOPY was only introduced in DOS 3.2 and the BACKUP options were extended for DOS 3.3). This may affect batch file operation (see Chapter 16).

■ Some commands can become decidedly awkward if you mix versions (for example, BACKUP and RESTORE from different versions should never be mixed).

The operating system name and version can be displayed with the *VER* command (Figure 6.3):

```
VER
```

The response is in the form:

```
MS-DOS version 3.30
```

or:

```
The IBM Operating System/2 Version is 1.00
```

The first part of the version number changes whenever there is any major change in the operating system; for example, DOS 2.00 introduced the concept of sub-directories while DOS 3.00 allows us to use high-capacity floppy disks. Minor changes and bug fixes are denoted by changes in the second part of the number.

If you discover that you are using the wrong version of the operating system the only way to install a different version is to reset the computer with Ctrl-Alt-Del.

```
[C:\]ver

The IBM Operating System/2 Version is 1.00

[C:\]
```

Figure 6.3 Checking the operating system version number

QUICK REFERENCE SUMMARY

This first part of the book has provided an introduction to DOS 3.3 and OS/2. The majority of the commands needed for the day-to-day running of the computer have been described in detail. Once these have been mastered you should be able to do most of the things that are needed for efficient use of the system.

The table in Figure 6.4 lists in alphabetical order the commands that have been mentioned so far, giving the page numbers of where they have been described and where further information may be found.

Part Two goes on to describe the complete set of operating system commands in detail; this is mainly a reference section, for users who feel confident enough to be able to use new commands without the need for a full tutorial. It also describes other features of the operating systems and their customisation.

Command	Description	Tutorial page no.	Main reference
BACKUP	Backs up data, usually from hard disk to floppy	111	173
CD	Changes current directory for any drive	90	155
CHDIR	See CD		
CLS	Clears the screen	119	189
COPY	Copies one or more files	97	177
DATE	Sets the date	120	189
DEL	Deletes one or more files	105	181
DISKCOPY	Copies entire floppy disks	73	139
ERASE	See DEL		
FDISK	Partitions a hard disk	69	134
FORMAT	Formats a disk	61	136
LABEL	Changes a disk's volume label	72	148
MD	Creates a sub-directory	93	153
MKDIR	See MD		
PROMPT	Changes the prompt	124	193
RD	Removes a sub-directory	94	156
REN	Renames one or more files	103	180
RENAME	See REN		
RESTORE	Restores files created by BACKUP	115	175
RMDIR	See RD		
TIME	Sets the time	122	191
TYPE	Displays the contents of files	107	182
VER	Displays the operating system version number	127	192
VOL	Displays a disk's volume label	72	147
XCOPY	Extended copying program	110	168

Figure 6.4 Basic command reference

PART TWO

THE OPERATING
SYSTEM
COMMANDS

7. *Disk-based Commands*

Part Two consists of a reference section, covering each of the DOS and OS/2 commands in turn. The commands are grouped according to their general use, and in each group they appear in a logical order.

Following this there is a reference section for various features of the operating systems. At the end of Part Two there is an alphabetical reference covering the commands and operating system features.

In the following chapters each command is briefly described. In each case the syntax of the command is given, along with details of which versions of the operating system it may be used with. The DOS version number indicates the minimum DOS version needed to use the command and it can be assumed that the command is available for all subsequent versions of DOS, unless otherwise stated. Enhancements that were added later are also indicated.

The conventions used in the syntax are as follows:

- Square brackets [ ] indicate that an item is optional.

- The vertical bar 'I' separates alternatives (e.g. ON I OFF implies either ON or OFF could be used).

- Any item that can be repeated is followed by '[...]' (e.g. for a list of filenames).

- Italics indicate a special element of the command.

The elements of the command that may be required are:

location	The location of the command (e.g. C:\DOS\)
drive	A drive specifier (e.g. C:)
drive1	The first drive specifier
drive2	The second drive specifier
path	A directory path (e.g. C:\, C:\WP\)
directory	A sub-directory name (e.g. BOOK, WP)

file	A file name (e.g. WP.EXE or *.EXE)
file1	The first file name
file2	The second file name
spec	A complete file specification, which may include a drive specifier, path and ambiguous filename, (e.g. C:, C:\WP, CONT.LST, C:\WP\BOOK\CONT.*)
spec1	The first complete file specification
spec2	The second complete file specification
spec3	The third complete file specification
date	A date in the standard format
time	A time in the standard format
number	A numeric value (e.g. 15, 100)

Other items, for individual commands, are self-explanatory. Note that the syntax given for each command excludes the parameters, which are listed below in each case.

This chapter provides a reference to those commands which are relevant to disks as a whole.

FDISK

Command:	FDISK
Effect:	Partitions a hard disk
Version:	DOS 2, OS/2
Type:	External
Syntax:	[*location*]FDISK [*drive*]
Parameters:	None

Before a hard disk can be used it must be divided into one or more partitions. This command creates or changes hard disk partitions. It is a fairly dramatic command, so should be used with care. After a partition has been created it must be formatted before it can be used.

There may be up to four DOS partitions, one of which is the primary partition; the others are extended partitions. The extended partitions may be further subdivided into logical drives. Each logical drive or primary partition must not exceed 32M.

This is a menu-based program, the structure of which is shown in Figure 7.1. Versions prior to DOS 3.3 had fewer

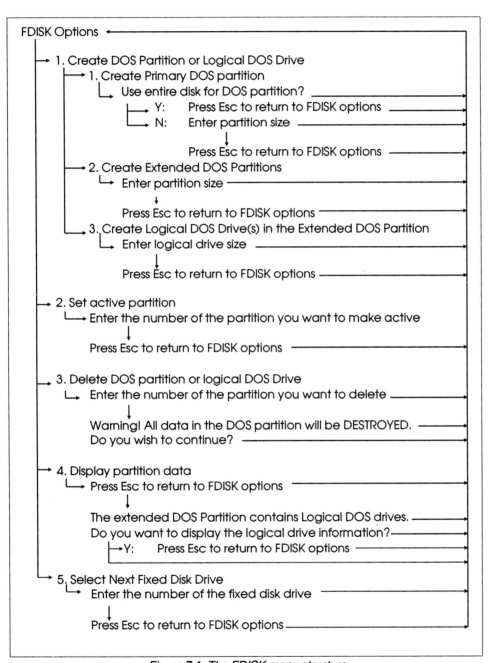

Figure 7.1 The FDISK menu structure

options than those shown. Versions up to and including DOS 3.2 allowed only a single DOS partition, with maximum size 32M.

Details of the operation of the first four options of this program were given in Chapter 3.

Option 5 only appears if the system has more than one physical hard disk and is used to select the disk to be partitioned.

FDISK should not be used with JOIN or SUBST.

FORMAT

Command:	FORMAT
Effect:	Formats a floppy or hard disk
Version:	DOS 1, OS/2
Type:	External
Syntax:	[*location*]FORMAT [*drive*]
Parameters:	/S System disk

/1   Single-sided (DOS 2; not OS/2)
/8   8 sectors per track (DOS 2; not OS/2)
/B   8 sectors per track, allowing space for system files (DOS 2, not OS/2)
/V   Volume label requested (DOS 3, OS/2)
/4   Quad density (DOS 3, not OS/2)
/4   Double-density (OS/2, not DOS)
/N:n Number of sectors is n (DOS 3.3, OS/2)
/T:t Number of tracks is t (DOS 3.3,OS/2)

This command formats a disk prior to use. In the case of hard disks, the disk must have been partitioned; the command formats the primary partition or logical drive. For floppy disks, the command performs both a low-level and high-level format. Any existing data is destroyed.

FORMAT always asks for confirmation that it is to proceed and gives you an opportunity to load a disk. When the format is complete the program displays the total disk space, the space taken by the system files (if any), the number of bytes in bad sectors and the number of bytes free on the disk. For floppy disks, it concludes by giving you the opportunity to format further disks.

A full description of the operation of this command was given in Chapter 3.

As a general rule FORMAT determines the number of sides, tracks and sectors from the drive type. The defaults can be overridden in certain circumstances. For example, /8 provides compatibility with DOS 1, which only create 8 sectors per track; /1 formats disks for use in single-sided drives.

If the /B parameter is included the system files can be added later with the SYS command.

The /N and /T parameters are useful for creating double-density disks in a high density drive.

The /4 parameter, implemented in DOS 3, allows you to create quad density 1.2M disks. The same parameter is used by OS/2 to produce a reverse effect, formatting a 360K disk in a 1.2M 5¼" drive. For this reason it is best to steer clear of this parameter and use /N and /T instead.

FORMAT should not be used with ASSIGN, JOIN or SUBST.

Examples

To format a floppy disk as a system disk, adding a volume label, enter:

    FORMAT A: /S /V

To prepare a 360K disk in a quad density drive, enter:

    FORMAT A: /N:9 /T:40

If you use this option you should stick to the combinations relating to the recognised disk formats, otherwise the disk may appear to be unreadable later.

SYS

Command:	SYS
Effect:	Transfers system files to a formatted disk
Version:	DOS 1, OS/2
Type:	External
Syntax:	[*location*]SYS [*drive*]
Parameters:	None

SYS adds the system files to a previously formatted disk. This disk either must be completely empty or should have space allocated for these files. FORMAT allocates space for system files with either the /S or /B parameter. The system is transferred from the disk in the current drive.

The need for this command arises from the fact that the system files must be placed at the start of the file space; such a disk can then be used to boot the system.

The scope of this command is limited. It is useful if you decide that one of a batch of blank, formatted disks must be a system disk, since it saves reformatting. It can also be used to downgrade a system disk to an earlier version of DOS. (DOS system files tend to increase in size with each version; the files must not be fragmented, so there is usually insufficient room to fit in a later version of DOS, but an earlier version will fit with plenty of spare space.)

SYS does not copy across COMMAND.COM (DOS 3.3) or STARTUP.CMD (OS/2) but the command processor can be added at any time since its physical location is unimportant.

Examples   If drive A is a system disk, containing the SYS program, the system files can be transferred to a disk in drive B with the command:

```
SYS B:
```

On a single-drive system the operating system prompts you to swap disks when the system files have been read into memory. The following message is displayed when the transfer is complete:

```
System transferred
```

System files can be transferred at any time, assuming space has been allocated.

DISKCOPY

Command:	DISKCOPY
Effect:	Copies the entire contents of one floppy disk onto another, formatting the target disk if necessary
Version:	DOS 1, OS/2
Type:	External
Syntax:	[*location*]DISKCOPY [*drive1*] [*drive2*]
Parameters:	/1 Copy one side only

DISKCOPY creates a replica of a floppy disk. The entire content of one floppy disk (the 'source') is copied onto a second disk (the 'target'), with the relative position of all data maintained on the disk. Therefore, if the files of the original disk were highly fragmented the same will be true of the copy. (To overcome the problems of fragmentation use either COPY or XCOPY.)

If the target disk is blank it will be formatted automatically. The format routine is a part of DISKCOPY; FORMAT.COM is not required. In this case the program displays a message to let you know that the target is being formatted. In any event, any data on the target disk is overwritten.

The data is copied across in a number of sections. On single-drive systems (where no drives are specified on the command line or both are the same), you are instructed to swap disks when the program is ready. It is very easy to get confused with single-drive copies, especially as no extra message is displayed when the copying restarts after a key press. Therefore, you should never remove a disk until you have checked that the drive light is off.

To avoid the dangers of accidentally overwriting an uncopied disk the source disk should always be write-protected.

After completing the copy the program offers you the chance to copy further disks. A full description of this command was given in Chapter 3.

The /1 parameter can be used to make copies of DOS 1 single-sided disks.

The source and target drives must be of the same type.

DISKCOPY should not be used with JOIN or SUBST.

Examples

To copy a disk using a single drive, enter:

```
DISKCOPY A: A:
```

To copy from one floppy to another, enter:

```
DISKCOPY A: B:
```

The copying process can be interrupted at any time by pressing Ctrl-Break; the target disk is then unusable until reformatted or used to make a further copy.

VERIFY

Command:	VERIFY
Effect:	Turns verification of disk-writing processes on or off
Version:	DOS 2, OS/2
Type:	Internal
Syntax:	VERIFY [ON|OFF]
Parameters:	None

As a general rule, when DOS or OS/2 write information to a disk there is no check that the data has been written correctly. This command provides one method for turning *write-verification* on. When the verification is switched on the operating system always checks each sector after it has been written to make sure that it can be read back into memory satisfactorily. The verification process does not compare the original data with the copy; it merely checks that the new data is readable.

Verification should be turned on when very important data is being written or when a disk or drive are thought to be suspect. Verification remains on until specifically turned off, or the system is rebooted. The default is that verification is OFF.

The main disadvantage of using VERIFY ON is that this slows down the operation of disk-writing operations to a considerable extent.

```
[C:\]verify
VERIFY is off.

[C:\]verify on

[C:\]verify
VERIFY is on.

[C:\]verify off

[C:\]verify
VERIFY is off.

[C:\]
```

Figure 7.2 The VERIFY command

Verification can also be affected by the /V parameter of the COPY and XCOPY commands. Alternatively, COMP and DISKCOMP can be used for a full comparison of files or disks.

Examples

Verification can be turned on with:

```
VERIFY ON
```

The current write-verification status can be ascertained by entering the command without parameters:

```
VERIFY
```

To turn verification off again use the third form of the command:

```
VERIFY OFF
```

If verification is OFF the COPY or XCOPY /V parameter turns it on temporarily; if verification is ON the /V parameter is ignored.

DISKCOMP

Command:	DISKCOMP
Effect:	Compares the contents of two floppy disks
Version:	DOS 1, OS/2
Type:	External
Syntax:	[*location*]DISKCOMP *drive1 drive2*
Parameters:	/1 Compare one side only (DOS 2, not OS/2)
	/8 Compare 8 sectors only (DOS 2, not OS/2)

This command is used to check the contents of two floppy disks for differences. It is appropriate either when a disk has been copied and it is thought that a fault may have developed, or the disks have become muddled and it is necessary to find out which disk is a copy of a particular original disk.

DISKCOMP is only any use when disks have been copied with DISKCOPY, since it makes the comparison sector by sector, rather than file by file.

The program ends with this message if no differences are found:

```
Diskettes compare OK
```

Otherwise, the tracks where differences have been found are listed.

The results are of little help to the user if errors are found. There is no way of knowing where files are stored, so it is impossible to tell which files are different or may be corrupt. To identify the files that are different you must use the COMP command.

DISKCOMP stops after it has found ten differences.

As for DISKCOPY, the comparison can be made using either one or two drives. The messages that are displayed are similar to those of DISKCOPY (except that the disks are described as 'first' and 'second' rather than 'source' and 'target').

DISKCOMP can compare floppy disks only. It should not be used with ASSIGN, JOIN or SUBST.

```
C>diskcomp a: a:

Insert FIRST diskette in drive A:

Press any key when ready . . .

Comparing 80 tracks
18 sectors per track, 2 side(s)

Insert SECOND diskette in drive A:

Press any key when ready . . .

Insert FIRST diskette in drive A:

Press any key when ready . . .

Insert SECOND diskette in drive A:

Press any key when ready . . .

Compare OK
```

Figure 7.3 Single-drive disk comparisons

Examples

To compare disks using two drives, enter:

```
DISKCOMP A: B:
```

To compare two disks using a single drive, enter:

```
DISKCOMP A: A:
```

The program prompts you to enter the disks as they are required (Figure 7.3).

CHKDSK

Command:	CHKDSK
Effect:	Checks the status of a disk or group of files
Version:	DOS 1, OS/2
Type:	External
Syntax:	[*location*]CHKDSK [*drive*] (DOS 1)
	[*location*]CHKDSK [*spec*] (DOS 2)

Parameters: /F   Fix errors by writing corrections to disk (DOS 2)

            /V   List files and detailed errors ('verbose' listing)   (DOS 2)

This very useful utility has three main tasks. Firstly, it provides us with basic information about a particular disk, including its capacity, free space and the number of bytes in bad sectors; also included in this data is the amount of space taken up by hidden files (such as the system files and some application program files) and the sub-directories. The space recorded as used by sub-directories is the space needed to store the filenames and related information, not the space used by the files themselves. The root directory space is omitted from the calculations. For DOS and for OS/2's real mode the command also shows the total of the computer's RAM and how much is currently free.

The second task of this command is to identify disk errors. In particular it looks for errors in the way in which file locations have been recorded. In these cases the message will either indicate that *lost clusters* have been found (in a number of *chains*) or that a file is *cross-linked*. A lost cluster is simply a section of a file that exists on disk but for which there is no entry in the directory; a chain is a string of linked clusters. A file becomes cross-linked when it is discovered that the same section of the disk is allocated to two different files. In both cases CHKDSK gives the option to convert the offending sections to separate files. This is only possible if the /F parameter was specified (otherwise you are warned before you start that corrections will be listed on screen but not actually written to disk).

Fragmentation

If you do decide to convert the missing chains to files, you will end up with a set of files called FILE000.CHK, FILE0001.CHK, and so on. The new files are unlikely to be of any use to you but it is usually worth checking; you can try displaying them with TYPE or reading them into a word processor. If they are no good it is as well to delete them. In any event, as long as the /F parameter was specified, the space that was previously occupied by the bad data will be freed and available for new data.

CHKDSK's third task is to check for fragmentation of files. Whenever a file is stored on disk the operating system always

```
C>chkdsk

 32428032 bytes total disk space
    55296 bytes in 2 hidden files
    45056 bytes in 17 directories
 13012992 bytes in 703 user files
   262144 bytes in bad sectors
 19052544 bytes available on disk

   655360 bytes total memory
   540976 bytes free

C>
```

Figure 7.4 Checking the disk status

uses the first available space. The first few files are stored one after another on a disk. As files are deleted the data area used on a disk develops 'holes'. The operating system uses these for files in preference to the unused area towards the end of the disk. The first gap in data may not be large enough for the entire file, so the operating system stores part of the file in the first gap, part in the second and so on until the file has been written away completely. It uses the directory and an area called the *File Allocation Table (FAT)* to link the parts of the file together (see Chapter 20 for more details). Such a file is said to be *fragmented*.

Fragmentation cannot harm your data but it can slow down the system quite considerably because the time taken to load a file into memory increases dramatically. The problem can become very noticeable on hard disks. You can check on fragmentation by including a file specification in the CHKDSK command. The command lists the files that are fragmented and in each case gives the number of fragments in the file (which it calls 'non-contiguous blocks').

There are two ways to deal with fragmentation. One is to buy one of the utility programs currently on the market that

```
C>chkdsk c: /f

63 lost clusters found in 1 chains.
Convert lost chains to files (Y/N)? y

 32776192 bytes total disk space
    79872 bytes in 26 directories
 32417792 bytes in 1454 user files
   129024 bytes in 1 recovered files
   149504 bytes available on disk

   655360 bytes total memory
   540976 bytes free

C>
```

Figure 7.5 Checking disk errors

```
Volume BACKUP   001 created 9 Mar 1990 5:18a

  1457664 bytes total disk space
        0 bytes in 1 hidden files
   458240 bytes in 10 user files
   999424 bytes available on disk

   655360 bytes total memory
   540976 bytes free

All specified file(s) are contiguous.

 32428032 bytes total disk space
    55296 bytes in 2 hidden files
    47104 bytes in 10 directories
 13213696 bytes in 721 user files
   262144 bytes in bad sectors
 18849792 bytes available on disk

   655360 bytes total memory
   540976 bytes free

C:\TEMP2\COMMAND.COM
    Contains 2 non-contiguous blocks.
```

Figure 7.6 Fragmentation of files

shuffle files around on disk until each file is in a single, unbroken block; this is the easiest method for hard disks. The other method is to use COPY, XCOPY or BACKUP to copy all files to a blank disk; these commands copy one file at a time, so the files will be in continuous blocks. This is really only practical for floppy disks. (Note that DISKCOPY preserves fragmentation of disks.)

The /V parameter lists all sub-directories and files and expands any error-messages.

Examples

To check the status of a disk use the command on its own (Figure 7.4):

    CHKDSK

The errors on a disk can be corrected as follows (Figure 7.5):

    CHKDSK C: /F

The level of fragmentation can be checked with a command in the form:

    CHKDSK A:*.*

This is illustrated in Figure 7.6.

VOL

Command:	VOL
Effect:	Displays disk volume labels
Version:	DOS 2, OS/2
Type:	Internal
Syntax:	VOL [drive] (DOS, OS/2 real mode)
	VOL [drive] [...] (OS/2 protected mode)
Parameters:	None

All disks created with versions of DOS greater than DOS 1 have the option for storing a volume label. This is simply a name for the disk as a whole; both floppy and hard disks can have volume labels.

The VOL command allows us to display the volume label for the current drive or a specified drive. The OS/2 version of the command allows more than one drive to be specified on the command line.

A volume label can be added by including the /V parameter in the FORMAT command, or with LABEL.

VOL can be used with all types of drive, including RAM drives, logical drives and network drives.

For a more detailed explanation see Chapter 3.

Examples

For DOS or OS/2 the volume label of a disk can be displayed on screen with:

```
VOL

VOL C:
```

The first option applies to the current drive, the second to drive C. OS/2 protected mode offers this enhancement:

```
VOL A: C:
```

This lists the volume labels for both drives A and C.

LABEL

Command:	LABEL
Effect:	Changes a disk's volume label
Version:	DOS 3, OS/2
Type:	External
Syntax:	[*location*]LABEL [*drive*] [*label*]
Parameters:	None

A disk's volume label can be changed with this command. The command line must specify the drive containing the disk, if it is not the current drive.

The program responds by displaying the current label and requesting a new label. The new label can be up to 11 characters long, selected from the same characters as for filenames (no spaces and no full stop).

To delete the current label altogether just press Return. Confirmation is required that this is what you want to do.

The process can be speeded up by including the new label on the command line. This is also a useful option for batch files.

Further descriptions of this command can be found in Chapter 3.

Examples　　To change the label of the current drive, enter:

```
LABEL
```

Type a new name and return.

To change the label of the hard disk to 'OS2DISK', enter:

```
LABEL C:OS2DISK
```

To delete the label of the disk in drive A, enter:

```
LABEL A:
```

When the program prompts you for a new name, press Return; when asked for confirmation, type 'N' and Return.

8. *Directory Management*

DOS 3.3 and OS/2 provide us with five commands for manipulating the root directory and sub-directories. Four of these we have met already in Chapter 4. The fifth, FASTOPEN, provides a method for faster access to files.

These five commands are described in detail below.

DIR

Command: DIR
Effect: Displays the contents of a directory
Version: DOS 1, OS/2
Type: Internal
Syntax: DIR [spec]   (DOS, OS/2 real mode)
              DIR [spec] [...]   (OS/2 protected mode)
Parameters: /P   Pause after each screenful
              /W   Wide listing of files only

Every disk has a root directory that contains details of files stored on the disk. This directory may contain sub-directories, which store details of other files. Each sub-directory may contain other levels of sub-directory, and so on. The DIR command lists the contents of the root directory or a sub-directory.

The command on its own lists all files in the current directory of the current drive. If it is followed by a file specification this may indicate a different drive, directory or group of files, or any combination of these.

The /P parameter forces the command to pause at the end of each screenful of information; /W produces a wide listing of filenames and extensions only.

The directory concludes with the total number of files and amount of space left on the disk (in bytes). Sub-directories always start with two special entries, representing the current and parent directories, these two 'files' are included in the file total.

```
[C:\]dir c:\wp\book\*.*

Volume in drive C has no label.
Directory of C:\WP\BOOK

.              <DIR>       8-03-90    5:01p
..             <DIR>       8-03-90    5:01p
CONTENTS LST      566      8-03-90    5:04p
ILLUS            2816      1-04-89    6:26a
CH7             22656     22-03-89    5:01p
CH9             37064     30-03-89   12:09p
CH8             11648     22-03-89    5:00p
CH10             9049     30-03-89   12:43p
CH11            25056     29-03-89   11:19a
CH12            12928     29-03-89   11:33a
CH13            40704      4-04-89   12:42p
    11 File(s)  18673664 bytes free

[C:\]
```

Figure 8.1 Sub-directory listing

OS/2 protected mode provides the enhancement that more than one directory can be listed at a time. A full description of this command is given in Chapter 4.

Examples

A listing of the current directory can be obtained by the command:

```
DIR
```

If the current directory is \WP\BOOK on drive C and C is the current drive, this is equivalent to:

```
DIR C:\WP\BOOK\*.*
```

The results of this command are shown in Figure 8.1.

A wide listing of the OS/2 external commands and associated files can be displayed a page at a time with the command:

```
DIR C:\OS2 /P /W
```

This is illustrated in Figure 8.2.

```
                              . .             4201     DCP    5202     DCP    ABIOS     SYS
ANSICALL DLL    BKSCALLS DLL    BMSCALLS DLL    BVSCALLS DLL    CLOCK01   SYS
CLOCK02  SYS    CMD      EXE    COMMAND  COM    COUNTRY  SYS    CPISPFPC  DLL
DISK01   SYS    DISK02   SYS    DMPC     EXE    DOSCALL1 DLL    DTM       DLL
FORMATS  TBL    HARDERR  EXE    ISPD     MSG    ISPM     MSG    KBD01     SYS
KBD02    SYS    KBDCALLS DLL    KEYBOARD DCP    MONCALLS DLL    MOUCALLS  DLL
MSG      DLL    NLS      DLL    OSO001   MSG    PRINT01  SYS    PRINT02   SYS
QUECALLS DLL    SCREEN01 SYS    SCREEN02 SYS    SESMGR   DLL    SHELL11F  AIF
SHELL11F AII    SHELL11F CNF    SHELL11F EXE    SHELL11F LIB    SHELL11F  PRO
STXTDMPC DLL    SWAPPER  EXE    VIOCALLS DLL    VIOTBL   DCP    F80000    BIO
FC0400   BIO    FC0500   BIO    F80100   BIO    CONFIG   SYS    SPOOLCP   DLL
ANSI     EXE    ANSI     SYS    APPEND   EXE    ASSIGN   COM    ATTRIB    EXE
CHKDSK   COM    COMP     COM    DISKCOMP COM    DISKCOPY COM    DOSCALLS  LIB
EDLIN    COM    EGA      SYS    EXTDSKDD SYS    FDISK    COM    FIND      EXE
FORMAT   COM    GRAFTABL COM    HELP     BAT    HELP     CMD    HELPMSG   EXE
JOIN     EXE    KEYB     COM    LABEL    COM    LINK     EXE    MODE      COM
MORE     COM    PRINT    COM    RECOVER  COM    REPLACE  EXE    SORT      EXE
SPOOL    EXE    SUBST    EXE    SYS      COM    TRACE    EXE    TRACEFMT  EXE
TREE     COM    VDISK    SYS    XCOPY    EXE    BACKUP   COM    BASIC     COM
BASICA   COM    COM01    SYS    COM02    SYS    CREATEDD EXE    MORTGAGE  BAS
MOUSEA00 SYS    MOUSEA01 SYS    MOUSEA02 SYS    MOUSEA03 SYS    MOUSEA04  SYS
MOUSEB00 SYS    MOUSEB01 SYS    MOUSEB02 SYS    MOUSEB05 SYS    OSO001H   MSG
PATCH    EXE    POINTDD  SYS    RESTORE  COM    SETCOM40 EXE    A
```

Figure 8.2 Wide listing of OS/2 sub-directory, by page

MKDIR (MD)

Command:	MKDIR *or* MD
Effect:	Creates a sub-directory
Version:	DOS 2, OS/2
Type:	Internal
Syntax:	MKDIR [*drive*][*path*][*directory*] (DOS, OS/2 real mode)
	MD [*drive*][*path*][*directory*] (DOS, OS/2 real mode)
	MKDIR [*drive*][*path*][*directory*] [...] (OS/2 protected mode)
	MD [*drive*][*path*][*directory*] [...] (OS/2 protected mode)

Parameters: None

This command is used to create a sub-directory. The rules for the sub-directory name follow those for filenames, though extensions are not usually given. If no path is given, the sub-directory is created in the current directory of the current drive. Otherwise, the path may specify a drive and/or directory path. If the first directory name is preceded by a '\' the path begins at the root directory.

MKDIR can include '..' in commands to represent the parent directory.

OS/2 protected mode allows the creation of several directories with a single command.

For further explanations, see Chapter 4.

Examples

A sub-directory called 'REPORTS' can be created in the \WP directory of drive C with the command:

```
MD C:\WP\REPORTS
```

If C is the current drive and \WP the current directory on C, this command can be abbreviated to:

```
MD REPORTS
```

If the current directory of C is \CALC\RESULTS, you can create a new directory at the same level as follows:

```
MD C:..\RESULTS2
```

The parent (C:\CALC) now has another sub-directory (C:\CALC\RESULTS2).

Using OS/2 we can create a series of sub-directories:

```
MD A:\DATA C:\DATA C:\CALC\RESULTS
```

New directories called 'DATA' are created in the root directories of both the hard disk and the floppy disk in drive A, and the \CALC directory on the hard disk has a new \RESULTS sub-directory.

CHDIR (CD)

Command: CHDIR *or* CD
Effect: Changes the current directory
Version: DOS 2, OS/2
Type: Internal
Syntax: CHDIR [*drive*][*path*]
            CD [*drive*][*path*]
Parameters: None

Each drive on the system has a current directory. This is the directory to which all commands refer unless we specify otherwise. The current directories are generally different for each drive. The default, when the system is booted, is the root directory in each case.

If the path that is specified does not include a drive specifier or full directory path then the current drive and directory are assumed.

CHDIR on its own, or with just a drive specifier, displays the current directory of the current or named drive.

CHDIR can use the '..' parent directory in commands.

For further information, see Chapter 4.

Examples

The current directory of the current drive and drive A can be displayed with the commands:

```
CD
CD A:
```

Do not confuse this second command with:

```
CD A:\
```

After this command, the root directory is the current directory of drive A.

The current directories can be changed as follows:

```
CD \WS\BOOKS
CD A:DATA
```

The first command changes the current directory to \WS\BOOKS for the current drive only. The second changes the current directory for drive A to the \DATA sub-directory of the current directory. For example, if the current directory of drive A was A:\PROGRAMS, it is now A:\PROGRAMS\DATA.

To move back up the directory tree one level use:

```
CD ..
```

The parent directory is now the current directory.

RMDIR (RD)

Command:	RMDIR *or* RD
Effect:	Removes an empty directory
Version:	DOS 2, OS/2
Type:	Internal
Syntax:	RMDIR [*drive*][*path*] (DOS, OS/2 real mode)
	RD [*drive*][*path*] (DOS, OS/2 real mode)
	RMDIR [*drive*][*path*] [...] (OS/2 protected mode)
	RD [*drive*][*path*] [...] (OS/2 protected mode)
Parameters:	None

Inevitably, some directories become redundant and need to be erased from the disk. RMDIR accomplishes this. As for the other directory commands, the command must specify the path leading to the directory to be deleted. If this does not include a drive specifier the current drive is assumed; if the first directory is not preceded by '\' it is assumed that the path to the directory to be deleted leads off the current drive.

You cannot delete the current directory and the directory must be completely empty. It must not contain any files or other levels of sub-directory. The '..' parent directory can be included in the path but cannot be deleted, or course.

OS/2 protected mode allows you to delete a series of sub-directories with a single command (although they must be specified individually; you cannot use wildcards).

Examples   The directory C:\CALC\RESULTS2 can be deleted with:

```
RD C:\CALC\RESULTS2
```

or:

```
RD RESULTS2
```

The second form of the command can only be used if C is the current drive and \CALC is the current directory of that drive.

Alternatively, if C:\CALC\RESULTS were the current drive and directory, the same directory could have been deleted with:

```
RD ..\RESULTS2
```

For OS/2 protected mode we can 'clean up' a disk with fewer commands:

```
RD C:\CALC\RESULTS C:\CALC\RESULTS2 \DATA
```

This deletes both sub-directories of C:\CALC and also the \DATA directory in the root directory of the current drive.

FASTOPEN

Command:	FASTOPEN
Effect:	Fast access to most recently used files
Version:	DOS 3.3
Type:	External
Syntax:	[*location*]FASTOPEN [*drive*][=*number*] [...]
Parameters:	None

This useful little command was introduced in DOS 3.3 but did not make it through to OS/2. The command is designed to speed up access to files and sub-directories by storing in memory precise details of the locations of the most recently used file.

When DOS needs to access a file, whether to read its contents or make changes, it must locate the file on disk. Using the directory path, it starts at the root directory, which contains the location on disk of the first sub-directory in the path; this sub-directory is read and from it DOS is able to locate the next sub-directory. This process continues until the last sub-directory is found. If a file has been specified, its location can be read from the last sub-directory. This process can take a comparatively long time.

For example, suppose the following command is entered:

```
TYPE C:\CALC\RESULTS\NOTES
```

DOS must read the root directory of drive C; the entry for CALC contains the location of the \CALC directory. DOS reads this directory and from it extracts the location of the \RESULTS directory. This directory must then be read to find the location of the file NOTES. If the sub-directories are spread about the disk (as is usually the case) three clusters of data must be read into memory before DOS can even begin to access NOTES.

FASTOPEN helps by storing in memory the actual location on disk of the most recently used files and sub-directories. The next time you want to look at the NOTES file DOS is able to go straight to it, cutting out all the directory searches. If the file is not in the list held by FASTOPEN then DOS must search through the directories as before but the new file and its location are added to the list. As a default, FASTOPEN keeps the locations of the last 34 files and/or sub-directories. As new files or directories are requested FASTOPEN replaces the oldest locations in the list with the newer ones.

When FASTOPEN is invoked the command must list all drives for which it is to be used. The number of entries in the list can be specified. These lists do not take up much space in memory (35 bytes for each item in the list) so we can afford to be generous.

FASTOPEN can only be used for hard disks. It may not be used with floppy disks, RAM disks or networked drives. It should not be used in combination with ASSIGN, JOIN or SUBST and it should only be invoked once during a session.

Examples

Access to a single hard disk can be speeded up with the command:

```
FASTOPEN C:
```

If there are a total of three logical drives but only drive C is used to any great extent, this can be indicated by:

```
FASTOPEN C:=200 D: E:
```

The locations of the 200 most recently accessed files and directories will be stored in memory, along with 34 each for D and E.

If C and D are accessed with equal regularity but E is rarely used the command could be:

```
FASTOPEN C:=100 D:=100
```

Here, a list of 100 files is maintained for C and D but no locations are stored for E.

9. *File Management*

There are a number of commands that affect individual files or groups of files. Half of these relate to the copying of files, in one way or another; the remainder provide a varied collection of routines to compare, rename, delete, display and change files, as well as a single command that attempts to recover a damaged file. Most of these commands have been described before but each is fully documented below.

COPY

Command:	COPY
Effect:	Copies or combines files
Version:	DOS 1, OS/2
Type:	Internal
Syntax:	COPY *spec1* [*spec2*]
	COPY spec1+*spec2*[+...] [*spec3*]
Parameters:	/A ASCII files
	/B Binary files
	/V Verification on

COPY is one of the oldest and most versatile of DOS commands. It is also one of the most frequently used. The command can appear in a number of different formats.

Copying files   At its simplest, COPY makes copies of one or more files in the same or a different directory, or on a different disk. The first file specification is the file or files to be copied; wildcards can be included and any file that matches is copied. If no drive is given, the current drive is assumed; if no path is specified, the operating system searches the current directory.

The second specification indicates the target for the copy. If no drive is given, the current drive is assumed; similarly, the copies are placed in the current directory if no other path is specified. If a filename is given, this is the name for the copy; otherwise the original filename is used.

You cannot have two files in the same directory with the same name. If you attempt to copy a file into its own directory with the same name, the operating system responds with the message that a 'file cannot be copied onto itself'. If the target name is the same as an existing file, then the old file is overwritten.

The second specification can also contain wildcards. These indicate those parts of the name that are to stay the same.

If the first specification includes wildcards the files that are found are listed as they are copied. (To turn this display off, use the NUL device described in Chapter 12.) The command always concludes with a statement of the number of files copied.

Other uses of COPY allow you to copy files to devices, as demonstrated in Chapter 12.

Combining files   COPY can also combine files by adding two or more files together. This is sometimes known by the rather ungainly term *concatenation*. The files to be combined are separated by '+' symbols. If two or more individual files are listed they are combined in the order given. The name and location of the resulting file is determined by the final specification, if there is one; if no specification is given, the first file in the list is replaced by the combined file.

If the second specification (following the '+') contains wildcards the files that match are all added to the first file; the results are stored in the file identified by the final specification, if there is one, or the first file named.

If all the specifications contain wildcards then the files are copied in pairs (or groups).

Some care is needed when combining files, as the results may not always be as you expect. It is a good idea to make copies of the files that may be changed before you start, deleting these extra files only when you are satisfied that the process has been completed satisfactorily. In particular, problems arise if the destination filename is included in the specification of the files to be combined (see the examples below).

Although you can combine different types of file it doesn't make a lot of sense to try and do so. Indeed, this command is only really useful for combining ASCII files (that is, files that contain pure text, with no control codes or special characters). When combining non-ASCII files you need the /B parameter (see below).

Combining files with 'nothing'

There is a potential problem when you want to combine a group of files that are defined by a single ambiguous specification but cannot think of a second specification to add. DOS helps out by allowing the second specification to be entered as ',,' (two commas). This special 'filename' is just there for padding. This facility is not available under OS/2.

An interesting side effect arises when the first specification is a single file. The copy process still goes ahead but the effect is that the date and time given for the file change to the current date and time. This only works for a single file but there is a routine in Chapter 18 to change the date and time for a group of files.

Parameters

One of the most important features of ASCII files is that they always end with a Ctrl-Z character. The /A parameter directs the command to treat the files being copied as ASCII files when it comes to determining the end of a file. The command copies those files only up to the first Ctrl-Z character; anything after that is not copied. (To get some idea of where this is, use TYPE with a filename; TYPE always treats files as ASCII and stops when it reaches this particular end-of-file marker.)

If /A is attached to the destination name the operating system adds a Ctrl-Z character to the end of the new file.

The /B parameter directs the operating system to treat files as *binary* files and determine the amount to copy from the size given in the directory, ignoring any end-of-file markers. If attached to the destination file, the operating system does not add an extra end-of-file marker. A binary file is one that can contain any characters, including all the non-ASCII control codes and special characters.

/A and /B are unusual in that they can be placed anywhere in the command line and may occur more than once. The two parameters are mutually exclusive. When either /A or /B is encountered the operating system assumes that the file immediately before the parameter is to be treated as that type and that all files that follow are to be treated the same, until another parameter is encountered.

If no parameter is specified, COPY assumes a default type. In particular, the operating system assumes that files are binary files during the normal copying process; this is also fine for

ASCII files, since the size in the directory should be correct and will include the Ctrl-Z character. When combining files the command assumes that the files are ASCII by default and copies only up to the first Ctrl-Z character, unless /B is specified.

The /V parameter makes the operating system verify that the file has been copied satisfactorily. It does this by reading the copy back to make sure that the result is readable. The parameter also slows down the copying process and is identical to that when VERIFY is ON.

Examples

A single file can be copied within a directory using the command:

```
COPY CHAP1.TXT CHAP1.OLD
```

A group of files starting with 'CHAP', and with TXT extensions, can be copied to files with the same name but different extensions, as follows:

```
COPY CHAP*.TXT *.OLD
```

These same files can be copied to the current directory of drive A with:

```
COPY CHAP*.TXT A:*.OLD
```

All TXT files can be copied from the \BOOK directory on drive A into the current directory of the current drive, with the names kept the same, as follows:

```
COPY A:\BOOK\*.TXT
```

Other examples of this command when used for copying were given in Chapter 5.

Two files can be combined as follows:

```
COPY CHAP1.TXT+CHAP2.TXT
```

The file CHAP1.TXT now includes the contents of both files (Figure 9.1). Alternatively, these files could have been combined into a single file called BOOK.ALL in the \FINAL directory:

```
C:\WP\BOOK>type chap1.txt
This is the text for CHAP1.TXT

C:\WP\BOOK>type chap2.txt
This is the text for CHAP2.TXT

C:\WP\BOOK>copy chap1.txt+chap2.txt
CHAP1.TXT
CHAP2.TXT
        1 File(s) copied

C:\WP\BOOK>type chap1.txt
This is the text for CHAP1.TXT
This is the text for CHAP2.TXT

C:\WP\BOOK>
```

Figure 9.1 Combining two files

```
COPY CHAP1.TXT+CHAP2.TXT \FINAL\CHAP.ALL
```

To combine a number of files, adding their contents to an existing file, use:

```
COPY BOOK.ALL+CHAP*.TXT
```

The file BOOK.ALL now contains its original text plus the contents of all the other files that match the ambiguous specification (Figure 9.2). If a target specification is given, the combined file takes this name and specification.

Note that the files are always copied in the order in which the command finds them in the directory. To change the order in the directory either use one of the commercial utility programs that include this facility or copy the files to a new directory, sorting them as you do so.

Some confusion can arise from the use of wildcards. Suppose that there are two sets of files, with extensions TXA and TXB. These can be combined into a single file as follows:

```
COPY *.TXA+*.TXB ALL.TXT
```

165

```
C:\WP\BOOK>copy book.all+chap*.txt
BOOK.ALL
CHAP1.TXT
CHAP2.TXT
CHAP3.TXT
        1 File(s) copied

C:\WP\BOOK>type book.all
This is the original text for BOOK.ALL
This is the text for CHAP1.TXT
This is the text for CHAP2.TXT
This is the text for CHAP2.TXT
This is the text for CHAP3.TXT

C:\WP\BOOK>
```

Figure 9.2 Combining a group of files

The file ALL.TXT is a combination of all the TXA files plus the TXB files (for example, CH1.TXA, CH2.TXA and CH1.TXB). However, the files are copied in pairs if wildcards are used throughout:

    COPY *.TXA+*.TXB *.TXC

The file CH1.TXC contains CH1.TXA+CH1.TXB, CH2.TXC contains CH2.TXA+CH2.TXB. If there is a file called CH3.TXA but not one called CH2.TXB, the command responds with a 'File not found' message.

Any of the specifications can, of course, include drive names and paths:

    COPY A:*.TXA+B:*.TXB C:\BOOK*.TXC

The TXA files on the current directory of drive A are combined with the TXB files in the root directory of drive B to form a set of TXC files in the C:\BOOK directory.

To combine all TXT files into a single file (under DOS 3.3), use the special ',,' filename:

```
C:\WP\BOOK>dir notes.*

 Volume in drive C has no label
 Directory of  C:\WP\BOOK

NOTES     DOC      191   1-03-90   8:15a
          1 File(s)  18655232 bytes free

C:\WP\BOOK>copy notes.doc+,,
NOTES.DOC
          1 File(s) copied

C:\WP\BOOK>dir notes.*

 Volume in drive C has no label
 Directory of  C:\WP\BOOK

NOTES     DOC      191   8-03-90   2:06a
          1 File(s)  18655232 bytes free

C:\WP\BOOK>
```

Figure 9.3 Changing a file's date and time

```
COPY *.TXT+,, TEXT.ALL
```

(If the ',,' were omitted, TEXT.ALL would just contain the last file copied.) Problems would also arise if the destination file had the same extension:

```
COPY *.TXT+,, ALL.TXT
```

The operating system creates a file called ALL.TXT and then tries to copy this new file as part of the process to combine the files. It does so but has to delete the original version, which may results in some loss of data.

Whenever the destination file already exists, the operating system issues a warning:

```
Contents of destination lost before copy
```

This message is rather late, because by the time the message is displayed there is nothing we can do about it.

The ',,' special filename can be used to change the date and time of a file:

```
COPY NOTES.DOC+,,
```

This is illustrated in Figure 9.3.

XCOPY

Command:	XCOPY
Effect:	Copies one or more files, with extended features
Version:	DOS 3.2, OS/2
Type:	External
Syntax:	[*location*]XCOPY *spec1* [*spec2*]
Parameters:	/A Copy modified files
	/D:*date* Copy files after specified date
	/E Copy empty sub-directories
	/M Copy modified files and clear archive attribute
	/P Prompt for each file
	/S Copy sub-directories
	/V Verify copies
	/W Wait before reading source files

This command provides an enhanced copying service. It is particularly helpful when we only want to copy files that have changed and when there are sub-directories to be copied.

In its simplest form, with no parameters, the command works identically to COPY.

/A directs XCOPY to copy only those files that have the archive attribute set (that is, they have been changed since they were last copied with XCOPY or BACKUP, or they are new files); /A does not affect the archive attribute. /M also copies these files but clears the archive attribute and is therefore more widely used.

/D instructs XCOPY to copy only those files that have a date the same as or later than that given.

/S copies the contents of any sub-directories, creating similar sub-directories on the target drive if necessary.

/E copies any empty sub-directories in the directory being copied (but is only effective if /S is also specified).

/P causes the command to issue a prompt for each file being copied. Press 'Y' to copy the file or 'N' to leave it.

/V switches verification on for the duration of the copy.

/W causes the command to wait before loading the original files. This gives you the opportunity to copy files from more than one disk.

Further discussion on this command can be found in Chapter 5.

Examples All files from the current directory can be copied to the disk in drive A with:

```
XCOPY *.* A:
```

Later on, you may want to copy only those files that have changed. If you have two backup disks (which is a sensible idea, since floppies have a tendency to corrupt unexpectedly), you can use different commands for each disk:

```
XCOPY *.* A: /A
XCOPY *.* A: /M
```

The first command copies all those that have changed; the second copies the same set of files and then clears their archive attributes.

If you add the /M parameter but there is insufficient space on the floppy disk for all the modified files, you can put in a new disk and repeat the command (by pressing F3). Only those files that did not fit on the first disk will be copied.

If a directory includes other sub-directories these can all be copied, with their contents, with a command in the form:

```
XCOPY C:\WP\BOOK A:\ /E /S
```

This command copies the entire contents of the \WP\BOOK directory, including any sub-directories. Empty directories are also copied. The disk in drive A will have the same directory structure as \WP\BOOK (Figure 9.4).

```
C:\WP\BOOK>xcopy c:\wp\book a:\ /e /s

Reading source file(s)...
C:\WP\BOOK\CH7
C:\WP\BOOK\CH9
C:\WP\BOOK\CH8
C:\WP\BOOK\PRELIMS\CONTENTS.LST
C:\WP\BOOK\PRELIMS\ILLUS
        5 File(s) copied

C:\WP\BOOK>dir a:

 Volume in drive A is BACKUP  001
 Directory of  A:\

CH7             22656  22-03-89   5:01p
CH9             37064  30-03-89  12:09p
CH8             11648  22-03-89   5:00p
INDEX          <DIR>        8-03-90   2:14a
PRELIMS        <DIR>        8-03-90   2:14a
        5 File(s)   1380352 bytes free

C:\WP\BOOK>
```

Figure 9.4 Copying files and sub-directories

REPLACE

Command:	REPLACE
Effect:	Replaces or adds files
Version:	DOS 3.2, OS/2
Type:	External
Syntax:	[*location*]REPLACE [*spec*] [*drive*][*path*]
Parameters:	/A Add files
	/P Prompt before replacing or adding
	/R Replace read-only files
	/S Replace in sub-directories
	/W Wait until disk is loaded

The REPLACE command replaces files on one disk with files of the same name from another disk. Alternatively, it adds any files to a disk that do not exist there.

The first item on the command line is the specification of the files to be copied (the *source*) including the drive and directory if necessary. This is followed by the destination drive and path. No filename is given in the last part of the command since the files cannot be renamed.

In its default state, with no parameters, REPLACE checks the destination for files that match those on the source disk. Only those files that exist in both locations are copied.

The /S parameter instructs REPLACE to copy the files to all sub-directories of the destination. If a file exists in more than one sub-directory, it is replaced in all those locations.

The /A parameter is perhaps the most useful, since this directs REPLACE to add any files that do not exist on the destination. No files are overwritten. Note that /A and /S cannot be used together.

As for XCOPY, /P causes REPLACE to issue a prompt for each file and /W makes it wait for a source disk to be loaded.

/R results in files with the *read-only attribute* set being overwritten as well. The read-only attribute can be set for any file and, in the normal course of events, stops the operating system from overwriting the file. For more information on attributes, see ATTRIB below.

Replace sets an ERRORLEVEL value when it finishes executing (Figure 9.5). For more on batch files, see Chapter 18.

Examples

Suppose that you have a backup disk and that only the relevant files are to be copied onto another computer. This can be achieved with:

```
REPLACE A:\*.* C:\PROGRAMS
```

Any files on C:\PROGRAMS for which there are corresponding files on drive A are replaced by the versions on floppy disk.

If some of the files on floppy exist on sub-directories of PROGRAMS, then the version on drive C can be replaced as follows:

```
REPLACE A:\*.* C:\PROGRAMS /S /P
```

The /P parameter results in the name of each file to be replaced being displayed; press 'Y' to replace it or 'N' to leave the original on drive C untouched (see Figure 9.6). The prompt is displayed for each matching file in each sub-directory.

ERRORLEVEL	Reason
2	No files matching the source specification
3	Invalid directory (source or destination)
5	Destination file is read-only (/R not specified)
8	Out of memory
11	Bad parameters
15	Invalid drive (source or destination)
22	Incorrect DOS version

Figure 9.5 REPLACE ERRORLEVELs

```
C:\PROGRAMS>replace a:\*.* c:\programs /s /p
 Replace C:\PROGRAMS\GLPSFG3.EXE? (Y/N) y
 Replacing C:\PROGRAMS\GLPSFG3.EXE
 Replace C:\PROGRAMS\GLSET9.EXE? (Y/N) n
 Replace C:\PROGRAMS\GLRDGTR3.EXE? (Y/N) n
 Replace C:\PROGRAMS\GLLIST3.EXE? (Y/N) n
 Replace C:\PROGRAMS\GLPLOT3.EXE? (Y/N) y
 Replacing C:\PROGRAMS\GLPLOT3.EXE
 Replace C:\PROGRAMS\MULTI.EXE? (Y/N) y
 Replacing C:\PROGRAMS\MULTI.EXE
 Replace C:\PROGRAMS\PROG2\GLPSFG3.EXE? (Y/N) y
 Replacing C:\PROGRAMS\PROG2\GLPSFG3.EXE
 Replace C:\PROGRAMS\PROG2\GLPLOT3.EXE? (Y/N) y
 Replacing C:\PROGRAMS\PROG2\GLPLOT3.EXE

5 file(s) replaced

C:\PROGRAMS>
```

Figure 9.6 Replacing files selectively

If the floppy disks contain old versions of files that already exist on the hard disk, as well as some new files, then these new files can be added as follows:

```
REPLACE A:\*.* C:\PROGRAMS /A
```

Only those files on A that do not yet exist on C:\PROGRAMS are copied.

BACKUP

Command: BACKUP
Effect: Creates backup disks
Version: DOS 2, OS/2
Type: External
Syntax: [*location*]BACKUP *drive1*[*path*][*file*] *drive2*
Parameters: /A   Add files to existing disks (DOS 3, OS/2)
        /D:*date* Backup files on or after given date
                (DOS2, OS/2)
        /F   Format before copying (DOS 3.3, OS/2)
        /L:*spec* Create or add to log file (DOS 3.3, OS/2)
        /S   Backup sub-directories as well
                (DOS 2, OS/2)
        /M   Backup modified files only
                (DOS 2, OS/2)
        /T:*time* Backup files at or after given time
                (DOS 3.3, OS/2)

This command creates or adds to special backup disks. The files are not stored in the normal way and can only be recovered with the RESTORE command. All disks are filled completely and automatically numbered by the command.

On entering the command you are asked to load a suitable disk and warned that any existing files on the disk will be overwritten. The specified files are then copied across until the floppy disk is full. Another disk is requested and the process continues in this way until all files have been backed up.

The /S parameter instructs BACKUP to copy the contents of all sub-directories while /M affects modified files only. /A adds the files to an existing backup disk while /F formats the floppies before it starts copying. If /F is included the FORMAT program must be in the current directory or in a directory pointed to by PATH.

/D and /T force BACKUP to check the date and time or the files and copy only those that were created on or after the date and time given.

/L creates a log file to record details of all files copied. This helps later on if files have to be recovered. The default name is

ERRORLEVEL	Reason
0	Command completed successfully
1	No matching files found to back up
3	Program interrupt by Ctrl-Break
4	Program ended with some other error

Figure 9.7 BACKUP ERRORLEVELs

BACKUP.LOG, and the file is stored in the directory being backed up unless otherwise specified.

If the destination is a hard disk a special \BACKUP sub-directory is used. This directory is created if it does not already exist.

BACKUP sets the ERRORLEVEL value before it ends. This can be used in batch files (see the example in Chapter 18). The ERRORLEVEL values and meanings are given in Figure 9.7.

Further descriptions of this command were given in Chapter 5.

BACKUP should not be used with APPEND, ASSIGN, JOIN or SUBST.

Examples

To copy a complete hard disk, including sub-directories, use:

```
BACKUP C:\*.* A:/S
```

Perhaps more useful is this command:

```
BACKUP C:\WP\*.DOC A: /S /F /M
```

This command copies all DOS files, in the \WP directory or its sub-directories, that have been changed or created since BACKUP or XCOPY were last used. All floppies are automatically formatted.

If a complete backup exists on floppy disk then this command may be used as part of the daily backup routine:

```
BACKUP C:\*.* A: /D:08-03-90 /A /M /S /L:C:\DAILY.LOG
```

Any files modified or created on or after 8th March 1990 are
added to the existing backup disks. Details of the files that
were backed up are stored in the file DAILY.LOG in the root
directory of drive C. This command would need to be edited
each day of course.

RESTORE

Command: RESTORE
Effect: Restores all files from disks created by BACKUP
Version: DOS 2, OS/2
Type: External
Syntax: [*location*]RESTORE *drive1* [*spec*]
Parameters: /A   Restores files modified on or after given
                   date (DOS 3.3, OS/2)
             /B   Restores files modified on or before given
                  date (DOS 3.3, OS/2)
             /E   Restores files modified at or before given
                  time (DOS 3.3, OS/2)
             /L   Restores files modified at or after given
                  time (DOS 3.3, OS/2)
             /M   Restore files that have been modified or
                  deleted (DOS 3.3, OS/2)
             /N   Restore files that have been deleted
                  (DOS 3.3, OS/2)
             /S   Restore sub-directories (DOS 3.2, OS/2)
             /P   Prompt for modified files (DOS 3.2, OS/2)

RESTORE recovers files from disks created by BACKUP. The
command can only be used for this type of file. The command
must specify the location of the backup disk and the
destination for the restored files. If the source is a hard disk,
RESTORE copies files from the \BACKUP sub-directory of the
root directory. The syntax is a little strange, as the names of
the files to be restored are given with the destination rather
than the source.

The command also asks for each backup disk in turn in the
same way as for BACKUP.

If sub-directories were backed up then the /S parameter must
be included. If there is any doubt about whether files have

ERRORLEVEL	Reason
0	Command completed successfully
1	No matching files found to restore
2	Some files not backed up because they were being accessed on a network
3	Program interrupted by Ctrl-Break
4	Program ended with some other error

Figure 9.8 RESTORE ERRORLEVELs

been backed up, add the /P parameter. RESTORE then issues a prompt whenever it encounters a file on the hard disk that has the archive attribute set. Press 'Y' to overwrite this file or 'N' to leave it. The DOS 3.3 and OS/2 versions of this parameter also issue a prompt for read-only files that are about to be overwritten.

The /M parameter, which arrived with DOS 3.3, copies only those files whose archive attribute is set; that is, any modified files are overwritten. Any files that have been deleted are also copied.

More useful is /N, which only copies files that no longer exist on the destination disk.

DOS 3.3 also added a new selection of parameters (/A, /B, /E, /L) that forces RESTORE To copy only those files that were created or changed before or after a given date or time.

RESTORE sets the ERRORLEVEL value, for use in batch files (see Chapter 18). The values and reasons for these being set are listed in Figure 9.8.

For a further description of this command, see Chapter 5.

RESTORE should not be used with APPEND, ASSIGN, JOIN or SUBST.

Examples   A complete hard disk can be restored with the command:

```
RESTORE A: C:\*.* /S
```

All files on the backup disks are restored to the hard disk, including files in sub-directories.

If the files backed up were from the \WP directory and were originally specified by *.DOC, these can be restored with:

```
RESTORE A: C:\WP\*.DOC /S /M
```

This version of the command overwrites only those files for which the archive attribute has been set. Alternatively, you can restore only those DOS files whose names begin with 'CH' with the command:

```
RESTORE A: C:\WP\CH*.DOC /S /P
```

This command prompts you before each file is restored.

If you want to restore only certain files then this may be most swiftly accomplished by deleting the redundant versions from the hard disk and entering:

```
RESTORE A: C:\*.* /S /N
```

Only those files that do not exist on the hard disk are restored.

COMP

Command:	COMP
Effect:	Compares the contents of pairs of files
Version:	PC-DOS 1, OS/2
Type:	External
Syntax:	[*location*]COMP [*spec1*] [*spec2*]
Parameters:	None

This command verifies that two files are identical.

If you enter the specifications of two individual files the program compares them byte by byte. Whenever it encounters a difference this is shown on the screen. The display is not very helpful; it gives the *offset* of the error and the values found in the files. The offset is the location of the error, measured from the start of the file; the first byte of the file is byte 0. The values are given in the *hexadecimal* format. A hexadecimal-to-ASCII conversion table is given in the Appendix. The program halts after it has encountered ten errors.

COMP always checks for end-of-file markers as the last character of each file (though these will usually only appear in ASCII files). A warning message is given if they are not found:

```
EOF marker not found
```

In some cases files have a different method of denoting the end of file and always record their file size in the directory in blocks of 128 bytes or more. This means that there may some rubbish after the end of the file; COMP will not realise that it has reached the end and will continue the comparisons for the first ten bytes of rubbish.

The second specification can be a drive name, in which case COMP searches the drive for a file with the same name as the first specification.

Both specifications can include wildcards; here, the files are compared in pairs. COMP displays the names of each pair as it starts the comparison. A message is displayed if a matching file is not found.

If the command is entered on its own you are prompted to enter the names of the two files to be compared (referred to as the 'primary' and '2nd' filenames).

The second specification can be a drive name. After the comparison is complete you are asked if you want to compare more files.

Note that COMP is specific to PC-DOS. Similar programs exist with most versions of MS-DOS but these may have a different name and syntax.

Examples

Two files with different names can be compared as follows:

```
COMP AUTOEXEC.BAT AUTOEXEC.OLD
```

Alternatively, the STARTUP.CMD files on drives C and A can be compared as follows:

```
COMP C:\STARTUP.CMD A:
```

```
C:\>comp

Enter primary file name
c:\startup.cmd

Enter 2nd file name or drive id
a:

C:\STARTUP.CMD and A:STARTUP.CMD

Compare error at OFFSET B
File 1 = 50

File 2 = 70

Eof mark not found

Compare more files (Y/N)? n

C:\>
```

Figure 9.9 Comparing files

These files could be compared by entering the command on its own:

    COMP

When asked for the primary filename enter the text 'C:\STARTUP.CMD' and for the second filename give 'A:'. This is illustrated in Figure 9.9. The only difference found was a byte with hexadecimal values of 50 and 70. These values represent the letters 'P' and 'p' respectively, so the difference is not significant in this case.

To compare two groups of files enter:

    COMP C:\WP*.DOC C:\BACK*.DOC

For each file located by the first specification a matching file is located in the second drive.

Alternatively, if the second set of files are on drive A the command would become:

    COMP C:\WP*.DOC A:

If any file on drive C is not matched on A a warning message is given.

RENAME (REN)

Command:	RENAME *or* REN
Effect:	Renames one or more files
Version:	DOS 1, OS/2
Type:	Internal
Syntax:	RENAME [*drive*][*path*]*file1 file2*
	REN [*drive*][*path*]*file1 file2*
Parameters:	None

The RENAME command changes the name of one or more files. The first specification identifies the files to be renamed and must include a filename or ambiguous filename. The second specification gives the new name(s) of the file(s). There is no point including a drive or path in the second specification since the files must stay in the same directory.

Any attempt to rename a file using a name that is already in use results in an error message. You cannot overwrite files with this command.

If the first specification includes wildcards, all files that match are renamed. Any wildcards in the second specification indicate those parts of the name that are to stay the same.

Examples

To rename STARTUP.CMD as STARTUP.OLD, enter:

```
REN STARTUP.CMD STARTUP.OLD
```

Since the main part of the name stays the same this could be abbreviated to:

```
REN STARTUP.CMD *.OLD
```

This is a safer method, since the danger of accidentally mistyping the name is reduced.

All files that match the specification TEXT*.DOC on C:\WP\BOOK can be renamed, with the first letter changed to 'N' and a BAK extension, as follows:

```
REN C:\WP\BOOK\TEXT*.DOC N*.BAK
```

Further examples were given in Chapter 5.

DEL (ERASE)

Command:	DEL *or* ERASE
Effect:	Deletes one or more files
Version:	DOS 1, OS/2
Type:	Internal
Syntax:	DEL *spec* (DOS, OS/2 real mode)
	DEL *spec* [...] (OS/2 protected mode)
	ERASE *spec* (DOS only)
Parameters:	None

This command deletes one or more files. The specification can be a single file or can include wildcards to identify a group of files. If you use the '*.*' specification or give a directory name with no file specification, the operating system responds with:

```
Are you sure (Y/N)?
```

Press 'Y' only if you want to delete all files in the directory. The directory itself is unaffected and can only be removed with RD.

OS/2 protected mode adds the enhancement that more than one group of files can be specified on the command line.

It is usually a good idea to check that the correct files are about to be deleted by first using DIR with the file specification. Having listed the files type 'DEL' and press F3; you will then be sure that only those files listed are deleted.

Take care if using DEL with ASSIGN, JOIN and SUBST, since those commands affect the way in which the operating system identifies files.

Examples

To delete all DOC files in the current directory, use:

```
DEL *.DOC
```

To delete the entire contents of C:\PROGRAMS the command is:

```
DEL C:\PROGRAMS
```

Further examples can be found in Chapter 5.

TYPE

Command:	TYPE
Effect:	Displays the contents of a file
Version:	DOS 1, OS/2
Type:	Internal
Syntax:	TYPE [*drive*][*path*]*file* (DOS, OS/2 real mode)
	TYPE *spec* [...] (OS/2 protected mode)
Parameters:	None

The TYPE command displays on screen the contents of a file. Usually, only ASCII files are displayed but any file can be shown. Non-ASCII files are only displayed up to the first Ctrl-Z (end-of-file) character.

To make the display pause either add the MORE command (see Chapter 12) or use Ctrl-NumLock or Ctrl-S to interrupt it.

OS/2 protected mode allows more than one file specification on the command line; each specification can include wildcards. In this case the name of the file is printed on the line above the text for that file.

Examples

A single file can be displayed with:

```
TYPE AUTOEXEC.BAT
```

Under OS/2 protected mode you can display several files at once:

```
TYPE C:\*.BAT C:\*.SYS
```

For more information, see Chapter 5.

ATTRIB

Command: ATTRIB
Effect: Displays or changes archive and read-only attributes
Version: DOS 3, OS/2
Type: External
Syntax: ATTRIB *spec* [+A|-A] [+R|-R]
Parameters: /S   Display or change attributes of files in sub-directories

Every file stored in the directory has half a dozen *attributes* stored against it. These tell the operating system that the entry may be a volume label or a sub-directory; they are used to identify hidden files and system files; and they mark files as archive and read-only.

The *archive attribute* is set when a new file is created or an existing file is changed. The *read-only* attribute indicates that a file is not to be changed and cannot be deleted.

The archive attribute is cleared by XCOPY and BACKUP if they have the /M parameter. It is also used by RESTORE. The attribute can also be cleared or set by ATTRIB. The command is followed by the specification of the files to be affected and then either +A to set the archive attribute or -A to clear it.

The read-only attribute is set in a similar way with +R; the files can be changed again if you use -R. Both attributes can be changed in one command.

The ATTRIB command with just a file specification displays the current attributes of the files.

The /S parameter instructs ATTRIB to repeat the command in all sub-directories of the directory that is specified.

For information on the other attributes, see Chapter 20.

Examples

The file STARTUP.CMD can be protected against accidental damage with the command:

```
ATTRIB STARTUP.CMD +R
```

```
[C:\]attrib c:\text\*.*
    A        C:\TEXT\CH7
    A        C:\TEXT\CH9
    A        C:\TEXT\CH8
    A        C:\TEXT\CONTENTS.LST
    A        C:\TEXT\ILLUS
             C:\TEXT\CHAP1.TXT
             C:\TEXT\CHAP2.TXT
             C:\TEXT\CHAP3.TXT
    A        C:\TEXT\BOOK.ALL
    A     R  C:\TEXT\NOTES.DOC
    A        C:\TEXT\CH10
    A        C:\TEXT\CH11
    A        C:\TEXT\CH12
    A        C:\TEXT\CH13

[C:\]
```

Figure 9.10 Displaying file attributes

The attribute of DOC files in the \TEXT directory can be
displayed with:

    ATTRIB C:\TEXT*.DOC

(See Figure 9.10.) The archive attribute can be set for these
files with:

    ATTRIB C:\TEXT*.DOC +A

These files are now ready to be backed up with XCOPY.

RECOVER

Command:	RECOVER
Effect:	Recovers files from a damaged disk
Version:	DOS 2, OS/2
Type:	External
Syntax:	[*location*]RECOVER [*drive*][*path*]*file*
	[*location*]RECOVER *drive*
Parameters:	None

184

This command attempts to recover a file from a disk that has developed a bad sector. If an attempt to access a file results in a 'Data error reading' message, this means that part of the file is stored in a bad sector. RECOVER reads this file but omits the bad sector. The bad sector is marked as such so that it cannot be used again. The file keeps the same name.

Although this can be a useful command it has some severe limitations. Obviously it is useless for any programs that are corrupted. You can recover certain data files but the success of the operation may be limited. If the start of the file is missing it is unlikely that the file will be of any use. If a middle section is corrupt then the file may be alright and this section can be re-entered.

The loss of the final section may be fatal if the program that created the file depends upon a particular type of end-of-file marker.

RECOVER always works in whole sectors (512 bytes). Therefore any recovered files will have a file size that is a multiple of 512 and there may be rubbish at the end of the file that has to be deleted. (If this follows the end-of-file marker it can be ignored anyway.)

After you have entered the command, RECOVER waits for you to load the required disk.

RECOVER, when used with a drive name, attempts to recover all files on a damaged disk. The files are left on the disk and all bad sectors are marked as such. Strangely, the files are all renamed and put in the root directory; the new names are FILE0001.REC, FILE0002.REC and so on. RECOVER cannot cope with sub-directories; these are also renamed as files.

If RECOVER runs out of root directory entries it stops. The recovered files can be copied off and deleted, and the process can then be repeated. As a general rule, it is easier to recover files by using RESTORE or XCOPY, assuming that up-to-date backups have been regularly maintained.

Examples   Suppose that the file 'CH1.TXT' in the \TEXT directory has become corrupt. Part of its contents may be recovered with:

```
RECOVER C:\TEXT\CH1.TXT
```

```
[C:\]recover c:\text\ch1.txt

Press Enter to begin recovery of the
files on drive C:.


512 of 2048 bytes recovered

[C:\]type c:\text\ch1.txt


        1.        Introduction to the Operating System

        The first section of this handbook is aimed at those who are new to
        the intricacies of computer operating systems. Much of the information
        given here will be familiar to those who have already worked with
        previous versions of MS-DOS or PC-DOS. For those who already
        understand the basic workings of the operating system, probably all

[C:\]
```

Figure 9.11 Recovering a file

```
[C:\]recover a:

Press Enter to begin recovery of the
files on drive A:.

16 file(s) recovered

[C:\]dir a: /w

 Volume in drive A has no label.
 Directory of  A:\

FILE0001 REC     FILE0002 REC     FILE0003 REC     FILE0004 REC     FILE0005 REC
FILE0006 REC     FILE0007 REC     FILE0008 REC     FILE0009 REC     FILE0010 REC
FILE0011 REC     FILE0012 REC     FILE0013 REC     FILE0014 REC     FILE0015 REC
FILE0016 REC
      16 File(s)     993280 bytes free

[C:\]
```

Figure 9.12 Recovering a disk

After the file has been recovered it can be displayed with the TYPE command (see Figure 9.11).

A complete disk can be recovered with:

```
RECOVER A:
```

The program displays the number of files that have been recovered. These can be listed with DIR (Figure 9.12).

10.   *General commands*

There are a number of commands that affect the general running of the system. Many of these are used to customise the system so that it suits your own particular needs. These are described in Chapter 13. The remainder of the general commands are all internal commands and are described below.

CLS

Command: CLS
Effect: Clears the screen
Version: DOS 1, OS/2
Type: Internal
Syntax: CLS
Parameters: None

This is the simplest of the operating system's commands. Its effect is to clear the screen and display the prompt in the top left-hand corner. Under OS/2 it affects only the current session.

CLS always changes the screen colours back to their default settings when an application finishes.

The greatest use of this command is in batch files, particularly after screen updating has been turned off with ECHO OFF (see Chapter 16) or when the default colours have been changed (Chapter 18).

If the ANSI driver has been installed this command is the same as the ANSI command Esc[2J (see Chapter 13).

DATE

Command: DATE
Effect: Displays and changes the current system date
Version: DOS 1, OS/2
Type: Internal
Syntax: DATE [*date*]
Parameters: None

The DATE command has two main functions: to display the current date and to change the date. The date is useful from a personal point of view (it can be handy if there is no calendar nearby) and, more importantly, because the date of any changes to a file are always stored in the directory.

The command on its own displays the current date and gives you the chance to change it. The day of the week is calculated for you. Press Return to leave the date as it was. Otherwise, enter a date in one of the following formats:

day-month-year   (European)

month-day-year   (American)

year-month-day   (Japanese)

The format is set by the COUNTRY code, which is described in Chapter 13. In versions of the operating system prior to DOS 3, the format is determined by the appropriate KEYB?? program. The DATE prompt always tells you what format to use (e.g. *dd-mm-yy* for the European format).

The day and month can be either one or two digits; they can be padded with 0's but this is not essential. The year is displayed as four digits but may be entered as either two or four figures. The range is 1980 to 2079; four-digit years must be given for 2080 to 2099.

The three parts of the date can be separated by dashes (-), slashes (/) or periods (.).

The command always checks that the date is a valid one and can cope with leap years. Do not try to enter a day of the week.

In most modern machines the date is stored in battery-backed memory so need rarely be entered; in others it should be entered every time the computer is switched on or reset. Some computers that maintain the date in their battery-backed memory only have a limit of 100 years (to 2079).

If there is no AUTOEXEC.BAT file (under DOS) you are automatically asked to enter a date. To overcome this, create a dummy startup file, as described in Chapter 16.

Note that if PC-DOS is used on a machine other than the IBM PC or IBM PC-AT the battery-backed date may not be properly set by the DATE command. On the IBM PC-AT, running PC-DOS, you may need to use the special SETUP program to set the date.

Examples   To check the current date enter:

```
DATE
```

Then press Return.

To find out which day of the week you will be holding your end-of-century party enter the two commands:

```
DATE 31-12-99
DATE
```

After checking the day re-enter today's date.

To change the date and time of a group of files to the current values, enter commands in the form:

```
COPY *.DOC+,,
```

Further examples are given in Chapter 6.

TIME

Command:	TIME
Effect:	Displays and changes the current system time
Version:	DOS 1, OS/2
Type:	Internal
Syntax:	TIME [*time*]
Parameters:	None

As for DATE, the TIME command can be used as your own personal clock or to change the system time. The time when files are created or changed is stored in the directory, so the current time should be kept as accurate as possible.

The command on its own displays the current time (to the nearest hundredth of a second). Press Return to leave it the same or enter a new time in the format:

hours:minutes:seconds

The hours can be one or two digits (0's can be added as padding but are not essential), and the 24-hour clock must be used. The minutes and seconds do not have to be included but, if they are, they must be two-digit numbers.

The command checks that the time is valid before it accepts it. Computers with battery-backed memory permanently maintain the current time; otherwise it must be set when the computer is switched on or reset. If there is no AUTOEXEC.BAT under DOS the operating system prompts you to enter the current time, regardless of whether or not the time is battery-backed.

Note that if PC-DOS is installed on non-IBM machines the time is often lost when the computer is switched on, even if it is battery-backed.

Examples   The current time can be displayed with:

    TIME

Press Return to leave it unchanged or enter a new time. The time can be set to 4:30 p.m. with the command:

    TIME 16:30

Press Return when the time is exactly 4:30.

Other examples are given in Chapter 6.

VER

Command: VER
Effect: Displays the operating system version number
Version: DOS 2, OS/2
Type: Internal
Syntax: VER
Parameters: None

This command is useful for checking that the correct version of the operating system is being used. It results in a one-line listing of the operating system name and version number. The first part of the version number increases with major changes to the operating system; the last two digits are the minor version number and are updated with any slight changes or bug fixes. The versions most commonly in use were listed in Chapter 1 (Figure 1.1).

For further details, see Chapter 6.

PROMPT

Command:	PROMPT
Effect:	Changes the system prompt
Version:	DOS 1, OS/2
Type:	Internal
Syntax:	PROMPT [*text*]
Parameters:	None

As a default, DOS displays the 'C>' prompt, while OS/2 has '[C:\]'. These prompts are displayed whenever the operating system is waiting for the user to enter a command. The 'C' in the prompt changes to reflect any change in the current drive.

This prompt can be replaced at any time by entering the PROMPT command, followed by a piece of text. In general, these items of text are printed precisely as shown; there are some special cases however. The '$' symbol is used to indicate a special code. For example, '$p' is replaced by the current pathname in the command (including the drive specifier of the current drive).

Upper and lower case characters are treated the same. A full list of codes is given in Figure 10.1.

Any spaces at the end of the prompt are ignored, unless you follow them with a *null code* (that is, any code that does not have any other meaning, such as $x).

PROMPT on its own restores the default prompt.

Under OS/2 each session starts with the default; you can have a different prompt for each protected mode session. OS/2 introduced some extra codes for the prompt.

Code	Effect	Versions
$a	& character	OS/2
$b	\ (vertical bar) character	DOS, OS/2
$c	(character	OS/2
$d	Current date	DOS, OS/2
$e	Escape character	DOS, OS/2
$f	) character	OS/2
$g	> (greater then) character	DOS, OS/2
$h	Backspace (equivalent to Ctrl-H)	DOS,OS/2
$i	Session bar	OS/2
$l	< (less than) character	DOS, OS/2
$n	Current drive	DOS, OS/2
$p	Current path	DOS, OS/2
$q	= (equals) character	DOS, OS/2
$t	Current time	DOS, OS/2
$v	Operating system version number	DOS, OS/2
$x	Null characater (other non-used characters have same effect)	DOS, OS/2
$_	Start new line	DOS, OS/2
$$	$ character	DOS, OS/2

Figure 10.1 The PROMPT codes

Examples

To set the prompt to include the current path and the time (hours and minutes only), ending with a '>' symbol, use this command:

```
PROMPT $t$h$h$h$h$h$h $p$g
```

To restore the original prompt, enter:

```
PROMPT
```

The prompt can be particularly useful in sending codes to the ANSI driver. For example, the ANSI code to clear the screen, which is the Escape character followed by [2J, can be used:

```
PROMPT $e[2J
```

The screen is now cleared every time the prompt is displayed. This command only works if ANSI.SYS has been installed (see Chapter 13). Other examples are given in Chapter 6.

11.   *Input and Output*

The computer must communicate with external devices if it is to be of any practical assistance to us. These include devices such as printers, plotters and modems, of course, but there are other devices that form part of the main system: in particular, there are the keyboard and screen.

This chapter looks at ways in which we can communicate with other parts of the system, the commands that are needed and the special instructions that are available.

THE DEVICES

The operating system is set up to recognise a number of particular devices when it starts up. You can expand this list by adding extra *device drivers*, which are special programs that allow DOS and OS/2 to communicate with particular devices (see Chapter 13).

The standard devices, which are listed in Figure 11.1 can be included in the commands we have seen so far to vary the way in which output is produced or input derived.

Each of these devices is identified by a three-letter code. For example, the *console*, consisting of the keyboard and screen, is represented by CON. To be precise, the name should be followed by a colon (as in CON:). This makes more obvious the link between these and the other standard devices - the disks - which are represented by a single letter and colon.

The names listed in Figure 11.1 are reserved by the system and may not be used as filenames or directory names. The device names can be included in commands as if they were filenames. Information is directed to the devices as if they were files on disk, or in some cases may be read from them. When a drive is included in a command it takes precedence over the default device for that command.

THE EXTERNAL PORTS

As an example, we can direct information to be printed by using the PRN device instead of a filename. PRN can be included in the COPY command, for instance:

```
COPY PREFACE.TXT PRN:
```

Device name	Description
CON	The console (keyboard and screen)
KBD$	The keyboard
SCREEN$	The screen
AUX	The standard serial port
COM1	The first serial port
COM2	The second serial port
COM3	The third serial port
PRN	The standard parallel port
LPT1	The first parallel port
LPT2	The second parallel port
LPT3	The third parallel port
CLOCK$	The internal clock

Figure 11.1 The standard devices

In this case the file is copied not to another file but to the parallel port. If there is a printer attached and on-line, the contents of the file PREFACE.TXT will be printed out. (The result will only be readable if PREFACE.TXT is an ASCII file.)

The PRN, AUX and associated names refer to the external ports rather than particular devices. For example, we can send the contents of the same file to the standard serial port with the command:

```
COPY PREFACE.TXT AUX:
```

This file is now sent to the modem, printer or whatever other device is connected to the serial port. If no device is connected the command eventually 'times out'. (When writing to any device the operating system keeps trying for a specific amount of time and then gives up with a 'Not ready error' message.)

THE CONSOLE   The console is a special device that combines what we usually think of as being two separate components, the screen and keyboard. When a command sends output to the console, CON is taken to refer to the screen; for input, the console is the keyboard. Again, this is of greatest use with the COPY command.

```
[C:\TEXT]copy con: notes.txt
Draft contents list completed
List of illustrations inaccurate - needs to be checked
chapter 1 - done
chapter 2 - done
chapter 3 - check
^Z
        1 file(s) copied.

[C:\TEXT]type notes.txt
Draft contents list completed
List of illustrations inaccurate - needs to be checked
chapter 1 - done
chapter 2 - done
chapter 3 - check

[C:\TEXT]
```

Figure 11.2 Creating a file from the keyboard

The contents of a file can be displayed on the screen as follows:

```
COPY PREFACE.TXT CON:
```

The file is copied to the screen rather than another file; the effect is identical to that of TYPE.

In a similar way, a file can be created by typing it in directly from the keyboard:

```
COPY CON: NOTES.TXT
```

This command copies anything typed at the keyboard into the file NOTES.TXT. When the command has been entered, the operating system waits for the user to type some text. To experiment with this, type a line of text and then press Return. The line is stored in the file and the operating system waits for another line to be entered. If you make any mistakes on the line that is being entered you can backspace over it but you cannot move back up to a previous line.

197

When the file is complete, press Ctrl-Z and Return. Ctrl-Z is the standard end-of-file character for an ASCII file and is recognised as such by the operating system. The new file can be displayed with the TYPE command (Figure 11.2). This is a good method for creating batch files (as described in Chapter 13).

Such files can only be changed by a word processor or text editor (such as EDLIN). However, you can add to an ASCII file as follows:

```
COPY NOTES.DOC+CON:
```

Any new text is appended to the file.

You can even make your expensive computer and printer act as if they were a humble typewriter with this command:

```
COPY CON: PRN:
```

The text is only printed when you press Ctrl-Z and Return. This can be a useful option if you want to produce envelopes, for example, without having to create a file.

OS/2 also has separate names for the keyboard (KBD$) and screen (SCREEN$), which work in an identical fashion to CON.

THE NULL DEVICE

There is a special device, called the *null device* and represented by 'NUL', which does not physically exist. NUL is used to get rid of any unwanted output. As a filename it is of little use, though its effect can be demonstrated by this command:

```
COPY NOTES.DOC NUL:
```

The file is 'copied' to the null device; in other words the operating system reads the file and does nothing with it. The original file remains intact.

The greatest use for NUL, and indeed for all the device names, is as targets for redirection; this topic is discussed in the next chapter.

BUILT-IN PRINTER COMMANDS

The operating system provides us with a number of methods for directing our output to the printer. Most applications programs include their own options for producing printer output; the next chapter describes how the output from any command can be directed to the printer; COPY can also be used to direct the contents of one or more files to the printer.

In addition, the operating system includes it own facilities for producing printer output. Two of these are described below.

THE PRINT-SCREEN FACILITY

When the computer is processing the output for the keyboard it is constantly checking for specific combinations of key presses. For example, Ctrl-Break interrupts a process, Ctrl-NumLock suspends an operation and Ctrl-Alt-Del resets the computer. Another key combination, Shift-PrtSc causes the computer to attempt to print the current screen display.

Press and hold the Shift key, then press the key marked PrtSc. As long as the printer is connected to the parallel port, switched on and on-line the system will attempt to print a copy of the display. Any special characters (such as the box-drawing characters) will only be printed if the printer has that capability.

The result of this process is called a *screen dump*. As it stands, Shift-PrtSc is only effective for text screens.

GRAPHICS

A number of programs hijack the print-screen operation for their own ends, for example to save a copy of the screen display as a file. One such program, *GRAPHICS*, forms a part of the operating system.

Command:	GRAPHICS
Effect:	Provides enhanced print-screen operation
Version:	DOS 1, OS/2
Type:	External
Syntax:	[*location*]GRAPHICS (DOS 1, DOS 2)
	[*location*]*GRAPHICS* [*printer*] (DOS 3, OS/2)
Parameters:	/B Print background (selected printers only) (DOS 3)
	/LCD Print images as on LCD screen (DOS 3.3)

199

/R   Reverse black and white attributes
                                   (DOS 3)

The GRAPHICS program should be loaded into memory before any screen is printed. Once installed in memory, GRAPHICS remains there until the system is reset. Whenever the Shift-PrtSc combination is pressed, the GRAPHICS routines are called instead of the standard routines.

GRAPHICS provides the enhancement that you can get a screen dump of graphics screens as well as text screens. Medium resolution screens result in a dump in up to four shades of grey (assuming the printer can cope with this); high resolution dumps are printed in black and white but sideways on the sheet.

For DOS 3 you can specify a particular printer type:

COLOR1	IBM colour printer with black ribbon
COLOR4	IBM colour printer with 3-colour ribbon
COLOR8	IBM colour printer with 4-colour ribbon
COMPACT	IBM compact printer (DOS 3.3 only)
GRAPHICS	Epson graphics printer or compatible
THERMAL	IBM thermal printer (DOS 3.3 only)

In general, GRAPHICS with no printer specified will work quite satisfactorily.

Three parameters are also available, depending on the version of the program. As a rule, the standard screen displays (white text on black background) are printed as black text on a blank page. /R reverses this; anywhere the screen display has no colour appears as black on the paper, anything white is ignored.

/B is applicable only to the COLOR4 and COLOR8 printers and results in the background being printed in the same colour as the display background. /LCD prints the screen as it would be shown on an LCD screen.

ECHOING
OUTPUT

Another useful option is to persuade the printer to 'echo' anything displayed on the screen. That is, any new text displayed on the screen is also printed on paper. This is achieved by the combination Ctrl-PrtSc; it can also usually be activated by Ctrl-P.

Anything displayed is now copied to the printer. This is particularly useful for getting a printout of a directory listing. Type the directory command and then press Ctrl-PrtSc, before pressing Return. The printout can be stored away with the disk for reference.

The printer echo is turned off by the same combination of keys.

THE MODE COMMAND

Command:	MODE
Effect:	Sets up devices
Version:	DOS 1, OS/2
Type:	External
Syntax:	[*location*]MODE LPT*n*:[*chars/line*],[*lines/inch*], [P	N]
	[*location*]MODE LPT*n*:=COM*m*
	[*location*]MODE COM*m*:*baudrate*,[*parity*], [*databits*],[*stopbits*],[P	N]
	[*location*]MODE [*display*],[R	L],[T]
	[*location*]MODE [*display*],[*lines*	R	L],[T]
	(OS/2 only)

Parameters: None

MODE is a complex command that can be used to set up the way in which various aspects of the computer operate. In particular it sets up the serial and parallel ports and the screen display. A further range of options relate to code pages, which are described in Chapter 13.

Each of the four versions of the syntax is described here. In those cases where options are separated by commas, only the commas up to the last option need be included in the command.

Note that MODE on its own displays the current settings for all devices.

SETTING UP PRINTERS

The first two options of the MODE command relate to the parallel printer ports, LPT1, LPT2 and LPT3 (if available). In the first case you can specify:

- The number of characters per line to be printed (80 for normal print, 132 for condensed print or wide paper)

- The number of lines per inch (either 6 or 8)

- Whether or not the computer gives up trying to send data after a time-out error

These options are only likely to be effective with Epson printers and compatibles.

The P option instructs the computer to keep on trying to send data to the printer even when it receives the 'printer busy' signal. This is particularly useful for slow printers which cannot keep up with the speed at which data is being sent and may tend to cause a time-out error unnecessarily. If there is something wrong with the printer the 'infinite loop' that is set up can be interrupted with Ctrl-Break. The retry option can be turned off with the N parameter.

The second option allows us to *redirect* the printer output by specifying that anything that would have gone to a particular parallel port will instead go to a specific serial port.

Examples

The command on its own (under DOS 3.3) displays help information:

```
MODE
```

The results are shown in Figure 11.3.

To set up the printer to produce 132 characters per line and 8 lines per inch, enter the command:

```
MODE LPT1:132,8
```

To override the time-out errors and leave the other parameters unchanged enter:

```
MODE LPT1:,,P
```

If all printer output is to be directed to the first serial port instead of the first parallel port, enter:

```
MODE LPT1:=COM1
```

```
C:\>mode

Invalid number of parameters
Valid Command Line Parameters are:
MODE COMn[ : ]baud[ ,parity[ ,word_size[ ,stopbits[ ,P]]]] Serial Setup
MODE LPTn[ : ]=COMn                                Device Redirection
MODE LPTn[ : ][ ch ][ ,[ ln ][ ,P ]]               Printer Setup
MODE md                                            Video Mode Setup
MODE [ md ][ ,a ][ ,T ]                            Video Alignment
MODE device CodePage PREPARE=(( cplist) filename )  Prepare code pages
MODE device CodePage SELECT =CP                    select/activate code page
MODE device CodePage [ /STATUS ]                   Display active code page
Where: n = Device Number,    P = Continuous Retry,    ch = Characters Per Line
        ln = Lines Per Inch,  md = 40 / 80 / MONO / CO40 / CO80 / BW40 / BW80
        a = Alignment Shift,  T = Test Pattern
      device=CON,PRN,LPT1,LPT2,LPT3,   cp=code page number
      cplist= list of code pages, Filename=file containing the code pages
Examples:
MODE COM1:9600,n,8,1         Set COM1 for 9600 baud,8 bits,no parity,1 stop bit
MODE LPT1:=COM1              Redirect LPT1 output to COM1
MODE MONO                   Set Video mode to monochrome
MODE CON CP PREP=(( 850,,437 ) EGA) Specify console code pages from ega

C:\>
```

Figure 11.3 Using MODE

This is useful if you want to produce screen dumps on a serial printer.

SERIAL DEVICES The third option for the MODE syntax sets up the parameter for the serial port. These parameters determine the way in which communications take place. The parameters need to be set up to suit the particular device that is connected to the port. Details should be available in the device's manual; this may require the setting of dip switches.

The parameters that can be given are:

■ The *baud rate*: this must always be specified. Acceptable baud rates are 110, 150, 300, 600, 1200, 2400, 4800, 9600 or 19200. (The 19200 value is valid for DOS 3.3 only.) The last two zeros may be omitted in each case.

■ The *parity*: N (none), O (odd) or E (even). This determines the type of error-checking.

■ The *data bits*: the number of *bits* (values of 0 or 1) used to encode each character that is sent. Acceptable values are

```
C:\>mode com1:1200,,7,1

COM1: 1200,e,7,1,-

C:\>mode com1:1200,e

COM1: 1200,e,7,1,-

C:\>
```

Figure 11.4 Using MODE with the serial port

7 (to send the standard ASCII codes, up to 127) or 8 (to send the extended ASCII characters, up to 255).

■ The *stop bits*: the number of bits used to signal the end of a character (either 1 or 2).

■ Whether or not the system is to ignore time-out errors: P to ignore, N to respond by halting.

If any of these items are missed out of the command the current values remain the same.

Examples   The current settings for the serial port can be displayed with the MODE COM1: command. To change the baud rate to 1200, data bits to 7 and stop bits to 2, enter:

```
MODE COM1:1200,,7,1
```

The format of the response is shown in Figure 11.4.

Parameter	Screen mode
40	EGA, 40 column
80	EGA, 80 column
CO40	EGA, 40 column, with colour enabled
CO80	EGA, 80 column, with colour enabled
BW40	EGA, 40 column, with colour disabled
BW80	EGA, 80 column, with colour disabled
MONO	MDA (always 80 column)

Figure 11.5 MODE screen options

To set the parity checking to 'even', enter:

```
MODE COM1:1200,E
```

The ports are reset to the defaults when the computer is rebooted.

CHANGING THE DISPLAY

The last option of the MODE command, in this section, changes the screen display. At its simplest MODE is followed by a parameter that sets the type of screen display, including the number of characters per line, the type of adapter, and the colours displayed. Adapters include CGA (Colour Graphics Adapter), EGA (Extended Graphics Adapter) or MDA (Monochrome Display Adapter). The parameters that can be applied are given in Figure 11.5.

In addition you may specify R or L as the second parameter, the result of which is to shift the display to the left or right of the screen; the screen is shifted one column in 40-column modes or 2 columns in 80-column mode. The third parameter, T, displays a test pattern for adjusting the screen. The pattern consists of a row of numbers.

The T parameter can only be used in junction with L or R. It cannot be used on its own.

OS/2 adds the enhancement of allowing you to specify the number of lines on the screen as the second parameter.

Examples

The screen can be set to 40-columns, with colour, as follows:

205

```
MODE CO40
```

Under OS/2, you can set the screen to 80-column colour, with 50 lines of text on the screen, as follows:

```
MODE CO80,50
```

The screen can be shifted left, with the test pattern displayed, using this command:

```
MODE CO80R,T
```

When this command is entered, you are asked if you can see the leftmost '0' in the pattern. If you enter 'N' the screen shifts right one column for 40-column displays or two for 80-column displays.

CTTY

Command: CTTY
Effect: Changes the current input/output device
Version: DOS 2, OS/2
Type: Internal
Syntax: CTTY *device*
Parameters: None

Occasionally you may want to control the computer from some sort of remote device. This may be another computer at the end of a telephone line or some device connected to the serial port. CTTY specifies that all input is to come from somewhere other than the keyboard and output is to be directed to the same place. Once the input/output device has been changed the keyboard becomes ineffective and the screen display remains static.

To restore normal operation specify CON as the input/output device. This must be done by the external device of course.

CTTY stands for 'Change TeleTYpe', which harks back to the days when communication with computers was through a teletype terminal.

Examples   If you want to control the computer from an external device or remotely via a modem, enter the command:

```
CTTY COM1:
```

All information arriving from the serial port will be treated as if it were being typed at the keyboard; all output is sent to the serial port.

Normal operation is resumed by sending the following command at the remote device:

```
CTTY CON:
```

The keyboard and screen now operate normally. If the remote device cannot send commands, for any reason, the only other way to get out of the situation is to switch off and then on again.

THE PRINT SPOOLERS

One of the most frustrating things about using a computer is having to wait while files are printed. Under DOS, as soon as an application starts printing the whole computer is tied up until the print run has finished. The operating system overcomes this to a certain extent with the PRINT command. This allows you to set up a *queue* of ASCII files to print. DOS then sends some of the data to the printer when it has nothing better to do, allowing you to get on with another task. This command is also available for OS/2.

OS/2 has to be very careful with printing. Obviously it is not possible to have a range of applications all running at the same time and all competing for the same printer. Therefore all output is handled by a *print spooler*, which prints the files in an orderly manner.

PRINT

Command:	PRINT	
Effect:	Prints files in the background	
Version:	DOS 2, OS/2	
Type:	External	
Syntax:	PRINT [*drive*]*file* [...]	
Parameters:	/C	Cancel a file
	/P	Print a file
	/T	Cancel all printing
	/B:*bytes*	Disk buffer size (DOS 3)
	/D:*device*	Printer device (DOS 3)

/M:*number*	Maximum ticks for PRINT (DOS 3)
/S:*number*	Program timeslice (in ticks) (DOS 3)
/Q:*number*	Number of files in queue (DOS 3)
/U:*number*	Maximum wait when printer is busy (in ticks) (DOS 3)

The PRINT command sets up a queue of files to print. The program sits in memory and runs permanently in the background once it has been invoked. To make any sense, the files must be ASCII files, which defeats the object to a certain extent; it is rare that we want to print a file with no special styles, such as bold or italic.

The program works by allocating timeslices between the foreground programs and PRINT. The default is that the foreground tasks take 8 ticks for every 2 allocated to PRINT.

To add a file to the queue, enter the command followed by a file specification. As soon as possible PRINT starts printing this file. When it finishes with one file it sends a form-feed character to tell the printer to start a new page, and then prints the next file.

Note that the files added to the queue must always be in the current directory of the specified drive. After adding the files, the current directory can be changed without affecting the queue. Wildcards can be used.

The first time the command is entered you are asked to give the device name. Press Return for the default, which is the standard parallel port, PRN.

A file can be removed from the queue by adding the /C parameter. This parameter cancels the preceding file and all that follow, until a /P parameter is encountered. /P only needs to be used if /C occurs earlier in the command line. /T cancels all printing. If a file is cancelled during printing a 'cancelled by operator' message is displayed.

PRINT always keeps you up to date with what is happening; PRINT on its own displays a report of the current queue.

DOS 3 introduced some extra parameters to allow more control over PRINT. /D allows the device to be specified on the command line. /B allocates a larger or smaller *buffer* for the file being printed. This is the area of memory where the data waits to be printed; increasing this buffer reduces the number of times PRINT must access the disk, since PRINT always fills the buffer completely when it is empty. The default buffer size is 512 bytes.

/M changes the number of ticks allocated to PRINT in each timeslice while /S changes the foreground programs' timeslice. /U changes the number of ticks that PRINT waits when the printer is busy. The defaults for these three parameters are 2, 8 and 1 respectively. The maximum in each case is 255, the minimum is 1.

Finally, /Q changes the maximum number of files allowed in the queue. The default is 10 and the number cannot exceed 32.

Note that if PRINT is run under OS/2, the SPOOL command should be entered first.

Examples   PRINT can be initialised, with the files CH1.TXT and CH2.TXT added to the queue, as follows:

```
PRINT CH1.TXT CH2.TXT CH3.TXT
```

If the printer is connected to the standard parallel port, press Return when asked for the device name (Figure 11.6).

For DOS 3, we can vary this initialisation as follows:

```
PRINT CH1.TXT CH2.TXT CH3.TXT /B:2048 /S:4 /Q:20
```

This command increases the buffer size to 2048 (4 sectors), halves the amount of time spent in the foreground task during each cycle, and increases the maximum queue length to 20 files.

If you want to take CH2.TXT and CH3.TXT out of the queue and add a series of DOC files instead, enter:

```
PRINT CH2.TXT/C CH3.TXT *.DOC/P
```

Alternatively, to cancel all files, enter:

```
C:\TEXT>print ch1.txt ch2.txt ch3.txt
Name of list device [PRN]:
Resident part of PRINT installed

    C:\TEXT\CH1.TXT is currently being printed
    C:\TEXT\CH2.TXT is in queue
    C:\TEXT\CH3.TXT is in queue

C:\TEXT>print /t
Errors on list device indicate that it
may be off-line. Please check it.

PRINT queue is empty

C:\TEXT>
```

Figure 11.6 Adding to the PRINT queue

```
PRINT /T
```

The queue is now empty and new files can be added.

SPOOL

Command: SPOOL
Effect: OS/2 print spooler
Version: OS/2
Type: External
Syntax: [*location*]SPOOL [*drive*][*path*]
Parameters: /D:*device* Device to print
        /O:*device* Output device

Many applications can be running at once, each of them with the capability to send output to the printer. Clearly, this must be controlled, and this is the job of SPOOL, the OS/2 print spooler.

SPOOL works in a similar way to PRINT, setting up a queue of files to print. This time, however, it does so by directing the output from the application to a temporary disk file; the temporary file is printed when its turn comes. The print files cannot be specified from the command line. Any type of data can be printed, including all special printer codes. SPOOL does not contain any facilities to cancel printing, however. The only way to do that is to switch off the printer when the file starts printing.

As a default, the command uses the \SPOOL directory to store its temporary files. When the command is invoked you can specify a different sub-directory if you wish.

Once SPOOL has been installed in memory it remains in full control of the printing operation until the computer is rebooted. Make sure, before you start, that there is sufficient room on the disk for all the files that you want to print.

The /D parameter tells SPOOL to which port the printer is connected (the default being LPT1) while /O gives the name of the printer device, which defaults to the device in the /D parameter. This second parameter is of little use in the normal course of events.

SPOOL must be run from a protected mode session. Once it has been activated it displays a message to say that it is running. It never relinquishes control of the session, so you must return to the session manager (with Ctrl-Esc) to do any other work. SPOOL.EXE is then permanently included in the list of sessions.

Examples
The print spooler is normally invoked with:

```
SPOOL
```

If a serial printer is connected and you want to use the \PRINTER directory for the spooled files, enter:

```
SPOOL \PRINTER /D:COM1
```

Making a mistake is something of a nuisance. The only way to change the SPOOL settings is by rebooting the computer.

12. Redirection, Pipes and Filters

There are many occasions when you do not want the output from a command to go to the normal output device or you wish to get input from an unusual source. In such cases there are a number of ways of changing the output and input devices. This process is called *redirection* and various aspects of it are described below.

REDIRECTING OUTPUT

In the normal course of events, the output from all commands appears on the screen. This output can be redirected by adding '>' to the command, followed by the new destination of the output.

For example, a directory listing can be directed to the printer rather than the screen with this command:

```
DIR C:\BOOK > PRN:
```

The operating system simply redirects the information to the new device for the duration of this command only. (The spaces around the redirection symbol are not essential but help to make the command clearer.)

The TYPE command is a favourite for redirection:

```
TYPE CH1.TXT > PRN:
```

The output can be redirected to a file, instead of a device:

```
DIR A: > FILES.LST
```

The file called FILES.LST now contains the directory of drive A, exactly as it would appear on the screen.

It is here that the NUL device comes into its own. Any unwanted screen messages can be directed to this device and therefore disappear altogether. For example, when copying files, the list of files being copied can be redirected:

```
COPY *.DOC A: > NUL:
```

All messages are suppressed (except the number of files copied, under some versions of DOS). This is particularly useful in batch files (see Chapter 16).

Appending data   A second redirection operator, '>>', allows us to add output data to an existing file. For example:

```
DIR B: >> FILES.LST
```

The directory of the disk in drive B is added to the existing contents of FILES.LST.

REDIRECTING INPUT

In a similar way to the above, we can redirect input with the '<' operator. The format of commands is exactly the same. For example, the SORT program needs to know where to get its data from; SORT can be directed to get its input from a particular file, as follows:

```
SORT < FILES.LST
```

This command sorts FILES.LST into alphabetical order. The potential for redirected input is more limited than that for output.

PIPES

In some cases we need to take the output from one process and redirect it as the input for another. This is called *piping* and essentially combines redirection of output and input. It is represented by the vertical bar character, '|'. For example, the output from a directory listing can be redirected to become the input for SORT:

```
DIR A: | SORT
```

The operating system first gets the directory listing and then directs this into SORT, where it is sorted before being output to the standard output device, the screen (Figure 12.1).

```
[C:\]dir a: | sort


     12 File(s)     973312 bytes free
Directory of  A:\
Volume in drive A has no label
AUTOEXEC BAT        60    4-04-89   10:12p
COMMAND   COM     25276   24-07-87   12:00a
GLDLMAN3  EXE     76304    3-04-89   12:00p
GLEDIT3   EXE     55120    3-04-89   12:00p
GLLIST3   EXE     55840    3-04-89   12:00p
GLPLOT3   EXE     21936    3-04-89   12:00p
GLPSFG3   EXE     79152    3-04-89   12:00p
GLRDGTR3  EXE     75504    3-04-89   12:00p
GLSET9    EXE     54240    3-04-89   12:00p
GROWLOG   BAT        28    4-04-89    9:55p
MULTI     EXE     33917   21-07-88    6:01p
READ      ME       3200   21-07-88    6:01p


[C:\]
```

Figure 12.1 A sorted directory listing

The redirection operators can be combined:

```
DIR A: | SORT > FILES.LST
```

The sorted directory is placed in the file FILES.LST rather than being displayed on the screen.

FILTERS

There is a special set of programs, called *filters*, whose effect is to modify a file in some way. The principle of a filter is that it takes the contents of a file, modifies it and then outputs it.

DOS and OS/2 are generally supplied with three filters.

MORE

Command:	MORE
Effect:	Filter to display output a screenful of data at a time
Version:	DOS 2, OS/2
Type:	External

```
Volume in drive C has no label.
Directory of  C:\

BATS         <DIR>      4-04-89    8:46p
COLLAGE      <DIR>      4-04-89    9:07p
DOS          <DIR>      4-04-89    8:36p
OS2          <DIR>      4-04-89    9:44p
PICS         <DIR>      4-04-89    8:52p
QB           <DIR>      4-04-89    8:39p
SYSTEM       <DIR>      4-04-89    8:38p
WP           <DIR>      4-04-89    8:46p
WS5          <DIR>      4-04-89   10:15p
A                 59    4-04-89    8:44p
TRE              256    4-04-89   10:22p
AUTOEXEC BAT      60    4-04-89   10:12p
COMMAND  COM   25276   24-07-87   12:00a
CONFIG   SYS      59    4-04-89    8:44p
COUNTRY  SYS   11254   24-07-87   12:00a
KEYBOARD SYS   19735   24-07-87   12:00a
TRE      SYS   32919    4-04-89   10:13p
TREE     TXT     472    4-04-89   10:15p
M        COM      16    5-04-89   11:05a
TASM         <DIR>      5-04-89   11:23a
-- More --
```

Figure 12.2 Displaying directories with MORE

Syntax: [*location*]MORE
Parameters: None

The MORE filter is simple but extremely useful. It takes its input from a file or command and displays it a screenful at a time.

The input is identified by the redirection operators. At the end of each page the program pauses, with '--MORE--' displayed on the last line. Press any key to display the next screenful.

Examples   A directory can be displayed a screen at a time as follows:

    MORE < DIR C:

The command more usually takes the form:

    DIR C: | MORE

The directory listing pauses when the screen is full (Figure 12.2).

This filter is particularly useful with commands such as TYPE:

```
TYPE CH1.TXT | MORE
```

In this case the output from the TYPE command becomes the input for MORE and the file is displayed a screenful at a time.

SORT

Command:	SORT
Effect:	Filter to sort input and display the results on the screen
Version:	DOS 2, OS/2
Type:	External
Syntax:	[*location*]SORT

Parameters:	/R	Sort in reverse order
	/+*number*	Sort according to specified column

The SORT filter sorts into order the contents of an ASCII file or the results of a previous command. It takes its input from redirection, in the same way as MORE. The input is sorted into order and then displayed on the screen. The filter decides on the order by sorting according to the ASCII values of the characters; that is, 'A' comes before 'B' but 'Z' is before 'a', since all capitals come before the lower case letters in the ASCII codes. The full set of ASCII codes is given in the Appendix.

This means that the results are not always as expected. As long as all characters are in the same case there will be no problem.

Numbers are also sorted as if they are characters, and all the numeric characters come before the letters.

After sorting according to the first character, any lines with the same first character are sorted on the next character, and so on. This also applies to numbers, which are sorted according to their ASCII codes rather than their numeric values. Each line of text (ended by a carriage return character) is treated as a separate item.

The /R parameter results in a sort that is in reverse order while /+*number* causes the sort to be based on the characters starting at a particular character position on the screen.

```
      35 File(s)  17172488 bytes free
  Directory of  C:\
  Volume in drive C has no label.
  8325222F              8    8-83-98    3:37a
  83252234              8    8-83-98    3:37a
  A                    59    4-84-89    8:44p
  AUTOEXEC BAT         68    4-84-89   18:12p
  BATS         <DIR>         4-84-89    8:46p
  COLLAGE      <DIR>         4-84-89    9:87p
  COMMAND  COM      25276   24-87-87   12:88a
  CONFIG   SYS         59    4-84-89    8:44p
  COUNTRY  SYS      11254   24-87-87   12:88a
  DOC                  25    5-84-89    4:51p
  DOS          <DIR>         4-84-89    8:36p
  KEYBOARD SYS      19735   24-87-87   12:88a
  M        COM         16    5-84-89   11:85a
  OS2          <DIR>         4-84-89    9:44p
  PICS         <DIR>         4-84-89    8:52p
  PROGRAMS     <DIR>         8-83-98    2:16a
  QB           <DIR>         4-84-89    8:39p
  SPOOLCP  DLL       9828   21-18-87   12:88p
  STARTUP  CMD         68    8-83-98    2:27a
  -- More --
```

Figure 12.3 Sorted directory, a screen at a time

Examples

To demonstrate the way in which the sort takes place, enter the following text with the COPY command:

```
COPY CON: TEST.TXT
Redirection
Pipes
and
Filters
123
17
^Z
```

(The ^Z indicates that you should end the file by pressing Ctrl-Z.) This file can now be sorted as follows:

```
SORT < TEST.TXT
```

The result is the following display:

```
123
17
Filters
```

```
[C:\]dir a: | sort /+10


       12 File(s)      973312 bytes free
GROWLOG  BAT       28    4-04-89    9:55p
AUTOEXEC BAT       60    4-04-89   10:12p
COMMAND  COM    25276   24-07-87   12:00a
GLPLOT3  EXE    21936    3-04-89   12:00p
MULTI    EXE    33917   21-07-88    6:01p
GLSET9   EXE    54240    3-04-89   12:00p
GLEDIT3  EXE    55120    3-04-89   12:00p
GLLIST3  EXE    55840    3-04-89   12:00p
GLRDGTR3 EXE    75504    3-04-89   12:00p
GLDLMAN3 EXE    76304    3-04-89   12:00p
GLPSFG3  EXE    79152    3-04-89   12:00p
READ     ME      3200   21-07-88    6:01p
 Volume in drive A has no label.
 Directory of  A:\


[C:\]
```

Figure 12.4 Directory sorted on extension and file size

```
Pipes
Redirection
and
```

We have already seen that a directory can be sorted. The results can be displayed a screenful at a time as follows:

```
DIR C: | SORT | MORE
```

The output from the directory listing becomes the input for SORT, the output of which then becomes the input for MORE (Figure 12.3).

Alternatively, the sorted directory can be printed:

```
DIR C: | SORT > PRN:
```

A directory can be sorted according to the file extensions (which start at the tenth character) as follows:

```
DIR A: | SORT /+10
```

Any files with the same extensions are sorted according to the file size. Since the sizes are padded with leading spaces the fact that the sort is based on ASCII values will still produce a numerical listing. (The space character has an ASCII value of 32, which comes before any other printable character.) However, the text at the top and bottom of the listing may not end up where you expect (Figure 12.4).

The directory of drive C can be sorted in reverse order of file size as follows:

```
DIR C:  | SORT /R /+14 > PRN
```

In this case the result is printed, rather than displayed on screen.

FIND

Command:	FIND
Effect:	Filter to find a piece of text in a file
Version:	DOS 2, OS/2
Type:	External
Syntax:	[*location*]FIND [*parameter*] [*spec*] [...]
Parameters:	/C Count occurrences
	/N Display line numbers
	/V Find lines that do not contain text

The FIND filter searches an ASCII file for a specific item of text. The text is placed in quotes and more than one file can be searched at a time. The filter displays any line that contains the text; as an alternative, the /V parameter directs FIND to display those line that do not contain the text. The search is *case-sensitive*; that is if the text contains capitals then it is only matched by text in the file that also contains the same capitals.

Note that FIND is unusual in that the parameters are placed immediately after the command name.

/N inserts a line number in front of the lines that are output while /C produces a count of the number of occurrences (taking account of multiple repetitions on a line).

This filter is really only suited to files that have a carriage return at the end of each line; whole paragraphs may cause problems.

```
[C:\TEXT]dir ! find "DOC"
CHAP1      DOC       65   8-03-90    5:15p
CHAP2      DOC       32   8-03-90    5:15p
CHAP3      DOC       32   8-03-90    5:16p
NOTES      DOC      191   8-03-90    2:06a
DOCUMENT   PRN       26   8-03-90    3:41a
LASTDOCT   TXT     9049  30-03-89   12:43p

[C:\TEXT]
```

Figure 12.5 Finding files in the directory

Examples

If the file CONTENTS.LST contains an ASCII list, you can search for the text 'filters' as follows:

```
FIND "filters" CONTENTS.LST
```

The phrase 'echo off' can be located in several files with a BAT extension as follows:

```
FIND /N "echo off" AUTOEXEC.BAT WP.BAT CALC.BAT
```

The name of each file is displayed above the lines where occurrences are found and, in this example, each line is given the number of the line in the file.

FIND can be used in conjunction with other commands. For example:

```
DIR | FIND "DOC"
```

The result is a display of only those line where DOC occurs in the filename (Figure 12.5).

221

```
[C:\TEXT]dir | sort /+10 | find "-" | find /v ">" | more

FIND                 61    8-03-90    3:59a
ILLUS              2816    1-04-89    6:26a
CH10               9049   30-03-89   12:43p
CH8               11648   22-03-89    5:00p
CH12              12928   29-03-89   11:33a
CH7               22656   22-03-89    5:01p
CH11              25056   29-03-89   11:19a
CH9               37064   30-03-89   12:09p
CH13              40704    4-04-89   12:42p
BOOK     ALL        169    8-03-90    5:17p
CHAP2    DOC         32    8-03-90    5:15p
CHAP3    DOC         32    8-03-90    5:16p
CHAP1    DOC         65    8-03-90    5:15p
NOTES    DOC        191    8-03-90    2:06a
CONTENTS LST        566    8-03-90    5:04p
DOCUMENT PRN         26    8-03-90    3:41a
NOTES    TXT        142    8-03-90    3:12a
CH2      TXT        512    8-03-90    3:02a
CH3      TXT        512    8-03-90    3:02a
CH1      TXT        512    8-03-90    3:02a
LASTDOCT TXT       9049   30-03-89   12:43p
```

Figure 12.6 Combining filters

The lines of text at the top and bottom of a directory listing (which all contain a lower case 'i') can be excluded as follows:

    DIR | /V FIND "i"

All filenames are listed in capitals so will never be excluded by this command.

A similar effect can be achieved by searching for the '-' in the dates:

    DIR | FIND "-"

In this case the blank lines are also excluded.

Finally, we might want to combine all of the filters:

    DIR | SORT /+10 | FIND "-" | FIND /V ">" | MORE

This command displays the directory, excluding the header and footer text and also excluding sub-directory entries, sorted according to extension and listed a screenful at a time (Figure 12.6). Note that the output from one FIND can become the input for another, so that quite complicated combinations can be searched for or excluded.

OS/2 ENHANCEMENTS

OS/2 adds a number of enhancements to the way in which commands can be entered. These provide a form of re-direction, in that the decision on whether to execute a second command depends on the result of the first.

The first command line operator is the '&' symbol. This allows you to put more than one command on a single line. For example, two sets of files can be copied with this command:

```
COPY *.* A: & COPY *.DOC B:
```

All files are copied to A; when the first command has been completed the next is executed, copying all DOC files to B. The uses of this operator are somewhat limited.

An alternative is the '&&' operator, which executes the second command only if the first was successful (that is, it does not return an error number). For example:

```
DIR DATA.LST && TYPE DATA.LST
```

The file is displayed in full only if the directory listing finds an entry of that name.

The companion to this is the '||' operator, which executes the second command only if the first command fails. This can be quite useful:

```
DIR DATA.LST || COPY B:DATA.LST
```

The file is only copied from drive B if it does not already exist.

You can have more than one of these *logical operators* by enclosing a pair of commands in brackets:

```
(DIR DATA1.LST && DIR DATA2.LST) || COPY B:DATA?.LST
```

The files are copied from drive B if either file (or both) does not exist in the current directory. The COPY command is only ignored if both DIR commands find matching files.

Finally, you may have an '&' on the command line due to some other reason; in particular, this character is a legal filename character. To avoid confusion, if the '&' appears in a filename it should be preceded by the '^' character.

These OS/2 enhancements can be an advantage in batch files but they are unlikely to be used frequently.

13. *System Customisation*

When you first switch on the computer the system is set up with a variety of defaults. For instance, the prompt has been selected for you, the computer expects to send output to the parallel port and the keyboard produces a specific character set.

We have already seen how to change the prompt and direct output to another port. This chapter describes many of the other features that can be changed.

CONFIG.SYS

One of the first things the operating system does is to check a special file in the root directory of the system disk. This file is called *CONFIG.SYS* and contains information about the *system configuration*. The information here is read into memory, where it stays permanently in place until the computer is switched off or reset.

CONFIG.SYS is an ASCII file, so can be displayed on the screen, as illustrated in Figure 13.1, with the command:

```
TYPE \CONFIG.SYS
```

You are free to change CONFIG.SYS to suit your own system. If you just want to add new items to CONFIG.SYS use:

```
COPY \CONFIG.SYS+CON:
```

To make changes to existing items, edit it with a suitable text editor. Any changes made to CONFIG.SYS only come into effect when the system is reset.

ELEMENTS OF CONFIG.SYS

There are a great many items that may affect the configuration. Some of these are listed in Figure 13.2.

You do not have to have a CONFIG.SYS file and, if you do, not every item has to be given a value. However, for many of those that are not included the operating system automatically allocates a default value. Any value you give replaces the default.

```
[C:\]type config.sys
country=044
codepage=437,850
devinfo=kbd,uk,\keyboard.dcp
devinfo=scr,ega,\viotbl.dcp

[C:\]
```

Figure 13.1 Displaying CONFIG.SYS

Each item, or *variable*, appears in CONFIG.SYS in the form:

```
variable=value
```

In the case of DEVICE and DEVINFO, more than one entry can be included.

SET

Command:	SET
Effect:	Displays or changes environment variables
Version:	DOS 2, OS/2
Type:	Internal
Syntax:	SET [*variable*=[*value*]]
Parameters:	None

Some of the variables in the configuration list can be changed with the SET command. SET on its own displays the current configuration. If it is followed by a variable and value, the new variable takes effect straight away; it only stays in effect until the system is reset.

A variable can be temporarily removed from the configuration with a command in the form:

Variable	Operating system	Default value	Use
BREAK	DOS, OS/2	OFF	Frequency of checks for Ctrl-Beak key
BUFFERS	DOS, OS/2	2 (DOS) 3 (OS/2)	Number of disk buffers
CODEPAGE	DOS, OS/2	437	Extended character set
COMSPEC	DOS, OS/2	Root dir.	Location of command processor
COUNTRY	DOS, OS/2	001	Country code
DEVICE	DOS, OS/2	(None)	Installable device drivers
DEVINFO	DOS, OS/2	(None)	Code-page switching for a device
DPATH	OS/2	(None)	Search path for data files
DRIVPARM	DOS, OS/2	(None)	Block device configuration
FCBS	DOS, OS/2	4,0	Number of file control blocks
FILES	DOS, OS/2	8	Number of file handles
IOPL	DOS, OS/2	NO	Input/output protection level
LASTDRIVE	DOS, OS/2	E	Last drive that can be accessed
LIBPATH	DOS, OS/2	\	Directory containing DLL files
MAXWAIT	DOS, OS/2	3	Maximum time for processes to wait
MEMMAN	DOS, OS/2	NOSWAP,MOVE (Floppy) SWAP,MOVE (Hard disk)	Memory swapping restrictions
PATH	DOS, OS/2	(None)	Search path for executable files
PRIORITY	DOS, OS/2	DYNAMIC	Priority of processes
PROTSHELL	DOS, OS/2	(None)	Prot. mode command processor and automatic execution file
PROTECTONLY	DOS, OS/2	NO	Set to YES to run protected mode applications only
RMSIZE	DOS, OS/2	(Varies)	Memory available for real mode
RUN	DOS, OS/2	(None)	Background file to be run or startup
SHELL	DOS, OS/2	COMMAND.COM	Real mode command processor
STACKS	DOS, OS/2	0,0	Number and size of interrupt stacks
SWAPPATH	DOS, OS/2	\	Directory for segment swapping
THREADS	DOS, OS/2	48	Maximum number of items that can be run concurrently
TIMESLICE	DOS, OS/2	(None)	Minimum and maximum time available to each process

Figure 13.2 Elements of CONFIG.SYS

```
C:\> set
COMSPEC=C:\COMMAND.COM
PROMPT=$p$g $x
PATH=\

C:\> set path=c:\;c:\dos

C:\> set
COMSPEC=C:\COMMAND.COM
PROMPT=$p$g $x
PATH=c:\;c:\dos

C:\> set path=

C:\> set
COMSPEC=C:\COMMAND.COM
PROMPT=$p$g $x

C:\>
```

Figure 13.3 Using SET to change the environment

> SET *variable=*

The number of variables that can be affected by SET is limited.

Examples   The current environment can be displayed with the command:

> SET

The current display path can be changed with the command:

> SET PATH=C:\;C:\OS2

The path can be deleted altogether with:

> SET PATH=

For more on the path, see the PATH command below. The effect on the configuration of such a command is illustrated in Figure 13.3.

Code	Effect
`Esc[HEsc[J`	Clears screen
`Esc[K`	Clears to end of line
`Esc[2J`	Clears to bottom of screen\
`Esc[`*n*`m`	Set colour (*n*=1: intense; *n*=30 to 37: foreground; *n*=40 to 47: background)
`Esc[`*y*`;`*x*`H`	Moves cursor to (*x,y*)　　(col,row)
`Esc[`*n*`A`	Moves cursor up *n* rows
`Esc[`*n*`B`	Moves cursor down *n* rows
`Esc[`*n*`C`	Moves cursor right *n* columns
`Esc[`*n*`D`	Moves cursor left *n* columns
`Esc[s`	Save cursor position
`Esc[u`	Restore cursor position
`Esc[`*y*`;`*x*`R`	Get cursor position
`Esc[6n`	Get device status
`Esc[`*a*`;`*b*`p`	Redefine ASCII character *a* by ASCII *b*
`Esc[0;`*f*`;"`*s*`";13p`	Redefine function key *f* by string *s*

Figure 13.4 The ANSI.SYS codes

DEVICE DRIVERS

Any device connected to the computer requires a special program to handle communication between the computer and the device. Such a program is called a *device driver*. The operating system includes a number of default device drivers for handling the keyboard, screen, serial and parallel ports and disk drives. For anything else we must install a separate device driver. The installation must take place when the system is booted and the names of any device drivers to be installed must be included in CONFIG.SYS, in the form:

```
DEVICE=driver.SYS
```

In this command, *driver* is the name of the device. All device drivers have a SYS extension. If the device driver is not in the root directory, a path to the file must be specified.

ANSI.SYS　　　The operating system has very limited facilities for screen and keyboard handling (in the default CON device). ANSI.SYS is a replacement console-handling device driver. The driver works by checking all output to the screen for special codes. If it finds one of these codes it carries out a predefined process; otherwise, it lets the default driver carry on in the normal way.

These special codes begin with the Escape character and the '[' bracket, followed by one or more letters or numbers. It is important to note that upper and lower case letters are treated differently for ANSI codes.

Many programs use the ANSI codes, so require you to include the following command in CONFIG.SYS:

```
DEVICE=ANSI.SYS
```

The ANSI.SYS codes are shown in Figure 13.4.

Often the easiest way of sending a code is through the PROMPT command, since this sends characters directly to the screen and has its own special code ($e) for the Escape character. For example, to modify function key F7 so that it executes the DIR command enter:

```
PROMPT $e[0;65;"DIR";13p
```

The PROMPT should be reset to its default immediately afterwards. Similar commands can be used to change the screen colours or move the cursor to a particular position.

RAM DISKS

It is sometimes useful to set aside a part of memory so that it behaves as if it were a disk drive. Files can then be transferred to this part of memory and accessed in the usual way. This is called a *RAM disk* and is allocated its own drive letter.

Access is faster, so this can be a useful place to store program files. Data files are very insecure, of course, and should not be left on the RAM drive in case the machine is switched off before they have been saved to a real disk.

RAM disks need their own device driver. This appears variously as VDISK.SYS and RAMDRIVE.SYS, and will include parameters to set the size of the disk and the number of entries allowed in the root directory. You may also be able to dictate where the RAM disk is placed in memory.

THE MOUSE   If a mouse is attached it must be installed before it will work. The type of installation depends on the variety of mouse. In some cases you need to run a special program (such as MOUSE.COM), in others you need to include the MOUSE.SYS driver in the CONFIG.SYS file.

COUNTRY INFORMATION

The operating system is able to supply a range of information for use in different countries. This includes such features as the format for the date and time and the symbol used for currency. For each country there is a three-digit code that selects the information. The formats supplied for each country are shown in Figure 13.5.

As a matter of interest, the country code is actually the international dialling code.

The country must be specified when the system is booted, using the COUNTRY variable of CONFIG.SYS; otherwise the USA format is assumed. The country cannot be changed later.

The format for the COUNTRY variable is:

```
COUNTRY=country,[codepage],[spec]
```

where

    country is the country code

    codepage is a code page number (see below)

    spec is the specification of the country information file

The country information file is assumed to be COUNTRY.SYS and to be located in the root directory of the system disk, unless specified otherwise. The code page defaults to 437. For DOS 3.0 to DOS 3.2 only the country code could be specified with the COUNTRY variable.

It should be noted that far more limited information was available for versions of DOS prior to 3.0. This information was supplied as part of the KEYB??.COM programs; there was no COUNTRY variable.

Country Code	Country	Date Format	Hour Format	Currency symbol
1	United States	mm-dd-yy	1 - 12	$
2	French/ Canadian	mm-dd-yy	1 - 12	$
3	Latin America	dd-mm-yy	0 - 23	
31	Netherlands	dd-mm-yy	0 - 23	*f*
32	Belgium	dd-mm-yy	0 - 23	F
33	France	dd-mm-yy	0 - 23	F
34	Spain	dd-mm-yy	0 - 23	Pt
39	Italy	dd-mm-yy	0 - 23	Lit.
41	Switzerland	dd-mm-yy	0 - 23	Fr
44	United Kingdom	dd-mm-yy	0 - 23	£
45	Denmark	dd-mm-yy	0 - 23	DKR
46	Sweden	yy-mm-dd	0 - 23	SEK
47	Norway	dd-mm-yy	0 - 23	KR
49	Germany	dd-mm-yy	0 - 23	DM
61	Australia	dd-mm-yy	0 - 23	$
351	Portugal	dd-mm-yy	0 - 23	esc
358	Finland	dd-mm-yy	0 - 23	MK
785	Arabic	dd-mm-yy	0 - 23	
972	Israel	dd-mm-yy	0 - 23	

Figure 13.5 Country-dependent information

NATIONAL KEYBOARDS

The way in which the keys on the keyboard respond depends on which country they have been set up for. The default is the American format, where Shift-2 produces the '@' symbol and Shift-3 gives '#'. If your machine has been supplied with a British keyboard, for example, these two key caps will actually show the symbols '"' and '£' respectively. To make the keys actually produce these characters on the screen you must run the appropriate keyboard program.

In versions of DOS prior to 3.3 there was a separate program for each keyboard. The name of this program consisted of 'KEYB' plus a two-letter abbreviation. For example, the UK keyboard was set up by running the KEYBUK program.

For DOS 3.3 and OS/2 there is a single KEYB.COM program.

Keyboard Code	Code pages	Country code	Country
BE	437,850	032	Belgium
CF	850,863	002	French/Canadian
DK	850,865	045	Denmark
FR	437,850	033	France
GR	437,850	049	Germany
IT	437,850	039	Italy
LA	437,850	003	Latin America
NL	437,850	031	Netherlands
NO	850,865	047	Norway
PO	850,860	351	Portugal
SF	437,850	041	Swiss/French
SG	437,850	041	Swiss/German
SP	437,850	034	Spain
SU	437,850	358	Finland
SV	437,850	046	Sweden
UK	437,850	044	United Kingdom
US	437,850	001	USA
		001	English/Canadian
		061	Australia

Figure 13.6 Keyboard codes and code pages

Command:	KEYB
Effect:	Sets up the keyboard for a particular country
Version:	DOS 3, OS/2
Type:	External
Syntax:	KEYB [*keyboard*] (DOS 3.0 - 3.2)
	KEYB [*keyboard*],[*codepage*],[*spec*]
	(DOS 3.3, OS/2)

Parameters: None

The format is similar to that for the COUNTRY variable, except that the country code is a two-letter code. Only certain code page numbers are allowed for each country code, as shown in Figure 13.6.

The file specification refers to the *keyboard definition file*, the default for which is KEYBOARD.SYS. The operating system

ERRORLEVEL	Reason
0	Program ended successfully
1	Invalid code number of page or bad syntax
2	Keyboard definition file not found
3	Keyboard driver could not be loaded
4	KEYB cannot communicate with CON
5	Code page has not been prepared with MODE
6	Code page is not in the keyboard definition file

Figure 13.7 KEYB ERRORLEVELs

searches the root directory unless otherwise specified. This file contains all the information needed to set up the keyboard for each country.

Note that you can switch to the default US layout by pressing Ctrl-Alt-F1 and back to the selected country with Ctrl-Alt-F2.

You should not use KEYB.COM in versions of DOS prior to 3.3 or KEYB??.COM for DOS 3.3 or OS/2.

KEYB sets the ERRORLEVEL when it has finished its work. These codes are listed in Figure 13.7; for information on how to use them, see Chapter 18.

The KEYB command should be included in your startup file (see Chapter 16).

Examples

The current keyboard definitions can be displayed with:

```
KEYB
```

A new layout can be installed as follows:

```
KEYB UK,850,C:\OS2\KEYBOARD.SYS
```

This sets up the keyboard for the UK, with code page 850.

SELECT

Command:	SELECT
Effect:	Creates a system disk for a specific country
Version:	DOS 3

```
A>dir

 Volume in drive A has no label
 Directory of  A:\

COMMAND  COM    25276  24-07-87  12:00a
DOS           <DIR>          3-08-90   8:21a
CONFIG   SYS       35  3-08-90   8:24a
AUTOEXEC BAT       78  3-08-90   8:24a
         4 File(s)    1222656 bytes free

A>type config.sys
COUNTRY=044,437,\DOS\COUNTRY.SYS

A>type autoexec.bat
PATH \;\DOS;
KEYB UK 437 \DOS\KEYBOARD.SYS
ECHO OFF
CLS
DATE
TIME
VER
```

Figure 13.8 The files created by SELECT

Type:	External
Syntax:	[*location*]SELECT *country keyboard*
	(DOS 3.0 - 3.2)
	[*location*]SELECT [*drive1*] [*drive2*][*path*]
	country keyboard (DOS 3.3)
Parameters:	None

The SELECT command is used to set up a system disk that is customised for a specific country. The command line must specify the country code and keyboard code. Permissible combinations of country and keyboard codes are shown in Figure 13.6. Note that some country codes are used for more than one keyboard, and some keyboard codes apply to more than one country.

For DOS 3.3 you may also specify the drive containing the original system disk; this can be either A: or B:, with A: taken as the default if no other is given. You can state a drive and path where the DOS external command files and other files are to be stored. If no drive is given, the files are stored in the root directory.

The SELECT command, for DOS 3.3, carries out the following processes:

1. The new disk is formatted as a system disk.

2. The system files are copied to the new disk.

3. A sub-directory is created for the DOS files (if one was specified).

4. A CONFIG.SYS file is created, containing the relevant COUNTRY variable.

5. An AUTOEXEC.BAT file is created, with the relevant KEYB command, and a PATH command if a path was specified in the command. It also includes DATE, TIME and VER commands.

There may still be some further customisation necessary. In particular, the external commands must be copied across manually.

Examples

A new system disk can be created for the UK, storing all operating system files in a DOS directory, as follows:

```
SELECT A: B:\DOS 044 UK
```

The files created during this process are shown in Figure 13.8.

CODE PAGES

All information is stored as a set of numerical codes. These codes make up the ASCII character set. Half of the codes (from 0 to 127) are an internationally-recognised set that should produce the same characters, whenever and however they are used. The other half (from 128 to 255) form the *extended ASCII codes*. Here the standardisation is not so widespread. These codes are used for the line-drawing characters, special symbols and foreign characters. The operating system includes a *code page*, which is simply a translation table for converting the numerical codes to characters that can be displayed or printed. There are five code pages, numbered 437, 850, 860, 863 and 865.

Versions of DOS prior to 3.3 were each supplied with a particular code page (437, 860, 863 or 865), depending on the country where they were to be used. DOS 3.3 introduced a new 'standard' code page, 850. It is intended that all new applications should work with this code page but in the meantime we have to cope with applications that use the earlier code pages. This is done through a method called *code page switching*.

When the system is started up you can specify which code page is to be used as the default, as part of the COUNTRY variable. Later on you can change the code page for a particular application.

In order to use a code page with a device, that device must support code page switching. Such devices - of which there are only a few at present - will need a special *code page information file*, with a CPI extension.

Before using the devices it may be necessary to install two device drivers as part of CONFIG.SYS:

```
DEVICE=DISPLAY.SYS
DEVICE=PRINTER.SYS
```

The first relates to the screen, the second to a printer. Additional parameters may be required for these device drivers.

MODE

Command:	MODE
Effect:	Sets up code pages
Version:	DOS 3.3, OS/2
Type:	External
Syntax:	[*location*]MODE *device* CODEPAGE PREPARE=((*codepage*) [*spec*])
	[*location*]MODE *device* CODEPAGE SELECT=*codepage*
	[*location*]MODE *device* CODEPAGE /STATUS
	[*location*]MODE *device* CODEPAGE REFRESH
Parameters:	None

The first version of this command prepares a device for code page switching; the second implements the code page; the third option displays the current status of code page switching for the device; the last option re-installs a code page if it is no longer available (for example, because a device has been temporarily switched off).

Code page switching should only be attempted if recommended by a particular application for a specific device.

Examples   A code page can be prepared and then selected as follows:

```
MODE CON: CODEPAGE PREPARE=((437,850) C:\DOS\EGA.CPI)

MODE CON: CODEPAGE SELECT=437
```

This sets up the EGA screen to accept two code pages, and selects page 437.

NLSFUNC

Command:	NLSFUNC
Effect:	Identifies country information file and supports code page switching
Version:	DOS 3.3
Type:	External
Syntax:	[*location*]NLSFUNC [*spec*]
Parameters:	None

NLSFUNC is used to define the country information file, if it is anything other than COUNTRY.SYS or in a directory that is not pointed to by the PATH command.

In addition, this command must be invoked before you can switch code pages with CHCP (see below).

NLSFUNC should only be invoked once.

CHCP

Command:	CHCP
Effect:	Changes the current code page
Version:	DOS 3.3, OS/2
Type:	Internal
Syntax:	CHCP [*codepage*]
Parameters:	None

The CHCP command can be used to select a new code page. The command should be followed by the code page to be selected. Before changing the code page it must have been prepared. Under DOS 3.3 this involves preparing a code page with MODE and then installing code page switching with NLSFUNC.

Under OS/2, you must include in CONFIG.SYS the variables CODEPAGE= (followed by the code pages to be used) and DEVINFO=. DEVINFO must be included for each device that supports code page switching.

COMMAND AND DATA PATHS

Many of the operating system's most useful utilities are available in the form of external commands. For the operating system to find them, you must precede each command with the location of the file. However, this is rather tedious and can be extremely frustrating.

DOS and OS/2 provide a simpler method of specifying a *path* which the operating system can search for the required command file. Another path can be specified when searching for data.

PATH

Command: PATH
Effect: Specifies a search path for program files
Version: DOS 2, OS/2
Type: Internal
Syntax: PATH [*drive*][*path*];[...]
Parameters: None

If no path is specified the operating system searches the current directory of the current drive for a program, command or batch file whenever an instruction is entered. If it cannot find a file with the correct name, the result is a 'Bad command or file name' message (or the OS/2 equivalent).

The PATH command provides a list of directories, on one or more drives, that should be searched before the operating system gives up. Each time you enter the PATH command the existing path is replaced by the new one. Each directory must be separated from the next by a semi-colon. If no drive is included in the path, the current drive is assumed, so may be different each time. To cancel the path altogether, just use a semi-colon and no directory. The PATH command on its own displays the current path.

The new order of precedence for searches now becomes:

■ Internal commands

■ Files in the current directory with EXE, COM, BAT or CMD extensions

■ Files in the directories specified by PATH

The operating system always checks each directory for files with all the possible extensions before moving on to the next directory in the path.

Note that you can produce the same effect with a PATH= directive in CONFIG.SYS.

Examples

If the external commands are in the \DOS sub-directory you can instruct the operating system to check this directory with the following command:

```
PATH C:\DOS
```

The operating system can be told to check the root directory of the current drive as well, with this command:

```
PATH C:\DOS;\
```

If some of your programs are stored in C:\PROGRAMS and various batch files to run other applications are in \BATS, these directories can be added to the path with:

```
PATH C:\DOS;\;C:\PROGRAMS;C:\BATS
```

Only after checking these directories does the operating system issue the 'Bad command or file name' message.

APPEND

Command:	APPEND
Effect:	Defines search path for non-executable files
Version:	DOS 3.2, OS/2 real mode
Type:	External
Syntax:	APPEND [*drive*][*path*];[...]
Parameters:	/X Include executable files
	/E Stores path as environment variable

APPEND has the potential to be a very useful command but unfortunately its performance is somewhat marred by bugs and side effects.

The main problem with PATH is that the operating system can find a program file but will not find any overlay files or data files that are not in the current directory.

APPEND works almost identically to PATH, but specifies a search path not for executable files (with EXE, COM and BAT extensions) but for all other files.

The major problem with APPEND is that if any file is changed it is always saved in the current directory, regardless of whether or not this was the directory in which it was first found.

APPEND can be made to search for executable files but only if the /X parameter is specified when the command is first executed; similarly, any APPEND path can be made into an environment variable if the /E parameter is used the first time.

The problem with the /X parameter is that operating system commands start behaving in peculiar ways. DIR, for instance, lists all files in all directories in the path, as if they were all in the current directory.

APPEND also causes problems with BACKUP and RESTORE. Therefore this command is really best avoided.

APPEND works only with OS/2's real mode; for protected mode data paths, see DPATH below.

Examples

To set a data path to \PROGRAMS and \DATA, and include searches for executable files, enter:

```
APPEND /X
APPEND C:\PROGRAMS;C:\DATA
```

Note that the APPEND command on its own displays the current data path.

DPATH

Command:	DPATH
Effect:	Defines search path for non-executable files
Version:	OS/2 protected mode
Type:	External
Syntax:	[*location*]DPATH [*drive*][*path*];[...]
Parameters:	None

```
[C:\]dpath
DPATH=

[C:\]dpath c:\;a:\;c;\data

[C:\]dpath
DPATH=C:\;A:\;C;\DATA

   [C:\]
```

Figure 13.9 Data paths in OS/2 protected mode

DPATH works in exactly the same way as APPEND, except that this command is for OS/2 protected mode only and has no parameters. Whenever a file is required, OS/2 searches all directories in the path until it finds the one it needs.

Examples   A path can be set to include the root directories of both the floppy and hard disks, and the \DATA directory of drive C, as follows:

```
DPATH C:\;A:\;C:\DATA
```

Note that OS/2 will always use a file in the C:\ directory in preference to one on drive A (if both have files of the same name), since the directories are always searched in the order given.

DPATH on its own displays the current directory path (see Figure 13.9).

DRIVE IDENTITIES

Most of the time the labels assigned to the disk drives are perfectly acceptable. However, there are odd occasions when it is helpful to be able to change the meanings of the drive letters.

Three commands are available to do just this. These are described below, though it should be stated that all three of them can cause as many problems as they solve.

ASSIGN

Command:	ASSIGN
Effect:	Re-assigns a disk drive label
Version:	DOS 2, OS/2 real mode
Type:	External
Syntax:	[*location*]ASSIGN [*label1*]=[*label2*] [...]
Parameters:	None

Most application programs allow you to work with your own particular drive configuration and do not force you to use specific drives for programs and data. Some applications, however - particularly the older ones - specify that programs and data must use certain drives. This can be frustrating, especially when you have upgraded to another machine. If the program will only access data on drive B, for example, and you now have a computer with a hard disk and only one floppy drive, this can cause problems.

ASSIGN helps out by relabelling the drives. The first drive label given is re-assigned to the drive represented by the second label. The operating system then treats the second drive as if it were the first.

You can re-assign more than one drive with a single command. Each time the command is used it completely revises the drive assignments; ASSIGN on its own restores the original drive settings.

Note that ASSIGN should not be used with BACKUP, DISK-COMP, DISKCOPY, FORMAT, JOIN, LABEL, PRINT, RESTORE or SUBST. The JOIN and SUBST commands are often a better choice but can also be problematical.

```
C>join a: c:\floppy

C>join
A: => C:\FLOPPY

C>dir c:\floppy

 Volume in drive C has no label
 Directory of  C:\FLOPPY

COMMAND  COM     25276  24-07-87  12:00a
DOS          <DIR>         3-08-90   8:21a
CONFIG   SYS        35    3-08-90   8:24a
AUTOEXEC BAT        78    3-08-90   8:24a
        4 File(s)  17113088 bytes free

C>join a: /d

C>join

C>
```

Figure 13.10 Re-assigning drives with JOIN

Examples

If you want to store all data on drive C but the program expects to find the files on drive B, the floppy drive can be re-assigned as follows:

```
ASSIGN B=C
```

All references to drive B (including operating system commands, such as DIR) will now be redirected to the hard disk.

JOIN

Command:	JOIN
Effect:	Re-assigns a drive to a sub-directory
Version:	DOS 3, OS/2 real mode
Type:	External
Syntax:	[*location*]JOIN [*drive1*] [*drive2*][*path*]
Parameters:	/D Deletes previous re-assignment

This rarely-used command works in a similar way to ASSIGN but this time re-assigns a drive to a sub-directory. The sub-directory must be in the root directory of the second drive and must be empty. If the sub-directory does not exist, JOIN creates it.

244

JOIN on its own displays the current re-assignments. The /D parameter is used to cancel a re-assignment.

JOIN can confuse other commands and should not be used with ASSIGN, BACKUP, CHKDSK, DISKCOMP, DISKCOPY, FDISK, FORMAT, LABEL, RECOVER, RESTORE, SUBST or SYS. JOIN should not be used with networked drives. One questions whether it should ever be used at all!

Examples
The disk in drive A can be accessed as if it were the \FLOPPY directory on drive C with the command:

```
JOIN A: C:\FLOPPY
```

Any refernces to C:\FLOPPY will result in drive A being accessed (Figure 13.10). References to drive A will result in an error message. To display the current assignments enter:

```
JOIN
```

To cancel this re-assignment, enter:

```
JOIN A: /D
```

Any other joins remain active.

SUBST

Command: SUBST
Effect: Re-assigns a sub-directory to a drive
Version: DOS 3, OS/2
Type: External
Syntax: [*location*]SUBST [*drive1*] [*drive2*][*path*]
Parameters: /D   Delete previous re-assignment

The SUBST command is the reverse of JOIN, and works in a similar way. This time the directory path can be re-assigned to a drive letter. The drive letter must be one that is not currently in use and must be a valid letter. (It may be necessary to increase the value of the LASTDRIVE variable in CONFIG.SYS.)

The main reason for using SUBST is so that older applications that cannot handle sub-directories can be used with a hard disk. It can also cut down on the length of commands but should not be used for this reason alone, because of the problems associated with it. SUBST on its own displays the current re-assignments. The /D parameter cancels a re-assignment.

When working under DOS 3.3, SUBST should not be used with ASSIGN, BACKUP, CHKDSK, DISKCOMP, DISKCOPY, FDISK, FORMAT, JOIN, LABEL, RECOVER, RESTORE, SUBST or SYS.

Examples

The sub-directory C:\WP\BOOK can be made to behave as if it were drive E as follows:

```
SUBST E: C:\WP\BOOK
```

Any references to drive E now affect C:\WP\BOOK. The re-assignment is cancelled with:

```
SUBST E: /D
```

References to drive E now result in an error message.

SYSTEM OPERATION

A number of other commands affect the general operation of the computer. Many of these need never concern the user but some may be helpful from time to time for particular applications. These commands are described below.

BREAK

Command: BREAK
Effect: Varies the number of checks for Ctrl-Break
Version: DOS 2, OS/2 real mode
Type: Internal
Syntax: BREAK [ON|OFF]
Parameters: None

In the normal course of events you can interrupt most processes by pressing the Ctrl-Break combination. However, the operating system only usually checks for this key combination when it performs some operation with the keyboard, screen or any external device connected to the ports.

The frequency of checks can be increased by switching BREAK ON. The operating system now also checks whenever it performs any disk operation. The disadvantage of doing this is that programs now execute more slowly. As a result, it is normal to leave BREAK OFF, which is the default state.

BREAK on its own displays the current Ctrl-Break status.

The default can be changed by including the BREAK=ON parameter in CONFIG.SYS.

Examples

The number of checks for Ctrl-Break is increased with the command:

```
BREAK ON
```

Enter the BREAK command on its own to display the current status of Ctrl-Break key checking.

CMD

Command:	CMD
Effect:	Loads secondary command processor
Version:	OS/2 protected mode
Type:	External
Syntax:	CMD [*location*]
Parameters:	/C *command* Run a command
	/K *command* Run a command and keep permanently in memory

It is sometimes useful to load a second copy of the OS/2 protected mode command processor into memory. This is particularly the case when the first copy is tied up because you are running a program or batch file and need to execute a further command.

This command is similar to COMMAND, below.

COMMAND

Command:	COMMAND
Effect:	Loads secondary command processor
Version:	DOS 2, OS/2 real mode
Type:	External
Syntax:	COMMAND [*locations*]
Parameters:	/C *command* Run a command
	/P *command* Run a command and keep permanently in memory
	/E:*bytes* Size of environment (DOS 3.2, OS/2)

COMMAND is the DOS and OS/2 real mode command processor. When entered as a command it invokes a secondary command processor (in the same way as for CMD, above).

Its greatest use is in batch files, as described in Chapter 16.

In the normal course of events the command processor remains in memory until the EXIT command is issued. If the /C parameter is added (followed by a DOS command) the command processor only remains in memory for as long as it takes to execute the command. /P combines the two options: the additional command is executed and the command processor then resides in memory until an EXIT command is given.

EXIT

Command:	EXIT
Effect:	Exits a command processor
Version:	DOS 2, OS/2
Type:	Internal
Syntax:	EXIT
Parameters:	None

This command exits a command processor and frees the memory it was taking up. In DOS and OS/2 real mode the command exits a secondary command processor; under OS/2 protected mode it also cancels redundant sessions and returns you to the Program Selector.

GRAFTABL

Command:	GRAFTABL
Effect:	Loads an extended character set
Version:	DOS 3, OS/2 real mode
Type:	External
Syntax:	[*location*]GRAFTABL
	[*location*]GRAFTABL [codepage I /STATUS]
	(DOS 3.3)
	[*location*]GRAFTABL [codepage I /STA I ?] (OS/2)
Parameters:	None

When running a graphics program you may find that the extended ASCII characters are not displayed on the screen. These are the characters in the range 128 to 255, including the box-drawing symbols and foreign characters. In such cases you need to load a graphics character table into memory; this is done with GRAFTABL.

ERRORLEVEL	Reason
0	New code page table installed
1	New code page table installed, replacing previous code page
2	No code page table installed, either now or previously
3	Invalid parameter
4	Incorrect DOS version

Figure 13.11 GRAFTABL ERRORLEVELs

DOS 3.3 and OS/2 also allow you to specify the extended character set for a particular code page; the alternative /STATUS or /STA parameters display the current GRAFTABL code page. This version of the program also returns an ERRORLEVEL value; the values and reasons are given in Figure 13.11. The OS/2 real mode version also provides a '?' option which displays the possible command line values.

Examples

To load the default code page table of extended graphics characters, enter:

```
GRAFTABL
```

To replace this with code page 860, enter:

```
GRAFTABL 860
```

The current setting can be displayed with:

```
GRAFTABL /STATUS
```

The GRAFTABL messages are shown in Figure 13.12.

HELPMSG

Command:	HELPMSG
Effect:	Display OS/2 help messages
Version:	OS/2
Type:	External
Syntax:	[*location*]HELPMSG *error*
Parameters:	None

```
C>graftabl

No version of Graphic Character Set Table is already loaded.

USA version of Graphic Character Set Table has just been loaded.

C>graftabl 860

USA version of Graphic Character Set Table is already loaded.

Portuguese version of Graphic Character Set Table has just been loaded.

C>graftabl /status

Portuguese version of Graphic Character Set Table is already loaded.

C>
```

Figure 13.12 Using GRAFTABL

OS/2 always starts its error messages with an error number. The HELPMSG command takes this error number and expands upon it, to provide an explanation of why it might have occurred and to suggest possible action.

Examples

If you try to run a non-existent program OS/2 responds with the message:

```
DOS0002: The system cannot find the file specified
```

Further explanation of this message can be obtained by the command:

```
HELPMSG DOS0002
```

The help display that results is shown in Figure 13.13.

PATCH

Command:	PATCH
Effect:	Patches an executable file
Version:	OS/2
Type:	External
Syntax:	[*location*]PATCH *spec*
Parameters:	/A Automatic update from file

```
[C:\OS2]helpmsg sys0002

SYS0002: The system cannot find the file specified

EXPLANATION: The file name in the command
does not exist in the current directory or search path
specified. Or, the file name was entered incorrectly.
ACTION: Retry the command using the correct file name


[C:\OS2]
```

Figure 13.13 OS/2 help messages

This command should only be used by programmers and experienced users. It allows you to make changes to the code of an executable file, providing a more straightforward method than DEBUG (see Chapter 14).

A change to a program is called a *patch* and is usually intended to fix a known bug. Some software producers will issue patches from time to time.

When the command has been entered you are asked for the location (in hexadecimal) of the first patch. The code at this point is displayed and you can write over the top of it. Press Return when the changes have been made. You are then asked if you want to make further changes and the program loops round until you answer 'N'. At this stage you are asked if you want to save the changes that have been made.

The /A parameter automatically patches a program from changes stored in a file.

Example   The program DISPLAY.EXE can be patched by entering this command:

```
PATCH DISPLAY.EXE
```

The new code can now be written to the program.

SHARE

Command:	SHARE
Effect:	Allows file sharing on a network
Version:	DOS 3
Type:	External
Syntax:	[*location*]SHARE

Parameters:	/F:*bytes*	Number of bytes for share codes
	/L:*number*	Number of locks

When files are shared on a network the program specifies the type of access that may be available to other users for each file. This is done through a number of *share codes*. Similarly, parts of a file may be *locked* when one user is processing them so that they cannot be changed by another user.

The default is that 2048 bytes are set aside in memory for share codes and that 20 file locks are allowed. SHARE provides the means to change these defaults if they are inadequate.

Examples   The space for share codes can be increased to 4096 bytes and the number of file locks to 30 as follows:

```
SHARE /F:4096 /L:30
```

This is only necessary if programs indicate through their error messages that the current values are insufficient or if an application's manual suggests that it is necessary.

MEMORY CONSIDERATIONS

The basic DOS system is limited to 640K memory. Anything beyond this is inaccessible to DOS unless we introduce some special methods of gaining access to it. Many applications now struggle to keep within the 640K limit and would welcome the chance to spread themselves out into greater areas of RAM.

This is one of the reasons for the arrival of OS/2. This new operating system has no limit and applications are free to operate in as much memory as they need. Two different terms are used to refer to the extra memory that can be available.

EXPANDED MEMORY

To overcome the 640K limit on DOS we need to add some *expanded memory* (or *EMS*). This is memory that is additional to the standard 640K and is addressed by a method known as *bank switching*. The process is really quite straightforward. An extra device driver is loaded into memory that oversees all access to memory. At any time it can direct the operating system to work with a section of memory outside the normal range by switching the address of a 64K section (or *bank*) from the expanded memory with a similar bank in the standard memory. DOS still thinks it is working within its normal address range but, in fact, it is operating on a totally new section of memory. By constantly switching banks we can, with some effort, expand the memory available.

There are several different expanded memory device drivers available. The first to be developed was the *LIM* EMS, so-called because it was developed by Lotus, Intel and Microsoft. This was limited to an additional 64K of expanded memory, which is neither here nor there. As a result a rival, *EEMS*, that could add a megabyte of memory, soon appeared.

Now, however, there is a new LIM version, called EMS 4.0, that appears to be gaining acceptance as an industry standard. (What happened to versions 2 and 3 is not clear!) EMS 4.0 provides the potential to add 32M of RAM and copes well with multi-tasking.

EXTENDED MEMORY

So much for DOS. OS/2 has no need for such convoluted thinking when it comes to addressing memory. This operating system is only able to run on 80286 and 80386 machines and these computers can easily access memory well beyond the old limits. In fact, the 640K limit on DOS was a fairly arbitrary one and there is no reason why one megabyte could not have been used; the 8088 and 8086 computers certainly had the ability to address that amount of memory; 640K was an artificial limit imposed by DOS.

For 286 and 386 machines the first megabyte is considered the bare minimum for satisfactory operation. Anything beyond this is known as *extended memory*. Such memory is accessible to OS/2 protected mode without any difficulties.

Therefore, if you are running under OS/2, the final modification to your system may be to include a DEVICE command for an expanded memory driver in CONFIG.SYS. This is necessary if you have fitted expanded memory and if you are running a program that can actually use it. Under OS/2 this should not be necessary.

14. *Utility Programs*

It is always difficult to know when an external command becomes a fully-fledged program. All external command are, of course, programs in their own right. However, they are inextricably linked to a particular version of the operating system; try to run an external command under a different version and you will invariably get the 'Incorrect DOS version' message. This, then, marks them as being different to normal programs; a standard application program should work quite happily with a range of operating system versions.

Programs such as LABEL are clearly worthy of the title 'command' since they do so little. Others, such as DISKCOPY, perform quite complex tasks. Some programs, however, have their own sub-set of commands and are really too complicated to be called commands. This chapter briefly considers four of these *utility programs*. These programs are supplied with most implementations of DOS.

EDLIN

In order to create or edit ASCII files such as CONFIG.SYS you need a text editor or word processor capable of creating such files. Text editors are much simpler than word processors, providing only limited facilities for editing ASCII files. One such text editor usually accompanies MS-DOS and PC-DOS: EDLIN.

To be frank, most people never use EDLIN and would only consider using it as a very last resort. There are many commercial utility programs with text editing facilities that leave EDLIN standing. However, it is there, and can be used in an emergency.

STARTING EDLIN

To put EDLIN into effect you need to specify a filename. You can include a complete file specification in the command line, as follows:

```
EDLIN C:\WP\BOOK\NOTES
```

If the file NOTES does not exist it is created; otherwise, its existing contents are read into memory. EDLIN is an external

```
C:\>edlin config.sys
End of input file
*1
        1:*BUFFERS=20
        2: FILES=20
        3: COUNTRY=44
        4: DEVICE=\SYSTEM\ANSI.SYS
*2
        2:*FILES=20
        2:*files=32
*4i
        4:*device=\system\randrive.sys
        5:*^C

*e

C:\>type config.sys
BUFFERS=20
files=32
COUNTRY=44
device=\system\randrive.sys
DEVICE=\SYSTEM\ANSI.SYS
```

Figure 14.1 Editing with EDLIN

program and must therefore be in a directory pointed to by PATH. EDLIN responds as follows:

```
End of input file
*
```

The '*' is the EDLIN prompt, indicating that it is waiting for a command. If the 'End of input file' message is not displayed the whole file would not fit in memory in one go. There are commands to read in extra sections of text and store text away to file.

Add the /B parameter if you want to load a file that 's not terminated by Ctrl-Z.

EDLIN COMMANDS

Each of the EDLIN commands consists of a single letter (upper and lower case are treated the same). For example, to list the whole file, enter the List command:

```
L
```

Command	Name	Syntax	Effect
A	Append	(*n*)A	Appends a number of lines to the file in memory from disk. (Use for large files after Write)
C	Count	(*l1*),(*l2*),(*l3*),(*n*)C	Copies the range of lines *l1* to *l2* in front of line *l3* (repeating them *n* times)
D	Delete	(*l1*),(*l2*)D	Deletes a range of lines
E	End	E	Ends and saves the file
I	Insert	(*l1*)I	Inserts text in front of specified line
L	List	(*l1*),(*l2*)L	Lists a range of lines
M	Move	(*l1*),(*l2*),*l3*M	Moves the range of lines *l1* to *l2* in front of line *l3*
P	Page	(*l1*),(*l2*)P	Lists a range of lines, making the last line listed the current line
Q	Quit	Q	Quits and abandons changes
R	Replace	(*l1*),(*l2*),(?)R(*s1*)^Z(*s2*)	Replaces string *s1* with *s2* in the range *l1* to *l2*. Include '?' for a prompt before each replacement
S	Search	(*l1*),(*l2*),(?)S(*s1*)	Searches for string *s1* in th range *l1* to *l2* and makes it the current line. Include '?' to continue search until 'Y' is pressed
T	Transfer	(*l2*)T(*f1*)	Transfers contents of file f1 into current file in front of line *l1*
W	Write	(*n*)W	Writes a number of lines to disk. (Use for large files)

Notes:	Items in (square brackets) are optional
	f1 is a file specification
	l1, l2, l3 represent line numbers
	n represents a number
	s1, s2 are strings of text
	^Z represents the Ctrl-Z character

Figure 14.2 EDLIN commands

As you will see, each line in the file is numbered. The '*' to the right of a line number indicates that this is the *current line*: the line that EDLIN operates on unless you specify otherwise. Line numbers can be included in commands as follows:

```
2,5L
```

This command lists lines 2 to 5. The '#' symbol denotes the last line of the file, as in:

```
3,#L
```

The '-' and '+' keys indicate lines before and after the current line:

```
-1,+1L
```

This lists three lines: the current line and one line on either side.

You can edit a line by entering its line number with no command (Figure 14.1). When editing and inserting you can accept a new line with Return, or reject it with Ctrl-Break. During editing the usual DOS editing keys (Ins, Del and the function keys) are available.

To leave EDLIN, enter the E command to end and save, or Q to quit and abandon. If the file is saved, the old version is automatically renamed with a BAK extension, deleting any previous version of that name.

The full set of commands is given in Figure 14.2. The best way to learn EDLIN is to experiment with it.

DEBUG

Assembly language programmers need to be able to make changes to their program files, often without wanting to go through the entire compilation process. It is also useful to inspect the contents of memory. The DEBUG utility provides these options.

As was the case with EDLIN, DEBUG is supplied with all versions of DOS but most modern assemblers provide far better facilities. However, a working knowledge of DEBUG is useful.

STARTING DEBUG

DEBUG can be put into effect either with or without a file being specified. It may therefore be in either of these forms:

```
DEBUG
```

```
C:\>debug config.sys
-d
202F:0100   42 55 46 46 45 52 53 3D-32 30 0D 0A 66 69 6C 65    BUFFERS=20..file
202F:0110   73 3D 33 32 0D 0A 43 4F-55 4E 54 52 59 3D 34 34    s=32..COUNTRY=44
202F:0120   0D 0A 44 45 56 49 43 45-3D 5C 53 59 53 54 45 4D    ..DEVICE=\SYSTEM
202F:0130   5C 41 4E 53 49 2E 53 59-53 0D 0A 1A 46 F8 26 8B    \ANSI.SYS...F.&.
202F:0140   47 04 2B 46 F8 29 46 F0-EB CF C4 5E F2 8B 46 04    G.+F.)F....^..F.
202F:0150   26 39 47 02 77 06 26 39-47 04 77 93 FF 46 FE 83    &9G.w.&9G.w..F..
202F:0160   46 F2 06 E9 6F FF 8B 5E-06 8B 46 F0 89 07 E8 05    F...o..^..F.....
202F:0170   93 5E 8B E5 5D C3 55 8B-EC 83 EC 12 56 E8 CB 92    .^..].U.....V...
-q

C:\>
```

Figure 14.3 Displaying a file with DEBUG

```
C:\>debug
-e 100 b2 07 b4 02 cd 21 cd 20
-d 100 108
202F:0100   B2 07 B4 02 CD 21 CD 20                            .....!.
-r bx
BX 0000
:0000
-r cx
CX 0000
:0008
-n bell.com
-w
Writing 0008 bytes
-q

C:\>dir bell.com

 Volume in drive C has no label
 Directory of  C:\

BELL     COM        8   3-08-90   9:13a
        1 File(s)  17096704 bytes free

C:\>bell
```

Figure 14.4 Creating a short program

Command	Name	Syntax	Effect
A	Assemble	A A address	Assembles code directly
C	Compare	C range, address	Compares memory in range with memory starting at address
D	Dump	D D range	Displays next 128 bytes or range
E	Enter	E address E address, data	Enters data at specified address
F	Fill	F range, data	Fills range with data
G	Go	G	Executes program from start or from address
H	Hexadecimal	H value, value	Adds two hex numbers and also subtracts second from first
I	Input	I port	Inputs value from port
L	Load	L address L address, sectors	Loads a file or disk sectors
M	Move	M range, address	Moves a range of memory to a new address
N	Name	N filename	Names a file to load or save
O	Output	O data,port	Outputs data to a port
P	Proceed		
Q	Quit	Q	Quits DEBUG
R	Register	R R register	Displays contents of registers
S	Search	S range, data	Searches range for data
T	Trace	T T=address T steps	Traces program, optionally from a specified address an/or a number of steps
U	Unassemble	U range	Unassembles a range of code
W	Write	W W address W address, sectors	Writes a section of code to a file or directly to disk

Figure 14.5 DEBUG commands

```
DEBUG PROG.COM
```

In the second case, the program file PROG.COM is loaded into memory.

DEBUG responds with its '-' prompt, indicating that it is ready to accept a command. DEBUG does not only work with program files. Try calling up a copy of CONFIG.SYS (by including its name on the command line) and you will get a better idea of how a file is displayed and edited.

DEBUG COMMANDS

As for EDLIN, DEBUG's commands each consist of a single letter (either upper or lower case). For example, to display the first 128 bytes of the main part of the file, enter the Dump command:

```
D
```

The response is a display in hexadecimal (Figure 14.3). Each line starts with the address in memory of that line, given as a segment:offset pair. The line ends with a display of the ASCII text derived from the 16 bytes. Only those bytes in the normal printable character range (32 to 127) are shown; the rest are represented by dots.

Figure 14.4 shows how a simple file (BELL.COM) can be created to make the computer beep.

The full set of DEBUG commands is given in Figure 14.5. Once again, experimentation is the best way to learn but be careful; DEBUG can have quite disastrous effects on files, so always start with a renamed copy of the file.

LINK

Assemblers such as *DEBUG* produce programs consisting of machine code that are ready to run. Larger programs may need to include sections of code that have been prepared separately. These are called *object files* (with an OBJ extension). These files must generally be converted to *relocatable* files before they can be executed. A relocatable file is one that can be placed any- where in memory and still execute satisfactorily. Such files are given an EXE extension. LINK converts object files to relocatable files. It also combines object files with standard program modules to form a single program file.

The LINK program will only be of interest to programmers.

```
C:\>link

Microsoft (R) Personal Computer Linker  Version 2.40
Copyright (C) Microsoft Corp 1983, 1984, 1985.  All rights reserved.

Object Modules [.OBJ]: bell
Run File [BELL.EXE]:
List File [NUL.MAP]:
Libraries [.LIB]: c:\qb\bcom30.lib

C:\>dir bell.*

 Volume in drive C has no label
 Directory of  C:\

BELL     EXE    26924   3-08-90    9:20a
BELL     OBJ      747   3-08-90    9:14a
        2 File(s)  17061888 bytes free

C:\>
```

Figure 14.6 Linking object modules

STARTING LINK When LINK is run it needs to know the following information:

- The name of the object files (assumed to have an OBJ extension, unless otherwise specified)

- The name of the run file (assumed to have an EXE extension)

- The name of the list file (assumed to have a MAP extension, unless otherwise specified)

- The name of any library files (assumed to have a LIB extension, unless otherwise specified)

The *run file* is the executable program file, with an EXE extension, that is created by this process.

A *list file* is a file that lists the names and sizes of the segments created in the executable file.

A *library file* is a collection of standard routines that can be combined with the original object file. Any references not

262

included in the original object files are extracted from the library file.

LINK prompts you for each of these files (or groups of files) in turn. It always offers a default (shown in square brackets). Press Return to accept this default. If more than one file is needed (for example, to link two object files), their names are joined together by a '+' symbol.

Figure 14.6 shows how the BELL.OBJ file (created with QuickBasic) can be linked to create BELL.EXE. Note the size of the EXE file!

The filenames can also be included on the command line. Each of the four items can be specified, separated by commas. LINK still prompts for any name not given. To bypass the remaining prompts end the command with a semi-colon. For example, the command may be entered as:

```
LINK PROG1+PROG2,,PROG;
```

The program links the files PROG1.OBJ and PROG2.OBJ; it prompts for the executable file name (suggesting the name PROG1.EXE); the list file is PROG.MAP; there is no prompt for a library file.

Our earlier example can be linked with:

```
LINK BELL;
```

As a third option, the text for the command line can be taken from an ASCII file; the name of the file should be preceded by an '@' symbol on the command line. For example, suppose that a file has been created that contains just a single line:

```
PROG1+PROG2,,PROG,,
```

If the file is called PROG.TXT, LINK can now be executed with the command:

```
LINK @PROG.TXT
```

This saves a great deal of typing and potential errors, especially for very complicated command lines. Alternatively, put the entire LINK command in a batch file; then you may also add commands to copy backup files, run the new program, delete unwanted list files and so on. These are very useful options if you need to LINK the same files a number of times.

Once the filenames have been supplied, the LINK process is automatic.

LINK PARAMETERS

A number of parameters can be included on the command line:

/D   Data is loaded at the top of the Data Segment (required for Pascal and FORTRAN programs)

/H   Loads the program as high as possible in memory. (Cannot be used with Pascal and FORTRAN)

/L   List file includes line numbers and relative addresses (from the start of the file) of each line of code in the original program. (Only effective when all lines are numbered, as in BASIC for example)

/M   List file includes all *public symbols* (names that appear in more than one object file)

/N   LINK does not search default library files for references that do not appear in the object file(s)

/P   LINK pauses after creating the run file, before writing it to disk (to allow disk changes)

/S:*bytes*   Increases the stack size to a specific number of bytes

LINK is a fairly advanced feature of the operating system and should only be used if you are familiar with the basics of assembly language programming.

EXE2BIN

Many of the smaller programs created for use in DOS or OS/2 real mode have an extension of COM. These programs can be run in the same way as EXE files but have several advantages. They do not include the large header section that is necessary for EXE files because they are small enough to fit all of the program and its data into a single 64K segment. For this reason, COM files use less memory than their EXE counterparts. COM files also start executing more quickly but once the program is running there should be no difference as far as the user is concerned.

The disadvantage of COM files is the limitation that is placed on program and data size.

An EXE file can be converted to a COM (or *binary*) file with the EXE2BIN utility. For example, the BELL program created earlier can be converted to a COM file as follows:

```
EXE2BIN BELL
```

If the EXE file is invalid for any reason or does not satisfy the criteria for COM files, the utility responds with a 'File cannot be converted' message.

As for the other programs in this chapter, EXE2BIN is really only for the experienced programmer.

15. Alphabetical Cross-reference

This part of the book has covered most of the commands and features of the DOS and OS/2 operating systems. Once you are familiar with the basics of these two systems you should be able to use this chapter as a cross reference. In order to help you find your way around this part of the book, this chapter contains tables that cross-reference the commands and topics covered so far. It also provides pointers to the subjects mentioned later in the book.

COMMANDS

There are a large number of DOS and OS/2 commands. Unfortunately it is not possible to provide an exhaustive list. While the core of commands always remains the same, every version of the operating system and every implementation has a slight variation in its repertoire.

The table in Figure 15.1 lists the commands that are covered in this book. The list may include some external commands that are not available on a particular implementation of the system, and some uncommon commands may have been excluded. However, you should find here everything you need for 99% of your computer operation.

Note that the batch commands, covered in the next part of the book, are not included.

OPERATING SYSTEM FEATURES

The operating systems include a wide spread of features, ranging from their command line syntax to their utility programs. To help locate a particular feature of the system these are listed alphabetically in Figure 15.2. For a more detailed reference, consult the index.

Command	Description	Main page no.
APPEND	Defines search path for non-executable files	240
ASSIGN	Re-assigns a disk drive label	243
ATTRIB	Displays or changes archive and read-only attributes	183
BACKUP	Creates backup disks	173
BREAK	Varies the number of checks for Ctrl-Break	246
CHDIR or CD	Changes the current directory	155
CHKDSK	Checks the status of a disk or group of files	143
CHCP	Changes the current code page	238
CLS	Clears the screen	189
CMD	Loads secondary command processor (OS/2 protected mode)	247
COMMAND	Loads secondary command processor (DOS, OS/2 real mode)	247
COMP	Compares the contents of pairs of files	177
COPY	Copies or combines files	161
CTTY	Changes the current input/output device	206
DATE	Displays and changes the current system	189
DEL or ERASE	Deletes one or more files	181
DIR	Displays the contents of a directory	151
DISKCOMP	Compares the contents of two floppy disks	142
DISKCOPY	Copies the entire contents of one floppy disk onto another, formatting the target disk if necessary	139
DPATH	Defines search path for non-executable files	241
EXIT	Exits a command processor	248
FASTOPEN	Fast access to most recently used files	157

Figure 15.1 Operating system commands

Command	Description	Main page no.
FDISK	Partitions a hard disk	134
FIND	Filter to find a piece of text in a file	220
FORMAT	Formats a floppy or hard disk	136
GRAFTABL	Loads an extended character set	248
HELPMSG	Display OS/2 help messages	249
JOIN	Re-assigns a drive to a sub-directory	244
KEYB	Sets up national keyboard	233
LABEL	Changes a disk's volume label	148
MKDIR or MD	Creates a sub-directory	153
MODE	Sets up devices	201
	Sets up code pages	237
MORE	Filter to display output a screenful of data at a time	215
NLSFUNC	Identifies country information file and supports code page switching	238
PATCH	Patches an executable file	250
PATH	Specifies a search path for program files	239
PRINT	Prints files in the background	207
PROMPT	Changes the system prompt	193
RECOVER	Recovers files from a damaged disk	184
RENAME or REN	Renames one or more files	180
REPLACE	Replaces or adds files	170
RESTORE	Restores all files from disks created by BACKUP	175
RMDIR or RD	Removes an empty directory	156
SELECT	Creates a system disk for a specific country	234
SET	Displays or changes environment variables	226
SHARE	Allows file sharing on a network	252
SORT	Filter to sort input and display the results on the screen	217
SPOOL	OS/2 print spooler	210

Figure 15.1 Operating system commands (continued)

Command	Description	Main page no.
SUBST	Re-assigns a sub-directory to a drive	245
SYS	Transfers system files to a formatted disk	137
TIME	Displays and changes the current system time	191
TYPE	Displays the contents of a file	182
VER	Displays the operating system version number	192
VERIFY	Turns verification of disk-writing processes on or off	140
VOL	Displays disk volume labels	147
XCOPY	Copies one or more files, with extended features	168

Figure 15.1 Operating system commands (continued)

Feature	Page number
Ambiguous filenames	38
API services	339
Appending data to files	198
Attributes of files	183
Background printing	207
Backing up disks	173
Backing up files	173
Batch files	277
BIOS	329
Boot record	318
Booting the system	41
Break key checking	246

Figure 15.2 Operating system features

Figure 15.2 Operating system features (continued)

Feature	Page number
File sharing	252
File types	39
Filters	215
Finding text in a file	220
Formatting disks	136
Graphics screen dumps	199
Help messages	249
Interrupts	339
Linking programs	261
Logical operators on command line	223
Memory management	30
Multi-tasking	28
National keyboards	232
Null device	198
Operating modes	29
Parallel ports	195
Parameters	51
Partitioning disks	134
Patching files	250
Paths	239
Pipes	214
Print spoolers	207
Printing the screen	199
Program Selector	54
Prompt	193
Re-assigning directories	245
Re-assigning drives	243
Recovering damaged files and disks	184
Redirecting input	214
Redirecting output	213
Renaming files	180
Replacing files	170
Restoring files from backup disks	175
ROM-BIOS	317
Root directory	77
Screen displays - by page	215

Figure 15.2 Operating system features (continued)

Feature	Page number
Secondary command processors	247
Serial devices	203
Serial ports	203
Setting up printers	201
Setting up the screen	205
Sorting files	217
Sub-directories	83
System configuration	215
System disks - creating	225
System files	64
Text editing	137
Time	191
Transferring the system	137
Typing files to the screen	197
Utility programs	255
Verification	140
Version number	192
Volume labels	147
Wildcards in filenames	38

Figure 15.2 Operating system features (continued)

PART THREE

BATCH FILES

16. *Introduction to Batch Files*

The amount of time spent entering operating system commands should be fairly small (as a proportion of the total time that the computer is switched on); if the machine is earning its keep, most of the time will be spent running applications. Even the time spent at the command line is mostly spent entering the same set of commands repeatedly.

Part Three of this book looks at ways in which we can automate this process. This saves time, reduces the number of typing errors and stops us having to remember complicated sequences of commands.

A sequence of commands, stored as a file, is called a *batch file*. This chapter introduces the concepts involved in batch file programming.

AUTOMATING COMMANDS

Suppose that you need to execute these commands in order to start up your word processor:

```
CD \WP
WP
```

On completion you may want to copy all changed files from the \WP\TEXT directory to floppy disk and then return to the root directory, as follows:

```
XCOPY \WP\TEXT A:\ /M
CD\
```

Getting all this right first time, every time, is almost impossible. For this reason DOS and OS/2 include the concept of batch files.

A batch file is simply a set of instructions for the operating system, saved in a convenient form. The commands are stored in an ASCII file in precisely the same format that they would be typed at the operating system prompt. The file is given a

```
C>type autoexec.bat
@echo off
path=\;\dos;\system;\bats
prompt $p$g
keyb uk
cls
date
time
cls
ver


C>
```

Figure 16.1 Displaying AUTOEXEC.BAT

BAT extension for DOS and OS/2 real mode, or CMD for OS/2 protected mode. The commands can be put into effect by simply typing the filename (without its extension) as a command. Each command is then executed in turn, as if it had been typed at the keyboard.

AUTOEXEC.BAT   DOS and OS/2 real mode allow for a special batch file called *AUTOEXEC.BAT*. This is the *automatic execution file*; under DOS, it is automatically run every time the computer is switched on or reset. The commands in this file are executed after CONFIG.SYS has been read into memory and before the prompt is displayed for the first time. To be of any use the file must be stored in the root directory of the system disk.

The file is useful for executing the various commands needed to customise the system. It may include a new prompt or a PATH command to set up a search path, for instance, or MOUSE and GRAFTABL commands to install the mouse and load a graphics character table.

You may also include DATE and TIME commands if the computer does not have a battery-backed clock. If there is no

AUTOEXEC.BAT file the system automatically prompts for the date and time; it does not do so if the automatic execution file exists. A sample AUTOEXEC.BAT file is shown in Figure 16.1. Note that, amongst other things, the file clears the screen when most commands have been executed and then displays the operating system version number.

You may also use AUTOEXEC.BAT to run a particular application.

STARTUP.CMD

OS/2 protected mode includes its own version of the automatic execution file. In this case the file is called STARTUP.CMD. It operates in exactly the same way as AUTOEXEC.BAT. When the system is switched on or reset the commands contained in STARTUP.CMD are automatically executed. However, in this case a protected mode session is automatically created if STARTUP.CMD exists; press Ctrl-Esc to display the Program Selector when the batch file has finished its work.

Note that under OS/2 you can still use AUTOEXEC.BAT. This batch file is automatically executed when you select the real mode session for the first time.

OS/2 can also set up another batch file that is executed every time a new session is created.

CREATING A BATCH FILE

By far the simplest way to create a batch file is through the COPY CON: command. In the word processing example earlier, a file called WP.BAT could be created as follows:

```
COPY CON: C:\WP.BAT
CD \WP
WP
XCOPY \WP\TEXT A:\ /M
CD \
^Z
```

Type Ctrl-Z (^Z) to end the file, as usual. Any existing file with the same name is overwritten. To abandon the new file without saving it, press Ctrl-Break instead of Ctrl-Z. Alternatively, create this four-line file with a text editor.

It is quite alright to use the name of an application for the batch file that runs it, as long as the application itself is not in the same directory or pointed to by PATH. However, you should not use the names of external commands in batch file names. For example, a batch file called BACKUP.BAT may seem reasonable but if it tries to call the BACKUP command you will end up with a continuous loop (since the file BACKUP.BAT in the current directory will be located before BACKUP.EXE in a different directory).

As a general rule it can be quite a good idea to have all the batch files for running applications in a single sub-directory, for example \BATS. If this sub-directory is included in the PATH list the applications can be run from anywhere, regardless of the current directory.

RUNNING A BATCH FILE

You can run a batch file just be entering its name as if it were a command. Using our previous example, you can run the word processor from the root directory of drive C by entering the command:

```
WP
```

The word processor is loaded and run. When you exit the program the files are automatically copied. The danger is that you may not have a disk ready in drive A and the process will collapse with the usual error messages; later on, in chapter 17, we can see how to pre-empt this sort of problem.

Interrupting batch files

Once a batch file has been activated it carries on through to the bitter end, unless it is interrupted for some reason. One way of stopping it is to press Ctrl-Break. Under DOS or OS/2 real mode the operating system responds with:

```
Terminate batch job (Y/N)?
```

Press 'Y' to halt the batch file or 'N' to allow it to proceed (Figure 16.2). If you do continue, the operation that was being processed is abandoned and the operating system continues with the next command.

Under OS/2 protected mode Ctrl-Break causes the batch file to be abandoned altogether and you are returned to the prompt.

```
C>copy con wpback.bat
pause
xcopy \wp\text a:\ /m
cd \
^Z
        1 File(s) copied

C>wpback

C>pause
Strike a key when ready . . .  ^C

Terminate batch job (Y/N)? y

C>
```

Figure 16.2 Interrupting a batch file

EDITING BATCH FILES

Like any other form of programming, it is unlikely that you will always get it right first time. Batch files, being simple ASCII files, can be edited of course. There are a number of ways to do this:

■ Completely re-type the batch file from scratch (suitable for small files only)

■ Use a text editor, such as EDLIN

■ Using a word processor, import the ASCII file, edit it and re-save it as an ASCII file

Once the batch file has been changed it is ready to be executed again.

CALLING BATCH FILES

Often you need to execute one batch file from within another. For example, suppose that you already have a routine for backing up word processor files, called WPBACK.BAT. This can be called in a batch file as follows:

```
CD \WP
WP
WPBACK
```

This is fine as long as the call to the second batch file is the last line in the first file. When a second file is executed in this way the first is abandoned, so anything after the call to the other batch file is ignored.

Suppose that the file were as follows:

```
CD \WP
WP \
WPBACK
CD \
```

The final command, to change to the root directory, would never be executed.

SECONDARY
PROCESSORS

DOS 2 overcame this problem by allowing a batch file to invoke a secondary processor (using COMMAND), and run the second file that way. If you add the /C parameter this ensures that the secondary processor only stays in memory for as long as it takes to run the second batch file.

The batch file in our previous command becomes:

```
CD \WP
WP
COMMAND /C WPBACK
CD \
```

After executing the WPBACK.BAT file, the secondary processor is removed from memory, execution continues with WP.BAT and the 'CD \' command is executed before the batch file terminates normally.

FILEPRNT.BAT - Prints a named file

```
cd \book\text
command /c prntcall
cd \
```

PRNTCALL.BAT - Prints a directory entry and the corresponding file

```
dir ch1.txt > prn
type ch1.txt > prn
```

Figure 16.3 Printing a file

The examples in Figure 16.3 shows how this approach can be used to print a file.

This solution can only be applied to BAT files (for DOS and OS/2 real mode). For the CMD files in OS/2 protected mode you must use CALL, described below.

THE CALL COMMAND

The method described above for calling another batch file is somewhat long-winded, so DOS 3.3 and OS/2 provide a further means, using the first of the internal batch commands.

Command:	CALL
Effect:	Executes a secondary batch file
Version:	DOS 3.3, OS/2 (batch files)
Type:	Internal
Syntax:	CALL *batchfile* [*parameters*]
Parameters:	None

Placing CALL in front of a batch command is exactly the same as using COMMAND but far simpler. The main advantage is that the system is not slowed down by having to load a secondary processor. Any parameters that would normally be added to the second batch command could be included in the normal way. (Batch parameters are described in Chapter 18.)

Under DOS 3.3 and OS/2 real mode the WP.BAT file given above becomes:

```
CD \WP
WP
CALL WPBACK
CD \
```

The only problem here is that this batch file will not work on any version of DOS prior to 3.3.

Because DOS 3.3 and OS/2 are so similar when it comes to batch programming, the protected mode equivalent of this example, WP.CMD, is identical. The effect is also the same. The only difference is that the second batch file is called WPBACK.CMD.

Batch files provide a simple means for automating frequently used processes; the next two chapters show how the batch files can be made much more powerful.

17.   *Batch Commands*

The batch files we have seen so far are fairly straightforward, and also somewhat limited. If these batch files are to be really useful - and helpful to the user - they need to be enhanced. It is beneficial to be able to give messages to the user, accept limited input or vary the way in which messages are displayed.

The operating systems include a number of special internal commands to do just this. We have already seen one (the CALL command); four others are described below.

Note that all of these commands can be entered directly at the system prompt but there is generally little point in doing so.

REM

Command: REM
Effect: Includes a remark in a batch file
Version: DOS 1, OS/2 (batch files)
Type: Internal
Syntax: REM [*text*]
Parameters: None

The REM command is used to include a remark in a batch file. Anything typed after the 'REM' is ignored by the operating system. As with all batch commands, the entire line of text, including the REM command itself, is displayed on screen as it is processed - unless we specifically turn off the display with ECHO, which is described below.

The REM command can be included in a batch file for a number of reasons:

■ To give messages to the user

■ To create some space between sections of the batch file

■ To remind the programmer of what the program is supposed to do

■ To temporarily remove a line from a batch file

```
AUTOEXEC.BAT

     rem This file can be adjusted to suit different situations
     rem
     path=\;\dos;\system;\bats
     prompt $p$g
     keyb uk
     rem
     rem   Include the next command if you want to be able to display
     rem   extended ASCII cahracters in graphics modes
     rem
     rem   graftabl
     rem
     rem   Include the next command if you want to be able to print
     rem   graphics screen dumps
     rem
     rem   graphics
     rem
     cls
     date
     time
     cls
     ver
```

Figure 17.1 AUTOEXEC.BAT with REM statements

The first is not a particularly good reason; there are some far better ways of communicating with the user, as we shall see. The second reason can be quite useful; a column of REM's gives a block of white space that serves well to break up a lengthy batch file into logical sections.

As for the third reason, someone once wrote: "REMarks are used by bad programmers who cannot remember what their code is supposed to do." This is rather harsh and more than a little unfair! It is probably true that most of us pride ourselves on not having too many remarks in any program, regardless of the programming language, but remarks are a useful addition.

It is all too easy to forget, after several months, exactly what a program does, especially if the syntax is particularly complex.

It may also be that the batch files are to be used or modified by someone else, and explanatory comments can speed up the process of understanding what is going on.

If a batch file is to be customised by another user you need a way of telling them exactly what commands they should put in the file and where they should appear. This is particularly the case for AUTOEXEC.BAT and STARTUP.CMD. An example AUTOEXEC.BAT file using REMs is shown in Figure 17.1.

Note that the examples in this book contain rather more explanatory REMs than are usually necessary.

Finally, you can temporarily take out lines that you think may be causing a problem or are no longer required, so that they can be re-instated easily later.

ECHO

Command:	ECHO
Effect:	Suppresses or displays screen text
Version:	DOS 1, OS/2 (batch files)
Type:	Internal
Syntax:	ECHO [ON I OFF]
	ECHO [*text*]
Parameters:	None

As it stands, the instructions in a batch file are displayed on the screen as if they were being typed at the keyboard. Sometimes this doesn't matter but all this text - especially if there are a large number of messages - can be confusing and untidy. The ECHO command provides a solution to this problem.

The command comes in a number of formats. ECHO OFF has the effect that all subsequent commands are suppressed, as far as the display is concerned. There will still be messages on the screen but even most of these can also be hidden from view by adding '>NUL' to the commands. Once you have done all this the only display is the occasional message (under some versions of DOS) such as '*n* File(s) copied'.

```
C>type echotest.bat
rem       This line is printed
echo off
rem       This line is not printed ...
echo      ... and this line is printed
echo on
rem       All text from here is printed
echo      Some of it is printed twice!

C>echotest

C>rem       This line is printed

C>echo off
     ... and this line is printed

C>rem       All text from here is printed

C>echo      Some of it is printed twice!
     Some of it is printed twice!

C>
C>
```

Figure 17.2 The ECHO command

ECHO OFF followed by CLS has the effect that the screen is cleared and virtually nothing else appears until the batch file has terminated and the prompt is displayed again.

You can turn the displays back on - if you really have to - with ECHO ON. Note that ECHO is always turned on automatically when a batch file terminates. ECHO as a command on its own displays a message telling you whether ECHO is ON or OFF.

ECHO can also give messages to the user, providing a far more satisfactory method than REM. Any text on the ECHO line is displayed, even when ECHO is OFF, but the ECHO command itself does not appear. (This option is rather pointless when ECHO is ON, since the command itself is displayed before it is executed, so the message actually appears twice; in such circumstances you may as well use REM.)

So, by turning ECHO OFF, we have a method of giving out messages on a clear uncluttered screen (Figure 17.2).

BACKS.BAT - Demonstrates use of ECHO when backing up files

```
@echo off
rem   The line above ensures that nothing is displayed unless we
rem   want it to be (assuming DOS 3.3 or OS/2)
rem
echo
echo      All updated files are being copied to drive A
echo      (You can interrupt this process at any time by pressing Ctrl-Break)
echo
rem
xcopy *.* a: /m >nul
rem
echo
echo      All files have been copied successfully
echo.
echo      Backup files are being deleted
echo.
rem
del *.bak >nul
rem
echo      Backup procedures are now complete
echo.
echo on
```

Figure 17.3 ECHO batch file

Blank lines

Displaying blank lines is always a problem. When ECHO is ON, a blank line in the batch file is treated as just a carriage return, and results in an extra prompt being displayed (in exactly the same way as when you just press Return). When ECHO is OFF, this is ignored of course.

Under DOS 2 it is possible to display a blank line by entering ECHO and two more spaces; this just echoes the two spaces.

Unfortunately, this does not work under DOS 3, which always gives blank spaces at the end of ECHO commands and therefore treats it as an ECHO command on its own, displaying 'ECHO is OFF' whenever there should be a blank line. This means that any old DOS 2 batch files will have to be updated if they are brought over to DOS 3, otherwise your displays will become really untidy and confusing.

For DOS 3, you can use this command:

    ECHO.

This special form of ECHO just displays a blank line; under DOS 2, of course, it displays a blank line with a full stop on it!

If you have to prepare the same batch to run under both systems, it is better to use the DOS 3 version. At least then the DOS 2 displays do not look too untidy.

Hiding ECHO   The 'ECHO OFF' command itself can be hidden, by preceding it with the '@' symbol, as follows:

    @ECHO OFF

This symbol can actually be placed at the beginning of any individual command, with the result that the echo is turned off for that one command only. This option was only introduced in DOS 3.3, so do not use it if your batch files are likely to be run in earlier versions of DOS.

The batch file in Figure 17.3 shows how ECHO may be used to give an idea of what a batch file is doing.

PAUSE

Command:	PAUSE
Effect:	Waits for user to press a key
Version:	DOS 1, OS/2 (batch files)
Type:	Internal
Syntax:	PAUSE [*text*]
Parameters:	None

If can be very disconcerting to find yourself rushing headlong through a sequence of commands, and desperately trying to locate the Ctrl-Break keys to stop the file before it does something dreadful. There are a number of occasions when you want to be able to pause in a batch file.

■   To give the user a chance to swap disks

BACKS2.BAT - Backup procedure with options to interrupt

```
@echo off
echo.
echo      All updated files are about to be copied to drive A
echo      You can interrupt this process by pressing Ctrl-Break; otherwise
pause
echo.
rem
xcopy *.* a: /m >nul
rem
echo      All files have been copied successfully
echo.
echo      Backup files are about to be deleted
echo      Press Ctrl-Break if you do not want these files deleted; otherwise
pause
echo.
rem
del *.bak >nul
rem
echo      Backup procedures are now complete
echo.
echo on
```

Figure 17.4 Interrupting commands with PAUSE

- To wait until a screen display has been read

- To get confirmation that an action is required

All this can be achieved with the PAUSE command. PAUSE on its own displays this message:

```
Strike any key when ready . . .
```

Nothing happens until the user presses a key (almost any key will do). This also provides an opportunity for the user to interrupt the process by pressing Ctrl-Break.

PAUSE can also be followed by a message, which is displayed in the same way as for ECHO. For example, you may tell the

```
C>backs2

All updated files are about to be copied to drive A
You can interrupt this process by pressing Ctrl-Break; otherwise
Strike a key when ready . . .

All files have been copied successfully

Backup files are about to be deleted
Press Ctrl-Break if you do not want these files deleted; otherwise
Strike a key when ready . . .

Backup procedures are now complete


C>
C>
C>
```

Figure 17.5 The effects of PAUSE

user what is about to happen and how it may be avoided as
follows:

```
ECHO About to format the disk in drive A
ECHO Press Ctrl-Break to stop or
PAUSE
```

This results in the following display:

```
About to format the disk in drive A
Press Ctrl-Break to stop or
Strike a key when ready . . .
```

Unfortunately there is no way of sampling the key that is
pressed, so no simple way within a batch file of getting a 'Yes'
or 'No' from the user. (The batch file at the end of Chapter 18
shows how this can be achieved.)

Figure 17.4 shows how PAUSE may be put to good use; the
results of the batch file are shown in Figure 17.5.

LABELS (GOTO)

Command: GOTO
Effect: Jumps to a label in a batch file
Version: DOS 2, OS/2
Type: Internal
Syntax: GOTO *label*
Parameters: None

Although the various forms of GOTO command have gradually disappeared from most programming language over the last few years, in favour of a more structured approach, it still remains the best way of jumping about in a batch file. The GOTO command simply directs the operating system to unconditionally switch its attention to some other point in the batch file, by telling it to jump to a specific label.

A *label* consists of a colon, followed by up to eight characters. Use the same rules as for filenames; you can have more than eight characters but the extras will be ignored. The GOTO command is followed by the label name without the colon, as follows:

```
GOTO LABEL1
REM This line is skipped
:LABEL1
REM Rest of batch file
```

You can jump in either direction, as follows:

```
ECHO OFF
GOTO MIDDLE
:START
ECHO This is the start
GOTO END
:MIDDLE
ECHO This is the middle
GOTO :START
:END
ECHO This is the end!
```

The result is this display:

```
This is the middle
This is the start
This is the end!
```

This rather pointless example at least serves to show how easily batch files can become entangled in 'spaghetti' (a programming term, describing the appearance of a program when lines are drawn in to demonstrate the jumps).

If a label cannot be found, or two labels are the same (perhaps because they have the same first eight characters), the operating system displays an error message.

GOTO comes into its own with the IF statement, described in the next chapter.

18.   *Using Variables*

The simple batch commands we have seen so far are fine for a few limited purposes but they do not really come into their own until we start using some of the operating system's more advanced features.

This chapter introduces the concept of variables and shows how loops can be devised and jumps can be made conditional.

COMMAND LINE PARAMETERS

Much of the time we do not want to write a batch file that is specific to a particular set of files: rather we need to be able to design a batch file that works for any file we care to mention. This is done by adding parameters to the command line.

Any item that appears on the command line can be represented in the batch file by a '%' symbol and a number. The number represents the position of the parameter on the command line; the first parameter is %1, the second is %2 and so on. Up to nine of these parameters can be included; %0 represent the batch command name itself.

These *variables* can be placed in any command, in any position. The command is expanded, by replacing the parameter with the actual value, before it is executed.

For example, consider the following batch file (called COPYA.BAT):

```
COPY %1 A:
COPY %2.DOC A:\DATA\%2.TXT
```

When this is run the command can be followed by two parameters, as follows:

```
COPYA LETTER.DOC FINAL
```

Before the commands are executed they are expanded to proper commands:

```
COPY LETTER.DOC A:
COPY FINAL.DOC A:\DATA\FINAL.TXT
```

Any extra parameters are ignored; any that are missing are treated as blanks and usually cause the batch file to issue an error message.

These symbols can appear in any part of the command; they can be included as text in an ECHO command or represent commands themselves. The parameters can include wildcards or be items of text. For example, suppose that this is the OS/2 batch file SAMPLE.CMD:

```
@ECHO OFF
ECHO This is the batch program %0
ECHO It is being used to %1 files to drive %2
@ECHO ON
%1 %3 %2:
%4
@ECHO OFF
```

Enter the command as follows:

```
SAMPLE COPY A *.DOC Finished
```

The result is:

```
This is the batch program SAMPLE
It is being used to COPY files to drive A
COPY *.DOC A:
        1 File(s) copied
Finished
```

The batch files in Figure 18.1 provide facilities for deleting and renaming sub-directories, and moving files from one directory to another.

Note that if there are any '%' symbols in filenames, any actual occurrences of the filename in the batch file should have the '%' symbol replaced by '%%' so that the operating system does not get confused. This is demonstrated by Figure 18.2, which should also prove that the '%' symbol is not a good idea in filenames!

SHIFT

Command:	SHIFT
Effect:	Shifts parameters left one place
Version:	DOS 2, OS/2 (batch files)
Type:	Internal
Syntax:	SHIFT
Parameters:	None

DELD.BAT - Deletes a sub-directory and its contents

```
@echo off
rem   The command should be followed by the name of the sub-directory
rem   but should not include a file specification
rem   e.g.  DELD BOOK  or  DELD C:\WP\BOOK
rem
echo.
echo       Deleting the directory %1, including all its files
echo       Press Ctrl-Break to abandon
rem
rem   The next command displays an 'Are you sure?' message
rem
del %1\*.*
rd %1
```

REND.BAT - Effectively renames a sub-directory

```
@echo off
rem   The command should be followed by the name of the sub-directory
rem   (as for DELD above)
echo.
echo       Moving files from the directory %1 to %2
md %2
copy %1 %2  >nul
echo       Completed
echo.
echo       About to delete the directory %1
echo       Press Ctrl-Break to abandon
del %1\*.*
rd %1
echo.
```

MOVE.BAT - Moves a group of files to a different directory

```
@echo off
rem   The command should be followed by a file specification
rem   and the name of the target directory
```

Figure 18.1 General-purpose batch files

```
        rem   e.g. MOVE *.DOC C:\BACKS  or  MOVE A:\FILE1 C:
        echo.
        echo     Moving files %1 to the directory %2
        copy %1 %2 >nul
        echo     Completed
        echo.
        echo     About to delete the original files %1
        echo     Press Ctrl-Break to abandon or
        pause
        del %1
        echo.


AUTOEXEC.BAT - Dummy startup file to do nothing

        @echo off


VOLS.BAT - Displays volume labels for floppy and hard disks

        @vol a:
        @vol c:
```

Figure 18.1 General-purpose batch files (continued)

The SHIFT command provides some additional help in supplying parameters, by renumbering the parameters. The effect is to shift all the parameters left one place. After the first SHIFT command %0 represents the first parameter, %1 is the second and so on; apply another SHIFT and %0 takes on the value of the second parameter, %1 is the third and so on. This is useful for a couple of reasons:

■ More than nine parameters can be added to the command

■ The same command can be applied to a string of parameters

As an example, the following OS/2 real mode batch file (ODIR.BAT) mimics the OS/2 protected mode DIR command (which allows more than one parameter on the command line):

```
C>type percent.bat
copy 90%%*.%%ge *.%1
ren 90%%*.%1 %2*.*
dir *.*

C>percent txt 85%

C>copy 90%*.%ge *.txt
90%PROOF.DOC
        1 File(s) copied

C>ren 90%*.txt 85%*.*

C>dir *.*

 Volume in drive C has no label
 Directory of  C:\PERCENT

90%PROOF %GE    1541 03-04-87   4:02a
85%PROOF TXT    1541 03-04-87   4:02a
       1 File(s)   11001856 bytes free

C>
```

Figure 18.2 Batch files with % symbols

```
:START
DIR %1
SHIFT
GOTO START
```

Enter the batch command as follows:

```
ODIR *.BAT A: \PROG\*.*
```

The effect is as if we had entered the following separate commands:

```
DIR *.BAT
DIR A:
DIR \PROG\*.*
```

Unfortunately, after this the program goes into a endless loop which can only be interrupted by pressing Ctrl-Break. (The batch file EDIR.BAT, described later, overcomes this problem.)

THE SET COMMAND

The operating system provides a second type of variable that allows us to represent the configuration variables in a batch file. The value of any configuration variable can be included in

299

a batch file by enclosing the name in '%' symbols. For example, suppose that the following command had been entered:

```
SET PATH=C:\;C:\DOS
```

The current path can be displayed by including this line in a batch file:

```
ECHO The current path is %PATH%
```

When the batch command is run the following message is displayed:

```
The current path is C:\;C:\DOS
```

Perhaps more useful is the batch file APATH.BAT:

```
@ECHO OFF
SET PATH=%PATH%;%1
ECHO New path is %PATH%
```

The result is that the first parameter on the batch command line is added to the current path. This means that we can temporarily update the PATH without having to replace it completely; indeed, we do not even need to know - or care - what the current PATH is.

Note that the configuration can contain any variable we like, not just the standard ones described earlier. For example, the following could be added to CONFIG.SYS:

```
DIREC=*.*
```

(This could also have been added to the configuration using SET.) This new variable has little use except in batch files, where a command might be entered as follows:

```
DIR %DIREC%
```

These variables can be useful for temproary storage, as illustrated in Figures 18.6 and 18.7.

FOR LOOPS

Command:	FOR...IN...DO
Effect:	Repeats a command for a group of parameters
Version:	DOS 2, OS/2 (batch files)
Type:	Internal
Syntax:	FOR %%*letter* IN (*parameters*) DO *command*
Parameters:	None

Frequently we want to repeat the same command for a group of files, which may, or may not, be suitable for representation by a single ambiguous filename. The FOR loop, provided for use in batch files, helps us do this.

Three items must be supplied for the loop:

■ A parameter, consisting of '%%' followed by a single letter (for example, %%A)

■ A list of files or other parameters, enclosed in brackets

■ A command that can include the %% parameter

The parameters are usually files and therefore take the following forms:

```
(letter.doc notes.txt)

(*.dat)

(a.doc *.b c.txt)
```

Any reasonable number of items can be included in the parameter list. The FOR command takes each of these in turn and gives its value to the %% variable before executing the command. For example, you can extend the DOS TYPE command so that it lists all BAT files as follows:

```
FOR %%A IN (*.BAT) DO TYPE %%A
```

If you wanted to precede these listings with the contents of a text file containing the names of the batch files, this command could be extended as follows:

```
FOR %%A IN (BATCH.LST *.BAT) DO TYPE %%A
```

301

The variable %%A first takes the value 'BATCH.LST' and then takes the name of each of the batch files in turn.

You can include a command line parameter in the FOR loop. For example, consider the batch file CPY.BAT:

```
@ECHO OFF
FOR %%A IN (%1) DO COPY %%A %2:
```

The batch command might be entered as:

```
CPY *.DAT B
```

The result is that %1 takes the value '*.DAT' while %2 becomes 'B'. The effect is to individually copy each of the DAT files to drive B.

The final command can be almost any valid command. However, you are restricted from 'nesting' FOR loops; that is, the command cannot be a further FOR loop. On the other hand, you are not restricted from calling a further batch file and passing variables to it. The batch files in Figure 18.3 display the contents of a group of files; for each file that is found the program displays the directory entry and then the file itself. Note that there are two options for the last line of this file. One is for use with all versions of DOS after DOS 2.0 and OS/2 real mode; the other is for DOS 3.3 and all OS/2 modes (though the BAT extensions must be changed to CMD for OS/2 protected mode).

As stated earlier, the list of parameters can include any text:

```
FOR %%A IN (A B C) DO DIR %%A:
```

```
FOR %%B IN (Here we are) DO ECHO %%B
```

The first example produces a directory listing for all three drives, the second displays three lines of text.

Note that if FOR is entered directly as a command (outside a batch file) only one '%' symbol should be used for the variable.

LIST.BAT - Lists the contents of a group of files

```
@echo off
rem
rem   The second batch file is called for each file specified by
rem   the LIST parameter (%1)
rem   The selected file (%%a) is passed across as a parameter
rem
for %%a in (%1) do call list2 %%a
rem
rem   Replace the command above with the line below if not DOS 3.3
rem
rem   for %%a in (%1) do command /c list2 %%a
```

LIST2.BAT - Prints the directory entry for a file and the file itelf

```
@echo off
rem
rem   Note that %1 for this program is the %%a parameter from LIST
rem
rem   First type the directory entry
rem
dir %1  >prn
rem
rem   Now type the file SPACING, which includes some blank lines and
rem   a row of dashes
rem
type spacing >prn
rem
rem   Finally, type the file itself
rem
type %1  >prn
type spacing  >prn
rem
rem   Control now returns to LIST
```

Figure 18.3 Calling batch files with the FOR command

THE IF COMMAND

Command: IF
Effect: Conditional jump to a label
Version: DOS 2, OS/2 (batch files)
Type: Internal
Syntax: IF [NOT] *condition command*
Parameters: None

The IF command provides us with the means to carry out commands only if a condition is true. There are three conditions that can be applied. For each of these the condition can be preceded by the word 'NOT', in which case the command is carried out only if the condition is false.

IF EXIST

The first condition is 'EXIST' followed by the name of a file. The command that follows is carried out only if the file exists. For example:

```
IF EXIST DATA.LST TYPE DATA.LST
```

In this case the file DATA.LST is displayed if it exists. If it does not exist, the command is ignored (and therefore there is no error message).

The command also works with wildcards:

```
IF EXIST *.DOC COPY *.DOC A:
```

The command to copy the files only goes ahead if there is at least one DOC file.

In a similar way, the command can also take parameters from the command line:

```
IF EXIST %1 REN %1 %2
```

The REN command takes effect if the file specified by the first parameter on the command line exists; in that case it is given the name supplied as the second parameter.

These commands can be combined to good effect. Here, the GOTO command can be particularly helpful:

```
IF EXIST %2 GOTO NOCHANGE
IF EXIST %1 REN %1 %2
:NOCHANGE
```

The renaming process only takes place if the first file named exists and the second file does not.

The 'NOT' version serves to complete a command only if the file does not exist:

```
IF NOT EXIST %1 ECHO There is no file called %1
```

The 'NOT' version is particularly useful in installation processes, where it can be used to skip to an error message section if the required files cannot be found.

IF ERRORLEVEL During the earlier sections of this book we saw that a number of commands return an ERRORLEVEL value when they end. This value can be checked by the IF ERRORLEVEL command. The error number must be specified and the command is carried out only if the actual ERRORLEVEL number that was last returned is at least as great as the number specified. For example, the command might take this form:

```
IF ERRORLEVEL 3 ECHO Greater than or equal to 3
```

If the error number is 3 or higher, the following message is displayed:

```
Greater than or equal to 3
```

For this reason the ERRORLEVELs are usually processed in reverse order (otherwise a command to be carried out on ERRORLEVEL 0 will be executed in all events). Figure 18.4 gives the basis of a general batch file for processing the error levels for any command; all you need to do is replace the text. Figure 18.5 gives a routine for providing a regular backup procedure. Finally, Figure 18.6 provides a more sophisticated routine that takes its error messages from a text file.

Note that the ERRORLEVEL returned by a command is held in memory until another command or program terminates with a new ERRORLEVEL. Many application programs also return ERRORLEVELs; the general routine in Figure 18.4 should tell you whether a particular application does this; run

```
ERRORS.BAT - General error level processing

    @echo off
    rem
    rem   Can be expanded for any number of error levels
    rem
    if errorlevel 2 goto error2
    if errorlevel 1 goto error1
    echo   Error message 0
    rem   or carry out some action relevant to error 0
    goto end
    :error1
    echo      Error message 1
    rem   or carry out some action relevant to error 1
    goto end
    :error2
    echo      Error message 2
    rem   or carry out some action relevant to error 2 or greater
    :end
```

Figure 18.4 General ERRORLEVEL processing

it each time an application terminates and see if different messages appear in different circumstances.

The 'NOT ERRORLEVEL' condition results in the command being executed only if the error is less than that given.

IF ==

The final IF command is the 'IF ==' version. This command compares two items of text and carries out the command only if they are the same. It is most useful when one part of the text is supplied as a command line parameter.

For example, consider the batch file XC.BAT:

```
@ECHO OFF
IF '%2'=='/Y' XCOPY %1 A: /P
IF '%2'=='/N' XCOPY %1 A:
```

The batch command can be executed in two different ways:

```
BACKERR.BAT - Backup routine with error-handling

    @echo off
    echo     Copying all files in \WP or its sub-directories
    echo     that have beeen created or changed since last backup
    echo.
    backup c:\wp\*.doc a: /s /f /m
    echo.
    if errorlevel 4 goto error4
    if errorlevel 3 goto error3
    if errorlevel 1 goto error1
    rem
    rem   Otherwise, it must be error level 0
    rem
    echo     Command completed successfully
    goto end
    :error1
    echo     No files found to back up
    goto end
    :error3
    echo     Program interrupted by Ctrl-Break
    goto end
    :error4
    echo     Program terminated - error unknown
    :end
```

Figure 18.5 A regular backup routine

```
XC *.DAT /Y

XC *.DAT /N
```

In the first case the files are copied to drive A with prompts; in the second case there are no prompts.

You can also test for the *null* string (that is, an empty string, with nothing in it) by putting quotes around both sides of the equals symbols:

```
IF '%1'=='' ECHO No parameter
```

307

```
ERRORM.BAT - General error handling with messages taken from a file

    @echo off
    rem
    rem   Name of error message file must be specified on command line
    rem   e.g.  ERRORM BACKUP.MSG  (errors for BACKUP command)
    rem
    rem   Note that in this case the errors are handled from 0 upwards
    rem
    if errorlevel 0 set error=0
    if errorlevel 1 set error=1
    if errorlevel 2 set error=2
    if errorlevel 3 set error=3
    if errorlevel 4 set error=4
    if errorlevel 5 set error=5
    rem
    rem   %error% now holds the error number, which should appear in the text
    rem   on the relevant line of the file identified by %1
    rem
    find "%error%" %1
    set error=


BACKUP.MSG - Sample error message file

    Error  0  :   Command completed successfully
    Error  1  :   No files found to back up
    Error  3  :   Program interrupted by Ctrl-Break
    Error  4  :   Program terminated - error unknown
```

Figure 18.6 General purpose error-handling

If there is no parameter on the command line the message is displayed. This can be used to improve on our earlier ODIR.BAT file. The enhanced version, EDIR.BAT, takes the form:

```
@ECHO OFF
:START
IF '%1'=='' GOTO END
DIR %1 | MORE
PAUSE
SHIFT
```

YORN.BAT - Gets Yes or No answer form user

```
@echo    off
rem   create dummy directory
md \d$$$
rem   Put a file in it
copy yorn.bat \d$$$  >nul
rem   Display text - this can be changed to suit particular need
echo    Do you wish to continue (Y/N)?
echo on
rem   attempt to delete all files, so gives 'Are you sure?' message
rem   which is hidden by >NUL
@del \d$$$  >nul
@echo off
if exist \d$$$\yorn.bat goto no
rem   No files exist, so answer must have been Yes
rem   Insert action for Yes
goto finish
:no
rem   Insert action for No
rem   Delete file in dummy directory
del \d$$$\yorn.bat
:finish
rem   Delete dummy directory
rd \d$$$
```

NEWDATE - Changes date for a group of files

```
@echo off
echo.
rem
rem Only works for DOS, not OS/2
rem
rem New date and time can be specified on command line,
rem   after name of file(s) to be updated, or they can
rem   be entered separately.
rem e.g.  NEWDATE *.BAT 1-1-90 0:00  or  NEWDATE *.BAT
rem
```

Figure 18.7 Advanced batch files

```
if '%2'=='' goto enterdat
date %2
goto times
:enterdat
echo on.
echo Enter the new date for the files
echo.
date
:times
echo.
if '%3'=='' goto entertim
time %3
goto update
:entertim
echo Enter the new time for the files
echo.
time
:update
echo.
for %%a in (%1) do copy %%a+,, %%a  nul
echo.
echo Please re-enter to-day's date and time
date
time
```

Figure 18.7 Advanced batch files (continued)

```
GOTO START
:END
```

All the directories on the command line are listed, a page at a time, with a key press needed to take you on to the next directory. The batch program ends when there are no parameters left.

Other examples, using these more advanced commands, are given in Figure 18.7.

19. *Alphabetical Cross-reference*

Part 3 of this book concentrated on batch files in DOS 3.3 and OS/2. This chapter provides a cross-reference for the topics that have been covered.

Figure 19.1 lists the batch command alphabetically, and shows where descriptions and examples can be found.

Figure 19.2 describes the batch file concepts and shows where they are explained.

Finally, Figure 19.2 lists the most useful of the example batch files that were included in Part 3, giving page numbers and figure numbers when appropriate.

Command	Description	Page number
CALL	Executes a secondary batch file	283
ECHO	Suppresses or displays screen text	287
FOR...IN...DO	Repeats a command for a group of parameters	301
GOTO	Jumps to a label in a batch file	293
IF ==	Executes command if strings are the same	306
IF ERRORLEVEL	Executes command depending on error level value	305
IF EXIST	Executes command if file exists	304
IF NOT	Executes command if condition false	304
PAUSE	Waits for user to press a key	290
REM	Includes a remark in a batch file	285
SHIFT	Shifts parameters left one place	296

Figure 19.1 The batch commands

Feature	Page number
AUTOEXEC.BAT	278
Automatic execution file	278
Batch commands	285
Booting the system	278
Calling batch files	282
Comparing text strings	306
Conditional jumps	304
Creating batch files	279
Creating environmental variables	299
Creating space in batch files	285
Ctrl-Break key	280
Displaying blank lines	289
Displaying messages	288
Editing batch files	281
End-of-file marker	279
Environment variables	299
ERRORLEVEL	305
Errors returned by program	305
Existence of files	306
Interrupting batch files	280
Jumping to a label	293
Labels	293
Loops	301
Non-existence of files	305
Parameters	295
Pausing	290
Remarks	285
Running a batch file	280
Secondary processors	282
Shifting parameters	296
STARTUP.CMD	279
Suppressing commands	290
Suppressing the screen display	287
Temporarily removing lines from batch files	287
Waiting for a key press	290

Figure 19.2 Batch file concepts

Batch file	Effect	Page number
APATH	Extends directory path	300
AUTOEXEC	Automatic execution file (with REM statements)	286
	Dummy file - no action	297
BACKERR	Backup routine with error-handling	307
BACKS	Backs up files (with ECHO commands)	289
BACKS2	Backup with option to interrupt	291
DELD	Deletes a sub-directory and its contents	297
EDIR	Multiple directory listings	308
ERRORM	General error handling with messages taken from file	308
ERRORS	General ERRORLEVEL processing	306
FILEPRINT	Prints a normal file	283
LIST	Prints a group of files	303
LIST2	Prints a directory and file - called by LIST	303
MOVE	Moves files	297
NEWDATE	Changes date and time for groups of files	309
PRNTCALL	Prints a directory entry and file - called by FILEPRINT	283
REND	Effectively, renames a sub-directory	297
VOLS	Displays volume labels for floppy and hard disks	297
WP	Runs a program and copies changed files	282
WPBACK	Copies changed files - called by WP	282
YORN	Gets a Yes and No answer from the user	309

Figure 19.3 Summary of batch files

PART FOUR

PROGRAMMING

20.   *Disk Structure*

We have now covered in full the operation of DOS 3.3 and OS/2 from the user's point of view. This final part of the book looks at these two operating systems from a programmer's perspective. The last three chapters consider disks and their layout, the structure of the operating systems themselves and the programming services provided by DOS and OS/2.

This chapter describes the structure of the disks and the way information is stored on them; the directories and their construction; and the file allocation tables that are used to map the contents of a disk.

DOS vs. BIOS   The way in which the disk is formatted is determined by the computer's internal programs, the *ROM-BIOS (Basic Input Output System)*. The BIOS has a number of interrupts that programmers can access in order to format disks, read and write sectors and so on. All of these are duplicated in some form by the DOS interrupts and OS/2 services. It is far safer to use the disk operating system functions than those of the BIOS since compatibility with later versions of the operating system can be assured that way.

The actual layout and directory structure is a function of the operating system and of little concern to the ROM-BIOS.

DISK LAYOUT

As described earlier, no disk - either floppy or hard - can be used until it has been formatted. The formatting program marks out the tracks on the surface of the disk and divides these into sectors. All data areas are written to. The result is a blank disk, ready to receive data - as far as the user is concerned, that is.

In fact, no formatted disk is completely blank. The formatting process actually places a great deal of information on the disk to help it identify tracks and sectors and to prepare the root directory for file information.

In particular, the first few sectors of each disk are used for three types of information:

Byte	Meaning	Normal Range	
		Hard disk	**Floppy disk**
1	Track/cylinder	0 - ??	0 - 39
2	Side/Head	0 - 3	0 - 1
3	Sector	1 - ??	1 - 9
4	Number bytes (code)	0 - 3	0 - 3

N.B ?? = Number varies

Byte 4: number of bytes code	
Code	**Bytes/sector**
0	128
1	256
2	512
3	1024

Figure 20.1 Sector address marks

- The *boot record* is stored on Side 0, Track 0, Sector 1. This holds information about the structure of the disk and, on system disks, contains the code needed to load the operating system into memory.

- The *file allocation table (FAT)* is stored immediately after the boot record. This can take several sectors and it provides a map of how the remainder of the disk is allocated to files. There are two identical copies of the FAT.

- The directory follows on from the FAT and holds details of the files on disk.

Each of these sets of data is described further below.

Sector address marks

In addition to this main block of information, the formatting process includes a small amount of data at the start of each sector. This data, called a *sector address mark*, is used by the operating system to locate a sector and determine its size.

The built-in ROM-BIOS of the computer numbers the sides, tracks and sectors of a disk in a particular way. The sides are numbered 0 and 1 (for floppy disks) or 0 to 3 (for standard hard disks); high capacity hard disks with more platters are numbered accordingly. Similarly, the tracks on disks start at 0 on the inside and are numbered consecutively towards the centre; for example, the innermost track on a floppy disk is usually 39 or 79. Breaking with tradition, the sectors on each track are labelled from 1. Under this system, the third sector of the fifth track on the second side is labelled as Side 1, Track 4, Sector 3.

The sector address mark at the start of each sector holds these three values; a fourth byte contains a code that identifies the size of the sector (this is the number of bytes for storing data, excluding the sector address mark). The format of the sector address mark is given in Figure 20.1.

Normally, the sectors are numbered sequentially but, during the formatting process, you are at liberty to change the order. (This can be useful for some copy-protection methods.)

DOS and OS/2 numbering

It is worth mentioning that DOS and OS/2 have their own way of numbering sectors. A single number identifies each sector uniquely, starting from the outside and working through in the same order as that given by the BIOS. You can convert from the BIOS system to that of DOS with this formula:

DOS sector=

      BIOS Side x sectors per track)
  + (BIOS Track x sectors per track x number of sides)
  + BIOS Sector
  - 1

Conversions the other way are performed as follows:

BIOS Side =

    int ((DOS sector)/(sectors per track))
    mod (number of sides)

BIOS Track =

    int ((DOS sector)/(number of sides x sectors per track))

Offset (hex)	No. Bytes	Use
00	3	Jump instruction (long jump or short jump plus NOP)
03	8	Manufacturer name and DOS version and number
0B	2	Number of bytes per sector
0D	1	Number of sectors per allocation unit
0E	2	Number of reserved sectors
10	1	Number of FAT's
11	2	Number of root directory entries
13	2	Number of sectors on volume
15	1	Media type code
16	2	Number of sectors per FAT
18	2	Number of sectors per track
1A	2	Number of heads
1C	2	Number of hidden sectors
1E	-	Boot routine

Note: Bytes 0Bh - 17h are a copy of the BIOS parameter block (BPB).

Figure 20.2 The boot record

BIOS Sector =

((DOS sector) mod (sectors per track)) + 1

where int(x) is the integer part of x and x mod y is the remainder after x has been divided by y (the *modulo*).

THE BOOT RECORD

The first sector of every record contains a boot record, which is loaded into memory and executed every time the system attempts to boot from the disk. The boot record contains the following information:

- The first three bytes contain a JMP (jump) instruction, which points to the boot code

- The next part of the record contains details of the disk's structure

■ Following this is the *boot code*, which loads the operating system into memory.

The structure of the boot record is shown in Figure 20.2.

The boot code on a system disk loads and runs the system programs, which are stored in the first free space on the disk; for a non-system disk the code displays a 'Non-system disk' message, waits for a key press and then reboots.

THE DIRECTORY

The file directory consists of a list of 32-byte entries, with one entry for each file stored on disk. The structure of this entry is shown in Figure 20.3.

Because space for the root directory is fixed the number of entries is limited. Figure 20.4 shows the number of root directory entries and other related information for the more popular 5¼" disk formats.

Filename

The filename can be up to 8 characters long. Valid filename characters were given in Figure 2.1. Any unused characters at the end of the name are padded with spaces (ASCII 32).

The first bytes of this part of the entry may, as an alternative, hold one of these codes:

■ The null character (ASCII 0) to indicate that the entry has not yet been used

■ A full stop (ASCII 56), indicating a sub-directory entry

■ Two full stops (ASCII 56 twice), to represent the parent directory

■ The σ character (ASCII 229), which tells us that the directory entry has been deleted.

Note that when a file is deleted all that happens is that the first character of the name is replaced by an ASCII 229 code. The rest of the filename is recoverable, as is the file itself (assuming no new files have been added to the disk or

Contents of file directory entries	
Bytes	**Meaning**
0-7	Filename or entry code
8-10	Extension
11	Attributes
12-21	Reserved (unused)
22-23	Time stamp
24-25	Date stamp
26-27	Start cluster
28-31	File size

Figure 20.3 Structure of directory entries

		Size in sectors		Total	Entries	Cluster	
		FAT	Root directory	(Boot + FATx2 + directory)	in root directory	size	Data clusters
8 sector	SS DD	1	4	7	64	1	323
	DS DD	1	7	10	112	2	351
9 sector	SS DD	2	4	13	64	1	630
	DS DD	2	7	12	112	2	708
	QD	7	14	29	224	1	2371

Space allocations for FAT & root directory (5.25")

Figure 20.4 Root directory entries

existing files significantly changed). When a new file is created, it uses the first available space.

Extension   The extension can be up to 3 characters long, padded with spaces (ASCII 32).

Attribute   The *attribute byte* tells us what sort of entry it is. Each bit of the byte is set to indicate a different type of file or entry. The structure of this byte is given in Figure 20.5.

Bit	Meaning (if set)
0	Read-only file
1	Hidden file
2	System file
3	Volume label
4	Subdirectory
5	Archive
6-7	Not used

NB Under DOS 1 only bits 1 and 2 were used

Figure 20.5 The attribute byte

If the entry is a file it may be marked as read-only, hidden, archive or system, or any combination of these. For example, a value of 6 indicates a hidden system file while 7 makes this file read-only as well. Alternatively, the entry may be a volume label or sub-directory name.

Note that only the root directory may contain a volume label, and there can be only one of these.

Time stamp

The *time stamp* is updated when the file is created or changed. The current system time is stored here. The way in which the time stamp is stored (to the nearest 2 seconds), is shown in Figure 20.6. Note that the values are always stored with the low byte first (the standard method for storing 2-byte words when programming).

Date stamp

The date on which a file is created or changed is stored in the *date stamp*. The structure used here is shown in Figure 20.7. Again, the low byte is stored first.

Start cluster

All data is stored on disk a cluster at a time. The clusters are numbered sequentially (in a similar manner to the DOS and OS/2 sector numbering system) and the *start cluster* points to the first cluster of the file.

File size

The actual size of the file is stored in terms of bytes. Remembering that files are always allocated whole clusters at a time this means that there will be some wasted space at the

The time stamp word	
Bit	**Meaning**
15	)
14	)
13	) Hours
12	)
11	)
10	)
9	)
8	) Minutes
7	)
6	)
5	)
4	)
3	)
2	) Seconds / 2
1	)
0	)

Figure 20.6 The time stamp

end of each file. The sum of the directory listings will therefore not match the total disk size; for example, a 100-byte file reduces the amount of free space on a floppy disk by 1024 bytes even though its size is only shown as 100.

DOS and OS/2 provide various means for changing these entries. Some have already been discussed (such as the ATTRIB command and COPY *filename+,,*); other programming methods are provided by the DOS interrupts and OS/2 services, catalogued in Chapter 22.

SUB-DIRECTORIES

The root directory is stored right at the beginning of the disk and is allocated a specific amount of space. Because the size of each entry is fixed (32 bytes) there is obviously a limit to the number of entries that the root directory can hold. In the case of floppy disks, this is 112 entries. This limit includes sub-directories and the volume label, of course.

The date stamp word	
Bit	**Meaning**
15	)
14	)
13	) Year - 1980
12	)
11	)
10	)
9	)
8	) Month
7	)
6	)
5	)
4	)
3	)
2	) Day
1	)
0	)

Figure 20.7 The date stamp

Sub-directories have an identical structure to the root directory and are stored as data files, the main difference being the attribute that is stored for them in the parent directory. The advantage of sub-directories is that, in common with all files, their size is not fixed and therefore there is no limit to the number of entries they can hold.

The start cluster for the sub-directory name in the root directory stores the start point of the sub-directory. When a file is needed that is in a sub-directory the operating system reads in the sub-directory file and locates the relevant information. This directory may of course hold other sub-directories, which are stored as separate files.

The first entry (.) holds details of the sub-directory itself.

The start cluster of the second entry (..) in a sub-directory points back to the parent directory, completing the means of linking sub-directories in both directions. If the start cluster is given as 0 this indicates that the parent is the root directory.

FILE ALLOCATION TABLES (FAT's)

All space on a disk is allocated in terms of whole clusters. However, the way in which files are stored is not as obvious as it may seem. The operating system always uses the first available space, even if this is not large enough to take the whole file. The result is that files become fragmented.

The operating system uses an area called the *File Allocation Table (FAT)* to help it find the various fragments of each file.

Because the amount of space in the directory is limited, there is only room there to store the start point of the file.

The FAT contains an entry for each cluster on the disk. The start cluster in the directory shows where the first cluster is stored for that file. The value stored in the FAT for the first cluster points to the second cluster of the file, that of the second points to the third and so on. As a result you can follow through the chain of clusters for any individual file.

A special value is stored in any FAT entry to indicate that a cluster contains the end of the file.

Other special values are used to indicate clusters that have not yet been used and those that contain bad sectors (and are therefore unusable). The codes you are likely to encounter include:

000 or 0000	Cluster not yet used
FF7 or FFF7	Bad cluster (unusable)
FFE or FFFE	Reserved cluster
FFF or FFFF	End of file

Note that the first two entries of the FAT (representing clusters 0 and 1) are reserved. The first byte is a code that indicates the disk type (as shown in Figure 20.8).

The first data cluster after the directory - the point at which the first file can be stored - is cluster number 2.

Disk type, as indicated by first byte of FAT		
Disk type		**1st byte (Hex)**
5.25" 8 sector	SS DD	FE
	DS DD	FF
9 sector	SS DD	FC
	DS DD	FD
	QD	F9
3.5"	SS	FC
	DS	FD
	QD	F9
Hard disks	10Mb	F8
	20Mb	F8

Meaning of first byte of FAT	
1st byte (Hex)	**Disk type**
F8	Hard disk
F9	Quad density
FA	Not used
FB	Not used
FC	SS 9 sectors
FD	DS 9 sectors
FE	SS 8 sectors
FF	DS 8 sectors

Figure 20.8 FAT disk codes

Unfortunately, the FAT entries are stored in a rather complicated way. The size of the FAT entry varies, depending on the disk capacity:

■ Floppy disks and hard disks of less than 20M have 12-bit entries

■ Hard disks of 20M or more have 2-byte entries

The size had to be extended when high capacity hard disks were first catered for because a 12-bit entry can only take values up to 4096, and hard disks generally have many more clusters than this.

Matters are complicated by the fact that all values are stored as two-byte words, with the low byte first. For 2-byte FAT entries this is easy enough to unravel but for 12-byte entries it is much more complex, since each group of 3 bytes hold two entries. Therefore, the entry for cluster 2 is stored in byte 3 (the first 2 bytes are used for the disk information) and the top four bits of byte 4; cluster 3 takes the remainder of byte 4 and all of byte 5. When this data is stored, byte 4 comes before byte 3, so the components of the entries can become completely separated from each other.

Sorting this out can be quite a tricky task but once it has been accomplished you can create a map of the disk, showing where files are stored and how they are linked.

21. Operating System Structure

The operating system has a great deal of work to do. It has to control the use of memory, the storage of files on disk and all access to devices. In addition, it is responsible for running programs, error-handling and the interface with the user. This means that the operating system must be made up from a complex series of components.

Fortunately, the general design of DOS 3.3 and OS/2 is similar, which makes life much more straightforward for the programmer. That said, the way in which the operating systems can be accessed during programming does vary quite considerably. Whereas it was feasible in the past to write assembly language code that worked directly with DOS 3.3, the same is not true of OS/2. The complexity of this new operating system is such that most programming will inevitably be done through a high-level language, such as C. Even so, some knowledge of the inner workings of the operating system is helpful.

This chapter looks at the way in which the operating systems are put together, and at the various components.

THE SYSTEM FILES

The main operating system itself is comprised of three separate parts. Each of these deals with a different aspect of the computer's operation. The three parts are:

- The *Basic Input/Output System (BIOS)*, which deals with all communications between the CPU and the devices

- The *kernel*, which provides the link between an application program and the operating system BIOS

- The command processor, which contains all the internal commands and controls communication with users

The BIOS and kernel are the two system files that are generally hidden from the user. Each of these components is discussed below.

THE BIOS

The first system file on any system disk, immediately following the file directory, contains the BIOS. The file contains all that is needed to communicate with the hardware; in particular, it includes all the standard device drivers.

Whenever a program requests some action by a particular item of hardware, such as an instruction to print a character on the screen or get a key press from the keyboard, this request eventually finds its way to the BIOS.

It is the routines in the BIOS that convert the general instructions issued by other parts of the system into specific code that the hardware can understand. Having made the conversion the BIOS passes the instruction on to the device that has been specified. In most cases this involves routing the instructions through the relevant ROM-BIOS routines.

There is considerable variation in the way in which particular devices operate. The instructions needed to operate a similar device on another system may not be the same. For this reason, the BIOS tends to be different for different systems; instructions may arrive in the same format in each case but their translation needs to vary. Thus an operating system such as PC-DOS may have some peculiarities in the way in which it operates if it is run on any machine other than an IBM. (In particular, the operation of the clock can be affected.)

The BIOS is loaded into memory when the system is booted and remains there until the system is reset. The BIOS in MS-DOS is in a file called IO.SYS; under PC-DOS and OS/2 it appears as IBMBIO.COM.

THE KERNEL

The file that follows the BIOS is another system file, generally called the kernel. It is here that all requests for action by the hardware first arrive, when requested by an application. The kernel takes these requests and channels them to the appropriate part of the BIOS. Any response from the BIOS is returned to the applications.

The format of these instructions should be the same, regardless of the hardware. All code in this part of the system is supposed to be device-independent. For example, an instruction to send an item of data to the parallel port should be the same, no matter how the port is configured. This system file should therefore be identical on all systems (assuming they are running the same version of the operating system). Having said that, it is not a good idea to split the system files; they should always be transferred in pairs.

The kernel also resides permanently in memory, along with the BIOS. It is stored on disk as a file called MSDOS.SYS (for MS-DOS) or IBMDOS.COM (for PC-DOS and OS/2).

The two system files are transferred by the FORMAT command if the /S parameter is specified. They can also be transferred later using SYS. Note that in most versions of DOS the system files must be stored as unfragmented blocks. Therefore, for SYS to be successful, the space allocated to the system files must be large enough to take the files in their entirety. The practical result of this is that it is usually possible to downgrade a system disk without reformatting, but difficult to upgrade. The system files have tended to grow with each new version, so some juggling of disk space may be necessary before you use SYS. DOS 4 and OS/2 have broken with tradition, in that they will happily accept fragmented system files.

THE COMMAND PROCESSOR
The third part of the operating system is the command processor. This is the section of the system that the user sees. The command processor deals with all communications with the operator. It is responsible for accepting and processing commands, displaying the prompt and issuing messages to the user. In DOS the default command processor is called COMMAND.COM while the OS/2 version is CMD.EXE.

The command processor contains the code for the internal commands. It carries out whatever action is required, passing on all requests for input and output to the kernel.

This file is not hidden and has no specific place on the disk. Indeed, it can be replaced by a totally different program if you so wish. The SHELL directive in CONFIG.SYS determines the name of the command processor, if it is different to the default.

The command processor is sub-divided into three entirely separate sections:

- The *initialisation section*, which is only executed when the system is first started and gets the system up and running

- The *resident section*, a part of the processor that must be kept permanently in memory

- The *transient section*, which contains the internal command routines and may be temporarily overwritten.

Each section of the program performs a different set of tasks.

Resident section

The resident part of the command processor is read into memory first; this part of the program is stored in the first available space in the low end of memory and stays there throughout the time the computer is switched on.

Its first task is read into memory the other two parts of the program and to put into effect the initialisation section.

The resident part of the program also normally deals with all serious error-handling. This part has to be available at all times to handle situations such as a drive being empty or the printer being off-line. It is this part of the program that pops up, even in the middle of an application, with the 'Abort, Retry or Ignore?' type of message.

Initialisation

The initialisation section is only required when the system is first started. The main function of this part of the processor is to check for the existence of the startup files (such as AUTOEXEC.BAT) and automatically execute the instructions they contain.

This part of the operating system is stored in memory immediately after the resident portion; as soon as its work is completed it is overwritten by the next application to be read into memory.

Transient section

The transient part of the command processor holds the main substance of the program. It contains all the routines needed for displaying the prompt, taking information from the command line and processing commands. This part is responsible for loading and running applications; it also contains all of the code for the internal commands.

These activities are only required when the user is communicating with the operating system through the standard command line interface; none of them is needed when an application is running. Therefore, they can be overwritten, if necessary, once an application program has been started.

For this reason, the transient section is stored right at the top of memory. Applications that need the whole of memory will overwrite this section. After the applications have finished running, the transient part of the command processor must be loaded again. (Hence the requests, under DOS, to put in the disk with COMMAND.COM when an aplication finishes.) This is also one of the reasons that when you shell out of an application it needs to load a secondary processor.

Theoretically, it is possible to replace COMMAND.COM with a new command processor. Such a program could perform any range of tasks or provide a new interface for the user; the scope of the program is almost completely at the discretion of the programmer, as long as the new command processor is well-behaved and follows a few simple rules. Generally speaking, any other command processor should contain sections similar to those of the standard processors.

THE ENVIRONMENT

We have already seen that the file CONFIG.SYS sets up the system configuration. This file contains the operating *environment* and as such determines the conditions under which the system will operate. Although some of the less important aspects of the environment can be changed - such as the path and prompt - the major features cannot be varied once they have been installed. In particular, the environment dictates what command processor is to be used and where it is to be found, and results in the device drivers being loaded.

The environment file, CONFIG.SYS, is loaded into memory before even the command processor. The order of items in the environment is important, since they are processed sequentially. For example, the path must be set up before the device drives can be located, unless the appropriate lines of the configuration include the full drive and directory path.

The environment is stored in memory as an ASCII string, in precisely the same form as it appears in CONFIG.SYS, except that each line is terminated by a null character (ASCII 0) and the end of the environment as a whole is signified by two null characters.

DEVICE DRIVERS

Accurate communications between the CPU and the various devices to which it is connected are obviously critical to the operation of the system. This communication is carried out through the *device drivers*, programs whose task it is to convert the requests from the operating system into instructions that the devices can understand.

The device drivers fall into two main categories:

■ The *standard device drivers*, which form part of the operating system BIOS

■ The *installable device drivers*, which are added when the system is booted

We have very little control over the standard device drivers. These include the CON, NUL, COM1 and LPT1 devices, for example. They relate to devices that are fixed parts of the system.

The installable device drives, on the other hand, are totally within our control. It is the installable drivers that appear as files (with a SYS extension). These drivers must be installed when the system is first booted; the operating system loads them when the appropriate DEVICE directives are included in CONFIG.SYS. Installable devices include MOUSE.SYS, RAM-DRIVE.SYS and ANSI.SYS.

Each device - whether standard or installable - must be one of two types:

■ *Character devices*, which send and receive information one character at a time. These include the keyboard, screen, serial and parallel ports, and mouse. The null device is also classed as a character device.

Device	Type	Device Name
Null device	Character	NUL:
Console (keyboard & screen)	Character	CON:
First serial port	Character	COM1: or AUX:
Second serial port	Character	COM2:
First parallel port	Character	LPT1: or PRN:
Second parallel port	Character	LPT2:
Floppy disk drive	Block	Usually A: and B:
Hard disk drive	Block	Usually C:

Figure 21.1 The standard devices

■ Block devices, which send and receive data in blocks, usually of 512 bytes. These are used to control devices that deal with large amounts of data. They include the disk drives and other high-capacity storage devices.

There are various important differences between the types of device. Most importantly, perhaps, is the fact that each character device can only control a single device. A different device driver is needed for each parallel port, for example (LPT1, LPT2, etc.). Block devices, on the other hand, can control more than one device. Thus there is a single device driver to control all floppy disks connected to the system, assuming that they are all of an identical type. Any floppy unit that is different to that expected by the system may require its own device driver.

Character devices have device names (CON:, PRN:, etc.) while the block devices use drive labels (A:, B:, etc.). The standard devices are listed in Figure 21.1.

Installing devices   The devices are read into memory when the system is first installed, and remain there throughout its operation. They are stored consecutively, as a linked chain of routines. Each device has three main parts:

■ The *device header* contains information about the device driver. Amongst other things, it points to the start of the next device in the list.

335

Structure of MS-DOS device drivers		
Start Byte	No. Bytes	Purpose
0	4	Pointer to next device
4	2	Device attributes
6	2	Pointer to strategy routine
8	2	Pointer to interrupt routine
10	8	Device name
18	n1	Strategy routine
18+n1	n2	Interrupt routine

n1 = Length of strategy routine
n2 = Length of interrupt routine

Figure 21.2 Device driver structure

■ The *strategy routine* stores away the contents of the registers when the driver is called, so that they can be restored when the driver has finished its work.

■ The *interrupt routine* contains the main part of the device driver, which responds to the requests have been issued.

The structure of the device drivers is shown in Figure 21.2.

Whenever a call to a device is received the operating system searches through the drivers for the required device. It checks the name and, if this is incorrect, moves on to the next one, using the information at the start of the device header.

The *attributes* word in the device header contains various details of how the device driver can be used. The meaning of this word is detailed in Figure 21.3.

The request header

Whenever the operating system needs to communicate with a device it sets up a *request header*. This is a block of data that is used to pass information to and from the driver. The structure of the header is shown in Figure 21.4.

Bit	Character/ Block/Both	Use	Meaning if set (=1)	Meaning if clear (=0)
15	Both	Type of device	Character	Block
14	Both	IOCTL commands	Supported	Not supported
13	BLOCK	Format of disk	IBM	Non-IBM
12	CHARACTER	Output until busy	Supported	Not supported
11	Both	Device Open/Close and Removable Media commands	Supported	Not supported
10	Not used			
9	Not used			
8	Not used			
7	Not used			
6	Both	Get/Set Logical Device commands	Supported	Not supported
5	Not used			
4	CHARACTER	Int 29H for fast console I/O	Implemented	Not implemented
3	CHARACTER	Device is current clock	Yes	No
2	CHARACTER	Device is current null device	Yes	No
1	CHARACTER	Device is standard output device	Yes	No
0	CHARACTER	Device is standard input device	Yes	No

Figure 21.3 The device header attributes word

Perhaps most importantly, there are only a limited number of commands that the device is expected to deal with. The device driver returns a status word, indicating the success or otherwise of the operation.

Note that there are two ways of transferring data:

■ Standard input/output, where the device reads or writes data by directly accessing the internal ports

■ The IOCTL functions, which provide more sophisticated communications

The request header			
Offset	Bytes	Meaning	Set by
0	1	Length of header	DOS,OS/2
1	1	Unit code	DOS,OS/2
2	1	Command code	DOS,OS/2
3	2	Status	Driver
5	8	Reserved	
13	Variable	Set by op. sys.	DOS,OS/2

Figure 21.4 The request header

The *IOCTL* (Input/Output Control) functions are a more recent implementation (DOS 2) and provide standard methods of data-handling. The DOS interrupts include a single function to deal with this form of data transfer but this has many sub-functions.

22. Programming Services

The operating systems include a large number of routines that are used in all their commands to perform such tasks as writing text to the screen or getting characters from the keyboard. These routines are all available to the programmer and are listed in this chapter.

DOS INTERRUPTS

An *interrupt* is a signal to the CPU that some special action is required; when the CPU receives an interrupt signal it stops whatever it is doing and performs the required task. For example, every time a key is pressed, a keyboard interrupt is generated and everything else is temporarily suspended while the necessary action is taken.

The software can also produce interrupts, using the assembly language INT instruction. In particular, there are a large number of interrupts that form part of DOS and are accessible to programmers. These are really just subroutines that can be called from within a program.

Most of these are sub-functions of DOS interrupt 21h (decimal 33). They can be accessed within an assembly language program by the command:

```
INT 21h
```

Before calling the interrupt you should load the registers with the relevant values. The DOS interrupts are listed in Figure 22.1.

OS/2 SERVICES

OS/2 does not use interrupts but does have a similar set of routines available for the programmer. These are called the *Application Program Interface (API)* services. They can be called

Interrupt	Function	Service
20		Terminate program
21	00	Terminate program
	01	Keyboard input with echo
	02	Display character
	03	Get character from serial port
	04	Send character to serial port
	05	Send character to parallel port
	06	Keyboard input/ screen output
	07	Keyboard input without echo (without break)
	08	Keyboard input without echo (with break)
	09	Display string
	0A	Keyboard string input
	0B	Check keyboard buffer
	0C	Clear keyboard buffer, call interrupt 21h function
	0D	Reset disk
	0E	Change current drive
	0F	Open a file
	10	Close a file
	11	Find first matching file
	12	Find next matching file
	13	Delete a file
	14	Read sequential record
	15	Write sequential record
	16	Create a file
	17	Rename a file
	19	Get current drive
	1A	Set disk transfer area addrerss
	1B	Get FAT information for current drive
	1C	Get FAT information for any drive
	21	Read random record
	22	Write random record
	23	Get file size
	24	Prepare field for random record
	25	Set interrupt vector
	26	Create PSP

Figure 22.1 The DOS interrupts

Interrupt	Function	Service
21	27	Read random records
	28	Write random records
	29	Parse filename
	2A	Get date
	2B	Set date
	2C	Get time
	2D	Set time
	2E	Disk write verification
	2F	Get address of DTA
	30	Check DOS version number
	31	Terminate and stay resident
	33,00	Get control break
	33,01	Set control break
	35	Get interrupt vector
	36	Check free clusters
	38	Get or set country-dependent information
	39	Make directory
	3A	Remove directory
	3B	Change directory
	3C	Create a file
	3D	Open a file
	3E	Close a file
	3F	Read from file
	40	Write to a file
	41	Delete a file
	42	Move file pointer
	43,00	Get attributes of file
	43,01	Set attributes of file
	44	IOCTL functions
	45	Duplicate a file handle
	46	Force duplication of handle
	47	Check current directory
	48	Allocate memory
	49	Free memory
	4A	Modify allocated memory

Figure 22.1 The DOS interrupts (continued)

Interrupt	Function	Service
21	4B	Load/execute program
	4C	Terminate subprogram
	4D	Get return code of subprogram
	4E	Find first matching file
	4F	Find next matching file
	54	Check verification status
	56	Rename a file
	57,00	Get date & time stamp
	57,01	Set date & time stamp
	59	Get extended error code
	5A	Create a temporary file
	5B	Create a new file
	5C,00	Lock file
	5C,01	Unlock file
	62	Get PSP segment address
22		Terminate address
23		Break address
24		Critical error-handler address
25		Read sectors from disk
26		Write sectors to disk
27		Terminate & stay resident
2F		Access background program

Note: All values are hexadecimal

Figure 22.1 The DOS interrupts (continued)

directly by a program written in C, as long as the relevant OS/2 library file is linked in when the program is compiled.

A subset of these routines, called the *family API* services, result in programs that can be run in either real or protected mode. The BIND utility converts a program that normally runs only in protected mode into one that will run in either mode. The family API services are listed in Figure 22.2.

dosbeep	dosqfilemode	viogetphysbuf
doschdir	dosqverify	vioreadcellstr
doschgfileptr	dosread	vioreadcharstr
dosclose	dosrmdir	vioscrlock
dosdelete	dosselectdisk	vioscrunlock
dosdevconfig	dossetfhandstate	vioscrolldn
dosdevioctl	dossetfsinfo	vioscrolllf
dosduphandle	dossetfilemode	vioscrollrt
doserror	dossetvec	vioscrollup
dosfilelocks	dossetverify	viosetcurpos
dosfindclose	doswrite	viosetcurtype
dosfindfirst	kbdcharin	viosetmode
dosfindnext	kbdflushbuffer	vioshowbuff
dosmkdir	kbdgetstatus	viowrtcellstr
dosmove	kbdpeek	viowrtcharstr
dosnewsize	kbdregister	viowrtcharstratt
dosopen	kbdsetstatus	viowrtnattr
dosqcurdir	kbdstringin	viowrtncell
dosqcurdisk	viogetbuf	viowrtnchar
dosqfhandstate	viogetcurpos	viowrttty
dosqfsinfo	viogetcurtype	
dosqfileinfo	viogetmode	

Figure 22.2 OS/2 family API services

The DOS interrupts and OS/2 services provide the programmer with all that is needed to make fast and efficient programs.

Appendix

The ASCII character set

Dec	Hex	Char	Dec	Hex	Char	Dec	Hex	Char	Dec	Hex	Char
0	00	NUL	32	20	Space	64	40	@	96	60	`
1	01	SOH	33	21	!	65	41	A	97	61	a
2	02	STX	34	22	"	66	42	B	98	62	b
3	03	ETX	35	23	#	67	43	C	99	63	c
4	04	EOT	36	24	$	68	44	D	100	64	d
5	05	ENQ	37	25	%	69	45	E	101	65	e
6	06	ACK	38	26	&	70	46	F	102	66	f
7	07	BEL	39	27	'	71	47	G	103	67	g
8	08	BS	40	28	(	72	48	H	104	68	h
9	09	HT	41	29	)	73	49	I	105	69	i
10	0A	LF	42	2A	*	74	4A	J	106	6A	j
11	0B	VT	43	2B	+	75	4B	K	107	6B	k
12	0C	FF	44	2C	,	76	4C	L	108	6C	l
13	0D	CR	45	2D	-	77	4D	M	109	6D	m
14	0E	SO	46	2E	.	78	4E	N	110	6E	n
15	0F	SI	47	2F	/	79	4F	O	111	6F	o
16	10	DLE	48	30	0	80	50	P	112	70	p
17	11	DC1	49	31	1	81	51	Q	113	71	q
18	12	DC2	50	32	2	82	52	R	114	72	r
19	13	DC3	51	33	3	83	53	S	115	73	s
20	14	DC4	52	34	4	84	54	T	116	74	t
21	15	NAK	53	35	5	85	55	U	117	75	u
22	16	SYN	54	36	6	86	56	V	118	76	v
23	17	ETB	55	37	7	87	57	W	119	77	w
24	18	CAN	56	38	8	88	58	X	120	78	x
25	19	EM	57	39	9	89	59	Y	121	79	y
26	1A	SUB	58	3A	:	90	5A	Z	122	7A	z
27	1B	ESC	59	3B	;	91	5B	[	123	7B	{
28	1C	FS	60	3C	<	92	5C	\	124	7C	|
29	1D	GS	61	3D	=	93	5D	]	125	7D	}
30	1E	RS	62	3E	>	94	5E	^	126	7E	~
31	1F	US	63	3F	?	95	5F	_	127	7F	

ASCII control codes

Dec	Hex	Abbreviation	Meaning
0	00	NUL	Null character
1	01	SOH	Start of header
2	02	STX	Start text
3	03	ETX	End text
4	04	EOT	End of transmission
5	05	ENQ	Enquiry
6	06	ACK	Acknowledge
7	07	BEL	Bell
8	08	BS	Backspace
9	09	HT	Horizontal tab
10	0A	LF	Line feed
11	0B	VT	Vertical tab
12	0C	FF	Form feed
13	0D	CR	Carriage return
14	0E	SO	Shift out
15	0F	SI	Shift in
16	10	DLE	Data line escape
17	11	DC1	Device control 1
18	12	DC2	Device control 2
19	13	DC3	Device control 3
20	14	DC4	Device control 4
21	15	NAK	Negative acknowledge
22	16	SYN	Synchronisation idle
23	17	ETB	End transmission block
24	18	CAN	Cancel
25	19	EM	End of medium
26	1A	SUB	Substitute
27	1B	ESC	Escape
28	1C	FS	File separator
29	1D	GS	Group separator
30	1E	RS	Record separator
31	1F	US	Unit separator

Index